THE
HITCHHIKE

MARK PAUL SMITH

BQB
Virginia

First published in 2013 by Christopher Matthews Publishing, Bozeman, Montana under ISBN 9781938985089

Republished in 2020 by BQB Publishing (an imprint of Boutique of Quality Books Publishing Company, Inc.)
Christiansburg, Virginia

Printed in the United States of America

978-1-945448-76-8 (p)
978-1-945448-77-5 (e)

Library of Congress Control Number 2020938564

Book design by Robin Krauss, www.bookformatters.com
Cover design by Rebecca Lown, www.rebeccalowndesign.com

Editor: Caleb Guard

Dedication

To the women in my life:

My wife, Jo Ellen Hemphill Smith
My mother, Vaunceil Hulda Tiarks Smith
My sisters, Terri Vaun Lindvall,
Amy Maxwell Szwabowicz,
and Laura Lynn Eckstein

Special thanks to

My publisher, Terri Leidich of BQB and
WriteLife Publishing,
editor, Caleb Guard
and beta reader, Brenda Fishbaugh.

Table of Contents

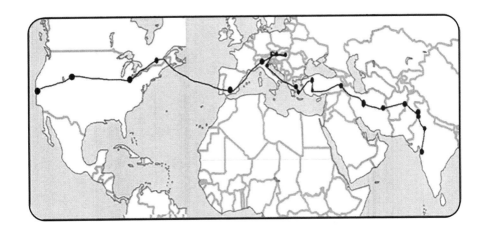

The Hitchhike

1. Monterey, CA
2. Golden, CO.
3. Fort Wayne, IN
4. Montreal, Canada
5. Lisbon, Portugal
6. Malaga, Spain
7. Milan, Italy
8. Vienna, Austria
9. Debrecen, Hungary
10. Innsbruck, Austria
11. Venice, Italy
12. Athens, Greece
13. Mykonos, Greece
14. Izmir, Turkey
15. Ankara, Turkey
16. Silifke, Turkey
17. Van, Turkey
18. Tabriz, Iran
19. Tehran, Iran
20. Mashad, Iran
21. Herat, Afghanistan
22. Kabul, Afghanistan
23. Lahore, Pakistan
24. New Delhi, India
25. Agra, India
26. Bombay, India

Preface

There was a time, not long ago, when you could walk to the highway, stick out your thumb, and catch a ride with a total stranger. Those were the days when sex was safe, and rock and roll was the rhythm of the revolution. Young people from all walks of life hit the road with nothing but packs on their backs to find enlightenment and somehow end the war in Vietnam.

When I left on my journey, I wasn't sure if I was an intrepid explorer or just another fugitive from justice. I had no idea I would end up meeting John Lennon, hitchhiking through the Iron Curtain, working on a collective farm in Hungary, living on a nude beach in Greece, nearly perishing in a storm at sea, smoking opium in Iran, finding my soul in the music of Afghanistan, smuggling turquoise over the Khyber Pass into Pakistan, and nearly dying from dysentery and the fury of my Argentinian lover in India.

I also had no idea that the women I would fall in love with along the way would completely change the direction of my life.

Peace and love,
Mark Paul Smith

CHAPTER ONE

Danny

SHE WAS LONG-LEGGED AND LEAN in her faded jeans and stylish sport jacket as she walked down the aisle of the jumbo jet airliner. Our eyes met and we smiled at each other. It was our second visual contact within an hour. Before boarding we'd shared a moment when she noticed we were each carrying a copy of the same book, *The Drifters*, by James Michener.

Now, I had to look down at my open book to keep from staring as she headed towards me. I saw her legs stop walking as I felt her hand on my shoulder. She whispered in my ear, "If you'd like a joint, come to the back of the plane."

She was on the move by the time I lifted my head to say, "I'll be there."

Rational thought gave way to confusion as I realized the potential for good fortune that had just fallen into my life. I hadn't

felt a woman's touch since California. The two-week hitchhike from the West Coast to Montreal had been a long, lonely adventure. Now, it was hard to keep from jumping out of my seat to follow her. *Don't be too eager* kept coming to mind, followed closely by *Don't make her wait too long.*

This was an interesting woman. Her English was perfect, but she had a soothing French accent. She didn't wear much makeup, not that she needed it. She was a natural—high cheekbones, full lips, and an aristocratic nose. Her face seemed tired, but her eyes flashed like neon reflections on a rainy street at night.

The plane took off in a massive rush of gravity force and jet scream. I felt excited and apprehensive at the same time, and not just about the miracle of flight or the woman I had just met. As I closed my eyes, it occurred to me I was taking off on a journey from which I might never return. I breathed deeply to settle the butterflies in my stomach.

We reached cruising altitude and the captain turned off the seat-belt and no-smoking lights. My thoughts collected from worrying about the future to focusing on the present opportunity. *Is she really waiting in the back with a joint?*

I waited, impatiently, and then waited some more. After what seemed like a long time but was probably less than twenty minutes, I took a few more deep breaths, unbuckled, and headed for the back of the plane.

She was all the way back by the lavatories. I could see her watching me closely as I walked down the aisle toward her. At six three, 185, with a bushy white boy Afro and leather-patched jeans, I was hard to miss.

"Hello again." I tried to sound casual. "Mind if I join you?"

She acted surprised but said, "Please do." She slid from the aisle seat to the window, leaving an empty seat between us as I collapsed awkwardly into her previous space.

"Whew," I exhaled and turned to stretch my hand in greeting. "I'm Mark."

She was already shaking a cigarette out of its pack, but took my hand briefly and said, "Nice to meet you, Mark." She began searching for her lighter like she had no intention of continuing the conversation. For an instant it felt like I'd made a terrible miscalculation. Was she just kidding?

"I'm Danny." She smiled as she lit up and took a drag. "Danny Trudeau to be complete." She blew out a huge plume of smoke over the seat in front of us. "What's your last name?"

"It's Smith. Mark Smith. Mark Paul Smith to be exact."

She laughed a little. "It sounds less like an alias when you put the 'Paul' in the middle." Then she looked suspicious. "Is it really Smith?"

"Swear to God." I held up my hands. "I know it sounds phony, but it's really my name. I've been a Smith all my life. My friends call me Smitty."

Danny chuckled, beginning to loosen up. "Well, I won't call you that, I promise."

"Thank you very much."

"So where are you headed, Mr. Mark Paul Smith?"

I didn't answer until it became obvious she was waiting for a response. "I have no idea, actually," I finally confessed. "How about you?"

"Oh, no, no, no." She turned slightly toward me. "You're not getting off that easy. Everybody's going somewhere and you're part of everybody; so, come on, where are you going?"

"Trudeau, let's see, that's French isn't it? How do you spell it?"

"Trudeau," she deadpanned, "T-R-U-D-E-A-U. It's French Canadian. Now don't try to change the topic." She blew out another plume of cigarette smoke for emphasis. Nobody but me paid any attention. The no-smoking light was off.

"Well," I started slowly, "if you must know, I'm going to Lisbon. That's as far as I'm flying. Then I'm going to bum around Europe."

"How long do you have off?" she asked as she realized I might not have a job. The woman was sizing me up. What a great role reversal. I played it coy.

"Off what?"

"Off work." She laughed. "You know what I mean."

"The best answer I can give is that I am currently unemployed, and I have no plans to actively seek gainful employment."

Danny looked at me carefully, took a drag, leaned back in her seat and observed, "So you're one of those hippies everybody's writing about. One of those spoiled Americans off to backpack through Europe on five dollars a day." She was teasing. "Staying in youth hostels and having free love and sit-ins to end the war." We both laughed. Then she straightened slightly and asked, "How old are you?"

I thought about lying, considering the downturn in the conversation, but answered honestly, "Twenty-two. How about yourself?"

"Damn, I knew it," she sputtered, stubbing out the butt of her smoke in the armrest ashtray. "You're too young." She sounded so desperately disappointed. It felt like the whole thing was falling apart before we had time to get started.

"Too young for what?" I laughed, trying to relax her. "Too young for you? You look younger than me."

She smiled appreciatively, acknowledging that I had at least enough sense to use well the only line capable of assuaging her doubt and salvaging the situation. "How old do you think I am?"

Clearly back in the game, I had to be careful. Guessing over thirty was not an option. Nor was guessing under twenty-two. "I'm going to say," making her wait for it, "I'm going to say twenty-six."

"Yes, yes." She chuckled. "You are very good. Actually, I'm twenty-seven. You can see I'm much too old for you." She searched my eyes. I was swimming in hers. They were sparkling hazel. For the first time since we'd met in the airport, we looked into each other.

"I'd say you're perfect for me." It unintentionally came out as a whisper.

She looked at me searchingly. My self-consciousness gradually morphed into a chuckle that turned into a heartfelt laugh, mostly at myself but also at the serendipity of our situation. Danny couldn't help but join in. Her smile erased the worry from her face.

"So, what about you?" I asked as our mutual sighs diminished. "Where are you headed?"

"I'm headed on to Madrid," she answered after a thoughtful pause. "This plane stops in Lisbon and then continues to Madrid."

"What's going on in Madrid?" I avoided the obvious fact that her itinerary would shortchange our encounter.

"Nothing really," she said sadly. "I've got two weeks off."

"Two weeks off what?"

"Two weeks off from a very terrible situation I'm sure you don't want to hear about."

"Try me," I encouraged her.

"No, no. It's too much too soon." She shook her head. "I'm not sure you really want to get to know me. I'm actually running away from a very bad scene. My work has been too much, mostly eighty hours a week, and I've had a horrible time with a man and . . . it's just too much. I can't talk about it all right now. I barely know you." She fumbled in her purse for another cigarette.

"Hey, hey," I soothed, waiting for her to look at me. "It's all right. We don't have to be in a big hurry here. It's a long flight. We can save the heavy stuff for later." She looked grateful as she pulled out her lighter.

"Hold that light," I suggested. "I've got a better idea. How about we smoke that joint you were talking about?"

Danny's smile came back, this time with a conspiratorial twinkle. "Do you think these overhead fans can handle the smoke?"

I looked up as if to carefully assess the ventilation system, knowing full well the little air blowers wouldn't do a thing to mask the heavy aroma of marijuana smoke. "I'm sure they can handle it quite well," I lied. "Besides, lots of people are smoking cigarettes back here in the smoking section."

She furrowed her brow and pursed her lips as she dug out of her stuffed black purse a quarter-ounce bag of what looked to be some pretty good reefer. I opened the plastic baggie and took a long sniff. "Ah, smells like the real deal here. I haven't smoked in days."

"Days? Has it been that long? Poor baby!" She produced a pack of Zig Zag rolling papers. "Can you roll?"

"Can I roll?" I grinned. "With one hand on the back of a Harley at sixty miles an hour. Yes, I can roll. How do you get Zig Zags in Canada?"

"We've got everything you do," she said indignantly as she watched me roll up two one-paper joints in quick succession. "Can you really do that one-handed on a motorcycle?"

"Actually, no," I said. "But as you can see, I've done this before. May I borrow your flame?"

Legal consequences never crossed my mind as I fired up that joint. I was already high on the real thing, chasing a woman. I took a big hit and passed it to Danny. She looked at the fans as if to question my earlier assessment. I nodded reassuringly and she took a tentative toke. We exhaled at the same time. It was good pot, the kind that takes you away, right away. Danny closed her eyes and started to relax. We didn't say much as we kept smoking, passing the joint back and forth.

Marijuana smoke was rolling up the passenger compartment of the plane like an inflatable parade balloon. Passengers couldn't help but notice the distinctive, pungent aroma. Some older folks became mildly alarmed at the unfamiliar smell, but no one hit the overhead call button. Some longhairs up about seven rows looked over their seats and motioned for us to pass it up. I just flashed them the peace sign. By now, Danny was laughing at nothing in particular. Her eyes were getting softer as she got farther and farther away from reality. "This is so great," she gushed. "I can't remember getting this relaxed or this high so fast."

I leaned back into the seat and closed my eyes. "We were high and going fast when we started."

Danny thought that hysterically funny. In fact, anything we said to each other led to more contagious laughter. We were stoned. Danny surprised me by lighting the second joint. "What do you think?" she asked as she passed it over.

I took a long drag and held it in until I choked up trying to exhale and speak at the same time. "I think two joints will get you higher than one."

We laughed so hard we were putting on a show that couldn't be ignored by our neighbors. People were craning their necks to see what all the commotion was about. We didn't notice. Our little get-acquainted party was turning into a smashing success. The high turned the plane into a dimly lit New Orleans jazz club. Saxophone solos somersaulting through my brain, and I half expected dancing hookers to come slinking down the aisle. The plane was rockin' like "Take the A-Train" in my brain. Danny slid into the seat next to me and took my hand. Her touch was warm and soft and inviting.

Meanwhile, the distinctive odor of marijuana had engulfed the first-class section and was easing through the door to the cockpit. A voice in the back of my head kept saying something was about to go wrong. Sure enough, our dazed reverie was shattered like a needle screeching across a vinyl record when I noticed somebody burst back through the first-class curtain. It was trouble headed our way; a man in a uniform who was in a hurry and obviously not happy as he waved his arms through the smoke.

Danny saw him too and snubbed out the half joint. Suddenly, nothing was funny anymore. No doubt, we were on our way to being arrested and thrown into some Spanish hellhole jail. Or worse. *Oh man, this is it. I'm busted. What was I thinking? This trip is over. Life as I know it is over. How could I have been such a fool?* My blood pressure rose, and my stomach clenched. My heart was racing. I glanced at Danny. She seemed strangely calm in the face of impending doom. I looked around. There was nowhere to run, nowhere to hide.

The steward looked plenty angry as he kept coming back, looking for the source of the problem. Finally, he spotted us. I didn't know how he knew it was us until he pointed his right index finger. "Danny,

I figured it was you. Jesus Christ! The whole plane is getting stoned, including the captain. He knows the smell. You know he knows. He sent me back here to put an immediate stop to it. You've got to cut it out. You're going to get us all fired!"

In a stunning reversal of expectations, the man was not threatening to cuff us, but pleading with this roguish girl. Danny maintained composure and spoke to him like a boss speaks to an employee. "Oh, Scott. Stop being so dramatic. We're just having fun. Nobody else seems terribly bothered."

Scott looked at me as if to say, "Could you please tell her to stop?" I shrugged and deferred to my obviously well-connected partner.

"Okay, Scotty," Danny said sternly. "I'll let you have your way. Even though you'll be spoiling all our fun. We'll stop smoking pot. But only on one condition." He waited with a knowing smirk until she continued. "And that one condition is you keep us in scotch for the rest of the flight." She winked at me and then at the steward.

"That I can do." He sounded immensely relieved.

Then it felt like Danny was pushing her luck when she added, "In fact, I think we're both ready for a double. That wouldn't be too much trouble would it? Would you be a dear and help us here?"

"Yes, I would be a dear," he said sarcastically and went off to get our cocktails. "I'm always a dear."

I watched him walk back to the food and beverage station, totally amazed at what had just transpired. I slowly turned to look at Danny, who was chuckling to herself, and said, "I am blown away. Who are you and what are you doing in the seat next to me?"

"We go way back" was all she said.

It was a good thing the steward had used the name Danny, because I had been in the process of forgetting it. After a short pause of breathtaking silence, I put the name to use. "Danny, what just happened here? Do you own the airline or what?"

She laughed, obviously pleased to have saved the day, and said,

"I've been with Canadian Pacific Airlines since college. Scott and I started out together but now I'm in the main office. I tell people what to do and they get mad at me and the customers get mad at me and my bosses get mad at me. They pay me a lot but it's not worth the stress. They work you to death, sometimes ninety hours a week and it's still not enough. That's why this is so good for me, getting away and meeting crazy people like you."

Her eyes softened to let me in. I put my hand on her right thigh. She was soft to touch even as she tightened up, took a sudden breath, and put her hand on mine. A look of alarm in her eyes slipped into relief as I squeezed her and slid both our hands down to her knee. "I'm not sure that's such a good idea," she said, referring to my sexual advance. I removed my hand as Scott returned with our drinks and a can of air freshener to spray the entire area with a sickly sweet drizzle.

"Enough." She laughed him off. "You're drowning us in that toilet water of yours." He left, shaking his head good-naturedly. Danny called out after him, "Bring us one every half hour 'til we pass out and then bring us one every hour."

The whole rear section of the plane loved that line and shared a communal laugh. Everyone was ready to join the party. Scott and the rest of the flight crew kept the drinks and snacks coming. People were in the aisle chatting each other up and having impromptu conversations over the tops of the seats, feeling strangely warm and free. Danny and I joined the banter from our seats but remained within the confines of our new, rosy little world.

"Who are you?" she asked as the flight began to quiet. "Can I trust you?" I could tell she was already thinking about getting off with me in Lisbon.

"I was wondering the same thing about you."

That seemed to assure her somehow. She started talking about herself. "My life is pretty much a mess. I'm stressed to the point of breakdown and not just from the job. My ex-boyfriend was much older. He was so cruel. You wouldn't believe it. He used to lock me in the closet! Our sex life was horrible. He only cared about himself. I don't know why I'm telling you all this." She rested her head gently against my shoulder.

Her touch was meltingly soft, and despite all the smoke and booze, her hair smelled fresh as a tropical garden, thanks to the miracle of modern shampoo.

We floated along together in contented silence for a lovely while. I thought about kissing her, then decided against it. *Best not to rush things. Or is time running out?*

Eventually, it seemed the only thing to do. I shifted her off my shoulder, took her head in my hands gently, and kissed her softly and slowly. She didn't fight the feeling or the moment. We both knew it was right. Her lips parted and we tasted each other. She was deliciously smoky and scotchy. Deep desires were rising within me.

"Goodness," she whispered as we paused. "You took my breath away."

"I'm sorry, I couldn't help myself."

Danny put her head back on my shoulder, this time putting her arm around mine. "I can't believe I'm doing this," she purred.

"If it feels good, do it," I said.

She stiffened momentarily. "I hate that saying."

I knew it was a stupid thing to say even as I spoke the words. "Yeah, me too. It's too selfish. What it should say is, 'If it feels right, do it.'"

She squeezed my arm. "Yes, yes, yes. That's what it should say. And that's what this is. It's just right. It feels just right."

We floated on into the night. The drone of the plane became hypnotic. Our fellow passengers had settled down for the duration. We waved off Scott. No more drinks needed. Our bliss was complete. We were on cloud nineteen. We were weightless and everything was pink and purple. *This is too good to end in a few hours. She's seriously considering jumping off her flight in Lisbon. Should I try to talk her into it?*

"Have you ever been to Europe?" she asked.

Realizing her need for more information, I opened up a bit. "Yes, I spent my junior year in Vienna and Budapest. It was a foreign studies program through DePauw University. All the classes were in English, but I tried to learn as much German as possible. By the end of the program I still wasn't very fluent."

"You say you were in Budapest? Isn't that behind the Iron Curtain?"

"Yeah, I guess our group was one of the first to do it. I don't know how they did it, but they got us in. It was some kind of big deal. Everywhere we went we were received like visiting dignitaries. I mean, we went to the Parliament and they sat us at these long, green, felt-covered tables with water and vodka at every setting and told us how important our program was to improving foreign relations. They took us to collective farms, the whole bit. The Hungarian students were eager to talk."

"What did you talk about?"

"Oh, a little bit about communism versus capitalism but mostly about rock and roll and the whole hippie movement. What they really wanted was our blue jeans. Talk about a hot commodity. Blue jeans were forbidden fruit in that country."

"I'll bet they loved yours with all those leather patches and embroidered names. By the way, who's Chucha?"

Ah yes, this woman is definitely screening me. In fact, she was turning the tables on me. As a hitchhiker, I had become practiced in the art of getting someone, anyone, to talk about his favorite topic, invariably, himself. Now, I was doing the talking and she was doing the interviewing.

I understood her need to know more about me, so I played along. "Actually, the jeans were pretty new in Hungary. I started sewing patches on them myself the next summer back in the States when I took a motorcycle trip around the West." I pointed to the leather patch above my right knee. "I remember sewing this one on myself in a campground beside Jenny Lake in Grand Teton National Park in Wyoming. As you can see, this was one of my first attempts with needle and thread."

Danny ran her fingertips over my stitches. "What made you take a motorcycle trip? Were you on your own?"

"I saw the movie *Easy Rider*. Ever see that movie?"

She looked up and into my eyes. "No, but I know it's about some drug dealers on motorcycles that get killed by some bad guys."

"They're not drug dealers. They're free spirits off to see the world and they get murdered by rednecks who don't like hippies."

"What's a redneck?"

"It's somebody who gets so mad his neck turns red."

"Mad about what?"

"Mad about all the social change of the sixties. They don't like women and blacks trying to be equal. And they don't like men growing their hair long and burning their draft cards."

Danny thought about the explanation for a moment. "So, you wanted to be a free spirit on your motorcycle?"

"Exactly, and I wanted to see the USA. When I was in Austria people asked me about places in America that I realized I had never seen."

Danny seemed satisfied with my rationale and returned her attention to my jeans. "I'll bet Chucha is a girlfriend and she sewed her name on herself. She looks like quite a seamstress." We laughed, but I didn't like the direction this line of inquiry was taking as she continued. "Oh and look. Linda has her own unique style. Stand up so I can see your other conquests."

"No, no, no," I protested. "It's not like that at all. These women are friends, not conquests. I've had men work on these jeans as well. And anyway, you're not getting in my pants that easily. I will put up a fight, you know."

"Oh, all right," she relented, amused by my conversational deflection. "I don't need to pry. It sounds like you've been quite the traveler, though."

Our good natured and intoxicated banter went on smoothly as we began feeling quite comfortable in each other's company. The unspoken question was whether she would get off the plane in Lisbon with me or fly on to Madrid. I learned enough about her work and love life to know she was in serious emotional trouble, perhaps on the edge of a breakdown. By that point it didn't matter. Danny had me on the hook like the smell of hamburger transported Wimpy in the Popeye cartoons.

She looked so peaceful when she closed her eyes. Even her breathing was sensual. I was fool enough to think that all she really needed was a little time with me.

Before it seemed possible, the rising sun began shooting golden rays through the clouds and into the plane. At first, this seemed confusing but then it dawned on me . . . we were speeding east, back into six hours of time zone change. It would be morning when we touched down in Lisbon.

The light intensified and began blasting orange and red into an electric armada of giant, cumulus nimbus clouds. The plane began its long descent. I took Danny's hand. She squeezed back gently. Suddenly, the thought of facing the Portuguese morning without her seemed unthinkable. The muscles in my lower back began to tense up.

How did six hours fly by so quickly? How had the world turned so much in such a short flight? Why am I so afraid to lose her?

The plane touched down and taxied to a stop on the tarmac. The seatbelt lights blinked off and the crew lowered a metal stairway to the ground. Danny got up with me and held my hand as we walked toward the door. *Is she going to say goodbye?*

Scott the steward grinned knowingly as Danny grabbed her two mid-sized suitcases from a crew closet and handed them to me. She was getting off the plane! I hadn't known until that instant whether she was coming with me or not.

"Have fun, you two," Scott called after us as we walked carefully down the steps. We turned around at the bottom and posed for his imaginary camera. In that moment we were ambassadors of love, lightheaded and tender to the touch.

We turned and headed off for customs, arm in arm, walking at least a foot off the tarmac. "You're sure I can trust you?" she asked with mock seriousness.

"I'll let you call my mother, if you want."

"That won't be necessary." She giggled, threw her arms around me, and kissed me hard on the lips. We were both caught up in the joyous prospect of a journey together. "Good morning, Portugal!" I shouted in triumph. "Bring on the bearded sailors in wooden sailing ships with soldiers in shining breastplates with long lances so we can conquer the natives." Danny squealed in delight at the bravado.

Customs quickly brought us down to earth. Danny was impressed and I was relieved when my backpack arrived on the baggage cart. The red, waterproof pack was loaded with four changes of clothes, a sleeping bag, cook kit, hatchet, flashlight, canteen, a zip-leather Bible, writing materials, and a black leather jacket. A two-man mountain tent was strapped to the top along with a nineteen-inch machete my father had brought me from Costa Rica.

"Wow," Danny observed, "you are ready for anything. Is that a machete I see?"

"You never know when you might need a little protection," I assured her.

"Oh my God," she said, "I'm going to end up in little pieces in some olive orchard."

Thankfully, neither my gear nor the weapon seriously concerned her. Even more thankfully, customs officials didn't search her purse as we glided through the checkpoint and got our passports stamped. My baggage didn't generate any interest or concern. They'd seen plenty of backpacks come through. They didn't even search me. Huge blade? No problem. Keep moving.

Danny did a quick money exchange and hailed a cab like the seasoned traveler she was. Before I knew what was going on, we were careening into Lisbon at a high rate of speed down cobblestone streets lined with palm trees and white stucco houses with dull-orange tile roofs. My head was spinning with new smells and the cacophony of a coastal city waking up. Danny rolled down her window and let her hair blow in the breeze. My skin tingled with appreciation and anticipation. *The woman knows how to live.*

Our driver was hairy and wiry and drove like a wild man. He darted in and out of dense traffic, narrowly missing little cars and leaning, canvas-topped lorries making their morning deliveries.

"I hope we make it to the hotel alive," Danny joked. "We want to go to the Paris Hotel," she told the driver. "Do you understand? The Paris Hotel?" He nodded happily and continued trying to win whatever race he thought he was running.

"The Paris Hotel." She spoke excitedly to me. "It's right on the ocean, but not too expensive. It's on a perfect beach in Estoril, a suburb west of Lisbon. The man at the money exchange told me all about it." I started to tell her I didn't have money for a hotel, but she waved me off as if money would be no concern.

The driver kept taking insane risks, bombing through intersections, his eyes as wide as the rearview mirror. We actually covered our eyes on several occasions, convinced a collision was inevitable. The driver cackled with glee and mumbled something reassuring in Portuguese. We were too high and tired and shaken up to do anything but give him the international thumbs-up sign.

Eventually, he screeched to a proud halt in front of a tall, eighteenth-century building with two-story marble pillars at the entry and men in white tuxedos helping us with our luggage. Danny paid for the cab and the room and a silver tray of meat and cheeses with two bottles of wine, which were delivered soon after we entered the room. "Don't worry about money," she said, sensing my unease. "This is too much fun. I've got money for both of us."

The fourth-story room had a small balcony with a magnificent view of a rocky bay on the Atlantic Ocean. Fishing boats bobbed on the sun-sparkled waves that rolled in with a low roar. Only a few blue umbrellas dotted the white sand beach. A gentle breeze blew back the silk curtains from the open glass doors to the balcony.

The room itself seemed a hundred years old: Persian rugs on wooden floors, a carved-wood antique dresser with glass handles, and a four-foot mirror on a swivel. The four-post bed piled high with pillows and comforters dominated the space. The bathroom had a clawfoot tub, a bidet, and a blue and white tiled floor.

"I feel like I've died and gone to heaven," I said as I exhaled a triumphant breath of salty air and took a seat on the balcony.

"We have," Danny purred into my ear as she sat on my lap. We kissed slowly and passionately. Our heads were spinning with the dizzying combination of lust and no sleep. I unbuttoned her top and began slowly kissing my way down her neck to her breasts. Amazingly, I hadn't noticed until that moment how full they were. She moaned her approval and arched her back. When I came up for air, she grabbed my head with both hands, then pulled me up to kiss her on the lips again. "I liked it when you kissed me like that on the plane," she whispered. "Do you like it too?"

As I was nodding my glazed approval she jumped up and ran into the room. I heard a commotion around the bed and wondered what she was up to. Then the front end of the mattress came tumbling out the doorway. She had me help her wrestle it out to stuff it flat on the balcony. Then she disappeared again, calling back, "Open up a bottle of wine."

I was pouring the wine when she came bouncing back out onto the balcony in nothing but flesh-colored panties to flop down on the mattress with a wonderful groan, rolling over on her back and holding up outstretched arms to the world. "Oh, God, I need some sun!"

Her nearly naked body was perfectly feminine. Her ankles were thin, her hips full but not broad, her breasts round and buoyant, her shoulders square but not muscular and her neck long and graceful. I took off all my clothes quickly and lowered myself lightly, so the full length of our skins barely touched. Every hair on our bodies instantly electrified. Her skin felt hot.

She was relieved to feel a gentle touch and pleased when I lay down beside her to say, "You are absolutely beautiful." She could feel my excitement.

"I hope we're not putting on too much of a show," she wondered aloud. "Not that I care at this point." I sensed this was a rare moment of expansion for Danny, something about this marvelous adventure made her feel so free, so confessional—she had opened several layers of emotional curtains to reveal herself to me.

"Don't worry." I kissed her ear. "No one can see us up here. This is the perfect love nest."

She was ready for everything, but I backed off, careful not to go too fast, and poured two glasses of wine. "I propose a toast to Portugal and all its promise of love and adventure."

"Here, here," she toasted, drinking nearly half her glass in one long pull. "This is so crazy. I love it. You make me feel happy. But what am I doing? I don't even know you."

"Yes, you do. We've known each other forever. I knew that the first time I saw you." She waited for more. "We probably know everything there is to know about a person when we first make contact. It's an intuitive thing. Our energy connects and we feel everything there is to feel without even knowing it. You know what I mean?"

Danny answered with an amazed smile. She was lost in the moment. "This place is so peaceful," she murmured. "It makes me feel like I'm taking a bath in the morning with nothing to do all day. And the sun. Feel how perfect? Look how it sparkles the wine." She held up her glass. "It's like liquid ruby." She looked deeply into my eyes. Without a blink, we were inside each other, looking through ourselves into infinite reflections of facing mirrors.

She rolled over on her stomach and I straddled her to rub her back. Her skin was soft. I stroked it lightly for a moment then let my fingers work their way into her muscles. "You're a little tight," I observed.

"Ooh, loosen me up," she cooed. "I need a deep massage."

"Portugal loves you," I said as I worked her entire body.

"Portugal loves us both," she said as she rolled onto her back and pulled me down to kiss her.

We made love to the rhythm of the ocean.

Once we came up for air, we turned cheek-to-cheek to gaze at the endless vista, each of us amazed at how quickly we had fallen for the other. The water was immensely calming and reassuring. Everything was right with the world. Danny bit my ear gently. We collapsed back on the balcony mattress. She felt like forever.

The sun beat down on our heaving bodies and beating hearts and lubricated skins. We felt like Bonnie and Clyde after a successful bank heist. Against all odds, we had gotten away with all the joy life has to offer.

Love is the perfect crime.

We passed out into a deep, exhausted sleep. Fortunately, the massive overhang on the hotel roof shaded us from the sun or we would have been burned to a crisp in the hours that we slept.

I woke up as the sun dropped lower on the horizon. It took a few moments to remember where I was. I heard Danny in the bathroom.

What an amazing turn of events. Twenty-four hours earlier, I had been totally alone and on standby in the Montreal airport, wondering if I'd even make the plane. Now, here I was with a commanding view of the Atlantic Ocean, in partnership with a gorgeous and intelligent French-Canadian woman. *Is this just luck or is the world opening up its secret treasures?*

I put on my jeans and stood up to survey the harbor. It was now filled with boats of all sizes. A deep breath brought about an "I wish my friends could see me now" moment. The ocean air was intoxicating and revitalizing. I was hungry and thirsty and only slightly hung over. Danny saw me reflecting and called out to me. "Let's go eat, I'm famished."

We showered and smoked a joint and watched the sun sizzle fabulously into the ocean, painting the horizon shades of red. Lights on the boats and on the shore were beginning to twinkle.

The walk to dinner was a twilight kaleidoscope of color and sound. Tile roofs glowed their last orange as the Portuguese moon rose like an eerie cartoon. Bicycles clattered on streets of stone, small cars with loud mufflers honked their horns, children squealed, and transistor radios blew tinny noises through red and green woven curtains and open windows of working-class apartments. We walked hand in hand for half an hour, away from the beach and into the night. It was fun to be together and off on such a romantic adventure. Fun until it was dark, and we were lost.

Danny was becoming uneasy on the dark side streets of Estoril. Poverty was a short walk from the high-priced, tourist side of town. We picked up the pace and set a course for the umbrella of light in the distance that illuminated the beach area. It didn't take long to return to the main drag. We decided to bypass the larger restaurants to avoid the tourist trap and chose one on a side street with the best music coming out.

We ducked under an awning and opened a tall wooden door to discover what was obviously a popular hangout. The locals stared at us curiously but seemed friendly enough. The waiter was welcoming and showed us to a table for two in the corner with a candle. No sooner did we sit down than we were engulfed in Fado music, Portuguese for "fate," folk songs about sailors and the sea and their wives left at home. The roiling melodies smacked us in the face like waves bursting over the bow, even though we couldn't understand the words. Two male musicians were singing, one playing a classical guitar, the other a large, round mandolin. They had the place jumping. The crowd sang along on the choruses and, every now and then, one of the patrons would jump up and sing lead. One song got the whole place dancing in a circle. Danny and I got up and did our best. She was beaming.

"I never would be here without you," she shouted over the celebration.

"Nor I without you," I yelled as I hugged her close enough to hear me. Our hearts were pounding for each other as we became one with the circle of dancers.

The band took a break and we sat down to try to order from a Portuguese menu. "How many escudos in a dollar?" I wondered, obviously concerned about prices.

"I think twenty-six," Danny answered. "But look, these prices aren't that bad. We can get a good meal for five dollars. A very good meal, as a matter of fact. Double that for the wine we're going to be drinking and we can get out of here for ten dollars each."

"Danny," I began slowly, "we're going to have to talk about money. As in, I don't have much and it's got to last me for a long time."

"I told you at the hotel not to worry about money. I've got enough for both of us and I don't have a lot of time to spend it. Besides, you're my tour guide and my sexual guru." She saw me stiffen and quickly continued, "No, no. I'm not saying you're my gigolo. I'm just saying I happen to have enough money for both of us. And I like the way you touch me."

Just then the waiter was serving a huge platter of shrimp to the table next to us. "Doesn't that look good?" She was obviously changing the topic and I didn't mind. She got the waiter's attention and managed to communicate to him in French that we wanted what he had just served. He nodded and left to put our order in.

When dinner arrived, I was horrified. My plate was overlapped with monsters from the deep. They still had heads on with long antennae and black, beady eyes and claws and tails. They were prawns, not shrimp. Up until that point, the only shrimp I'd ever eaten came curled up in cute little embryos without so much as a tail, served in a neat little row at the country club buffet. I'd never had to perform a full autopsy to get at my seafood. In fact, I had no idea where or how to begin.

Danny laughed playfully at my dilemma as she took charge of my plate like a fisherman and turned the creatures into something I could eat. The food was spicy and Mediterranean, crusty breads, and vegetables in olive oil. We ate heartily as the wine kept coming. We didn't get a chance to talk much once the string duo came back and got the crowd involved again with their performance. The music was melancholy and smoothly Mediterranean.

After several spirited songs, a woman the crowd seemed to know well got up to sing a solo. Everybody at the tables around us stood up as she draped a black shawl around her shoulders and began singing a beautiful song of lovelorn tragedy. Danny and I were spellbound by the woman's command of the emotional ballad, as were our fellow diners. I took Danny's hand as the singer wove her melodic web of a sad tale. Even the waiters remained motionless as she ended the song on her knees with her head on the floor. I looked at Danny. Tears were rolling down her cheeks. I felt my own tears welling. The sadness of the world was personalized by the woman's performance. The singer stood up to take a bow, and the room erupted from silence into a standing

ovation.Once we'd finished dinner and the musicians took another
break, Danny paid the bill with her credit card and waved off my offer
to contribute. I couldn't remember a more perfect dining experience.
Walking back to the hotel along the beach, she slipped into a pensive
mood. The moon was bright, and the waves were white capped as they
pounded out a deep rhythm on the shore. "You're lucky to be so free,"
she offered almost absentmindedly. "I wonder what it would be like to
not have any responsibilities. Or even to just be happy. What a freedom that would be."

I didn't respond. She needed to complete her thought. "That woman had me all the way when she was singing. She made sadness sound
so beautiful. I cried with her on that song. Everybody did. It felt good
to cry. But I've been crying too much lately. It hasn't felt good. I've
been feeling trapped and empty and wondering what's the point. Then
I meet you and, suddenly, it feels like life might be worth living. It
makes me think I need to break free from my life like you have."

I took her hand. We kept walking. I wanted to tell her the truth
about myself, but I couldn't do it. Besides, I didn't know what the truth
about me was going to turn out to be. I was anything but free.

"You know," I said, "Ever since I started out on this trip the most
amazing stuff has been happening. Things that never would have happened if I hadn't hit the road."

"Things like what?"

"Like a couple weeks after graduation from college I was in a
bookstore in Monterey, California, when I met John Lennon."

Danny stopped us both in our tracks. "Oh, come on."

"No, really. Swear to God. I was thumbing through a book of Ra-
phael prints in a bookstore. He was squatting down, looking at books
on a low shelf. The profile was unmistakable. It was John Lennon. I
couldn't believe it. I had to turn back to the art book, not knowing
what to do. I knew I'd never get another chance like this. There was no
one else in the store."

"Oh my God," Danny squealed. "This really happened! What did you do?"

"I took a deep breath and turned around and walked over to introduce myself. I said, 'Excuse me, are you John Lennon?' He looked up at me a little warily, so I quickly followed with, 'I just wanted to say I've really admired your work all these years.'"

"And then?" Danny was wide-eyed.

"That's when it happened."

"What happened?"

"He stood up."

"And?"

I held my right hand up a little below my shoulder. "And he was short. He was maybe five foot ten tops. I'm six three and the top of his head barely made it to my shoulders. My hero was shorter and smaller than me. He seemed almost frail."

She began walking down the beach again. "Oh, so this is some kind of guy thing."

"No, it was more than that. Once he stood up, he was nice, even friendly. He said, 'Well, if that's how you feel, then I'm definitely John Lennon.' He held out his hand. His handshake was firm. He said he was looking for books on radical politics, particularly on the history of communism. Well, that stuff is right down my alley. I majored in political science and studied socialism and communism in Hungary. So, there I was, advising John Lennon on leftist literature. I advised him to bear down on the Marx and hold the Mao."

"No, you didn't say that," Danny laughed.

"Okay, no, I didn't say that," I confessed. "I wished later on that I'd said something witty like that, but I didn't. Then Yoko came up and wanted to know what happened to all her cigarettes. Lennon looked at me like any henpecked husband and grinned."

"Was she just a total bitch?"

"No, not really. She was being good-natured about the whole thing.

They were probably tired from traveling but they were still having fun. The interesting thing was Lennon was hungry for knowledge. It made me realize that nobody really knows what's going on. Not even John Lennon. Meeting him was strangely liberating."

"What do you mean?"

I slowed slightly to formulate my thoughts. "I mean when you meet your hero and he's just another human being, it makes you realize you've got to be your own hero. You've got to write your own script. You can't rely on anyone but yourself. You start making the most of your life and paying attention to the people you meet because you know they have something to teach you or you wouldn't be meeting them."

"Hmm," Danny mused. "What do you think I have to teach you?"

She had been mostly quiet for the walk along the beach, letting me do the talking. Now, it was time to reassure her. I took both her hands in mine and pulled her close to kiss her softly on the lips, then the cheek, then the forehead. "You're teaching me that love is all around us and all we have to do is tap into it and the world is a wonderful place." I hugged her and lifted her feet off the sand. "You're reminding me that all you need is love, as John Lennon would say."

We laughed and walked back to the hotel where we stripped each other naked and slipped beneath crisp linens that smelled like the ocean. The waves pounded rhythmically on the rocks below.

"Just hold me," Danny sighed.

The next thing we knew, a brilliant coastal morning was blasting light through the balcony doors. Danny had awakened before me. Her eyes were shining in the sun as her head rested on the pillow. "Yesterday was perfect for me. I slept like a lamb. Your arm was around me and I could feel your skin all over me. It's been a long time since someone held me. I mean, held me gently. Do I feel good to hold?"

I kissed her on the nose. "You feel like velvet. We fit together perfectly. I don't think we rolled over once. Of course, the four bottles of wine might have something to do with that."

"Why are men so awful?" she asked suddenly.

"I don't think all of us are."

"I don't mean you." She squirmed. "I mean most men. They don't seem to understand women. All they care about is themselves . . . and being in control."

"Don't you think you're over generalizing?"

Danny sat up and adjusted the pillow behind her back so she could lean against the headboard of the bed. "No, it's not just me. Most of the women I know feel the same way. The men in their lives are like chores that need to be done. My friend, Janice, tells me that men are a necessary evil. Women need them for protection and money. Their men treat them like prostitutes, or slaves, depending on what they need at the moment." Her tone was low and bitter. She was glowering.

"Danny, what's this frustration I see on your forehead?" I rubbed the furrow in her brow. "How can you be sad on a morning like this? You haven't had time to get up on the wrong side of the bed."

She lightened up a bit. "At least I didn't have the nightmares last night."

"Nightmares? What kind of nightmares?" I waited a long time for an answer. The embroidered curtains on the balcony doors were gently waving their see-through reflections in the mirror. They billowed like nightgown sails on a ghost-pirate ship. Their motion was seductive. They made me think I might be dreaming. My mind wandered in the breeze until Danny broke the silence.

"I can't talk about my dreams. They are too terrible. The men in them are always chasing me or doing mean things to me or forcing me into cold, dark places. It all started when Arnold was hurting me and locking me in the closet."

I sat straight up in bed. "Locked you in the closet? That's criminal. And the dreams. I mean the nightmares. You know you can get help for this sort of thing."

"Oh, right. That's the American answer for everything. Pay somebody to listen to your problems and they're supposed to go away. What a joke. Besides, I've tried that, and it doesn't work. I'm just hoping that getting away from him will make the dreams go away. He never thought I could leave him. He laughed when I moved out. He said I'd be back. Then he started harassing me at work and at my new apartment. I called the police so many times they started not believing me. One night he tried to run me over with his car. Thank God somebody saw that and told the police and they arrested him. That's why I'm here."

She got out of bed and went to the bathroom. I braced myself for a rocky return. Instead, she emerged in a purple string bikini and said, "Let's hit the beach." She looked like a famous model, ready for a photo shoot.

We left Estoril after two blissful days. Danny rented a two-door Renault and we headed south for Torremolinos, Spain, a city romanticized in *The Drifters*.

It didn't take long for the glow of our new romance to wear thin in the cramped quarters of the little car. The two-lane, cracked blacktop road was winding down the windswept, mountainous coast of Portugal through orchards of red, elephant-skinned cork trees and vast, rolling grape and olive vineyards. The scenery was breathtakingly beautiful, but the driving was difficult. The road was a roller coaster.

Danny insisted on doing all the driving since she had paid for the car and listed herself as the only driver for insurance purposes. Money was obviously going to be an issue for her, no matter what she said initially.

For my part, I hated not being able to contribute any more than the occasional meal, having been taught how important it is in life to pay your own way. It also drove me crazy not being able to drive. I'd been king of the road since turning sixteen. Danny was not a very smooth driver, and I wasn't very good at keeping my mouth shut about it.

After our first day on the road we camped in a remote area among rows of small trees in an attempt to avoid being kicked off the land for trespassing. I set up the tent and made a fire from olive branches, hoping to make peace between us. Danny was impressed when I whipped out my cook kit and fried up a campfire stew of sausage, onions, and beans I'd purchased that afternoon in a wooden-floored grocery store filled with scales and bags of foodstuffs. It tasted better than the restaurant food she'd been paying for recently.

"I'm sorry I've been such a bitch today," she said quietly. Indeed, she'd been complaining about her back and her stomach most of the day, and she'd been getting inordinately upset every time my knee got in the way of the stick shift. Even so, her tired apology melted me.

"No need to apologize," I said. "It's tough driving a four speed all day when you're used to an automatic. And I guess I'm a pretty bad back seat driver even when I'm in the front seat."

She smiled weakly. "I remember when I was a little girl, the darkness frightened me so. I guess it still does. It's kind of mysterious out here. I mean, the stars are brilliant and bright, but you never know when somebody's going to come out of those trees with a gun and . . ."

"Hey, hey," I put my arm around her. "There's nobody out there. We're in the middle of nowhere. The last fishing village we passed was twenty kilometers ago. There's not even a farmhouse anywhere near here."

"What about the fire?"

"Don't worry. We're in a valley. Believe me, I know how to pick a secret campsite."

"What about the smoke?"

"Well, look at the smoke. See how peaceful it is? There's no wind. It rises up slowly to disappear into the stars. Watch the fire and the smoke and the stars and, before you know it, you won't be afraid anymore."

"That's some good advice." She used a twig from the fire to light another cigarette. She'd smoked nearly two packs that day as she went on and on about how stressful her job had become. She was having trouble unwinding but the fire seemed to be doing the trick at last. "I don't feel afraid when I'm with you. You amaze me. Here you are with no money and no job and no place to go and not one thing in the world seems to bother you. I envy that so much."

I put a few sticks onto the fire. "Well, actually, I do have some place to go."

Her head snapped to face me. "I knew it. I knew you weren't telling me everything. Hah! I thought so. Everybody has some place to go. So where is it you have to be?"

I played with the fire before answering, not pleased with having to give myself away. I finally answered with a sigh, "I've got to be in Debrecen, Hungary, by July 22nd."

"July 22nd? That's what, twenty days from today? How are you going to get there? That's a long way from here. And Hungary? That's behind the Iron Curtain. What do you think you're going to do? Just walk through the Berlin Wall? People get shot for that!"

"I've got a visa already and I won't be going through Berlin."

"I don't care what kind of paperwork you've got." She sounded seriously concerned. "The only way into the Soviet Bloc is to fly and even then, it's almost impossible. I know lots of people who get detained at the airport and then sent home. Important people who own companies. Unbelievable! It's 1972, the Cold War is still going strong, and you think you're going to thumb a ride into Communist Hungary, and everything will be fine. What are you doing in Hungary anyway?"

I looked up at the stars. "I'm the United States representative at an international youth work-study camp."

Danny was dumbfounded. "A what?"

"An international youth work-study." Her mouth fell open and her eyes were wide with astonishment, so I explained. "It's about forty students from all over the world who live at the dorms in the university in Debrecen for about a month and work on a collective farm. It's a program to promote international understanding."

"How did you possibly get into this thing?"

"When I was in Hungary during college, I made some friends in Budapest and they told me about the camp, and I applied and got appointed.

"I'm the only American going. There are people from Poland and Ecuador and Italy and all over. It should be a blast."

"If you ever get there."

"Oh, I'll get there all right. You know me."

"Well, apparently I don't know you as well as I thought I did. Now I know you're absolutely crazy." She pushed me down on the tarp I'd spread between the fire and the tent. "You're a spy, aren't you? Go ahead, you can tell me. You're a secret agent. Kind of a James Bond type without the car or the gun."

We laughed and smoked a joint and made love slowly and passionately. The night was warm. The fire danced on the trees and the tent. The stars grew brighter as the fire faded. We fell asleep on our backs looking up, only to be awakened by the chill as the fire burned down to embers. I put the tarp in the tent and threw the sleeping bag over us. We used our jackets for pillows.

The next morning Danny woke up in a wretched mood. Her back hurt from sleeping on the ground. Her stomach hurt from too much sausage and wine and bottled water. Worst of all, she had to take a crap and there wasn't a toilet within ten kilometers. Somehow, she hadn't looked far enough down the camping trail to realize this moment was bound to come. I handed her a couple paper napkins from my short supply.

Danny started cursing in French and stomped off to disappear into the orchard. Many minutes later she reappeared, looking immensely relieved but with a new sense of resolve.

"See, that wasn't so bad, was it?"

"Take me to a hotel," she said firmly. "I need a shower and a bath and a bed and a breakfast."

We ended up driving to Albufeiro, mostly in silence, where Danny paid for an expensive room. Our partnership for the road was clearly in jeopardy. The original plan was for her to pay for the car and I would provide food and lodging by cooking over a campfire and setting up camp. One night of outdoor living had been enough for Danny.

She remained curious and somewhat suspicious about my wild and free lifestyle. She kept asking if there was something I wasn't telling her. In fact, the more time we spent together, the more I was feeling like a fraud for not telling her the truth about myself. She kept quizzing me about my past and plans for the future as we explored Portugal. Somehow, at dinner on our fifth night together, while I was complaining about the prices, she boxed me into a confessional corner.

"You say you've only got $250 left and that money has to last you for eight months?" she cross-examined. I nodded reluctantly, realizing my mistake. "What happens in eight months?" she demanded.

"I don't know," I lied.

"Oh, yes, you do know," she bore down. "You said it like something definite was going to happen. So, what is it?" I tried to change the topic or ignore her altogether, but she was not having any of it. She waited for an answer.

"Danny," I hung my head and decided to come clean, "I'm not the man I pretend to be."

"Why have you been pretending?"

"That's a good question," I answered. "I've been realizing through knowing you that I'm embarrassed to tell you what I really am."

"So, what are you?" She waited for an answer.

"In eight months, I report to jet school for the United States Air Force. I'm actually a second lieutenant in the Air Force. I'm what they call a pilot candidate."

Danny remained silent until I looked up. "I don't believe it." She crossed her arms defiantly.

"Well you can believe it," I assured her. "I got my officer's commission the day I graduated from college. In fact, the Air Force gave me a full ride through college on an ROTC scholarship."

"What is this ROTC?"

"Reserve Officer Training Corps. You go to college like everybody else, but you also take military classes so when you graduate, you're an officer. I went to basic training the summer after my sophomore year and did airborne jump school for my senior winter term project. I earned my jump wings and my private pilot's license during senior year. After graduation they offered eight months leave if you signed up for it before you had to report to flight school. I signed up and here I am. I've got orders in my pack to report February 20, 1973, to Vance Air Force Base in Oklahoma."

She listened in stunned silence as the truth of my situation sunk in. On one hand she was impressed and somewhat relieved to find out I might be a man of some professional substance after all. On the other hand, she felt deceived.

"So, you're not the carefree, free-love hippie you pretend to be?"

"I don't know about that." I shrugged.

"You lied to me," she accused. "Why did you lie?"

"Wait a minute," I protested. "I never lied to you. Everything I've told you is true. I just haven't told you everything."

"Why not?"

That was a fair and good question. One that deserved an answer I hadn't formulated as yet. "I guess it's because I want to be free," I began awkwardly. "I know I shouldn't go back to the Air Force. Over the past few years I've developed strong anti-war feelings. What we're doing in Vietnam is so wrong I can't stand it. It's a senseless slaughter. I don't think I can be part of it anymore. I used to go to the peace demonstrations in my uniform until they created a rule that said you couldn't do that. I tried to quit after my summer motorcycle trip before my senior year, but they talked me out of it. For one, I saw the flight suit and I knew I had to learn to fly. Flying jets has been a dream of mine since as long as I can remember. For another, I wanted to keep the scholarship."

Seeing me searching through my confusion softened Danny. "Why don't you just quit?"

I drained my wine glass. "You don't just quit the United States Air Force, especially after they've paid for your last three years of college. The deal is I owe them six years of active duty after graduation. That's the commitment you sign up for when you accept the scholarship. If you don't report for active duty on time, they declare you AWOL and throw you in jail."

"What's AWOL?"

"Absent without leave."

"They've got funny little names for everything, don't they?"

"Yes, and they've got a funny little name for me if I don't go back."

"What's that?"

"Deserter."

"What happens to deserters?"

"They get shot."

Danny gasped and then recovered. "Or you could go to Canada. Isn't that where all the deserters are going?"

"I'm not going to desert my country."

She poured me another glass of wine. "Then what are you going to do?"

"I don't know yet. I'll just keep traveling. I've got some time before I have to make my decision."

Danny thought for a moment. She was an intelligent person. Nothing slipped by her unnoticed. "So, you're telling me you're going to hitchhike through the Iron Curtain into Hungary with your United States military papers in your backpack?"

"How did you know I had my orders in my pack?"

"You just told me."

I took a big gulp of wine and smiled recklessly. "I guess I better hope they don't search me, huh?"

Danny didn't respond to my cavalier attitude. Instead, she observed thoughtfully, "I think I know the real reason you haven't told me about yourself. I think you're ashamed of being in the Air Force and I think you're ashamed of what they want you to do in Vietnam."

It took some time for her assertion to sink in, but I eventually had to admit, even to myself, that she was exactly right. "You're probably right," I said glumly.

Admitting my shame, even to myself, afforded no relief. It felt like a hundred pounds of guilt had been thrown onto the load I had been carrying around. Less than a month earlier, in June of 1972, I had received my commission as an officer. Shortly thereafter, I hit the road. Maybe I was running away. Maybe I was off to find a reason to resign my commission. I had a sinking feeling in the pit of my stomach that I would eventually return home and serve my time in the Air Force. I'd tried to quit in college but ended up staying in for the scholarship money and my dreams of flying.

The years 1968 through 1972 had been a tough time to wear a military uniform on campus. Even at DePauw University in Greencastle, Indiana, I'd joined most of my friends in becoming at least part-time hippies. We became progressively more anti-war as the nation erupted into near civil war over the Vietnam "conflict." Shocking news footage had been coming into our homes since high school. By 1968 and the Tet Offensive, the evidence was becoming clear that the Viet Cong were fighting for their country's independence and that the United States was the foreign aggressor. Once the draft became a birthday-lottery system that wiped out exemptions for college kids, it wasn't just poor kids going off to die for their country. The Baby Boomers took to the streets to protest the injustice and the mounting death toll.

It wasn't all about politics. By 1969, the lines had blurred between the sexual revolution and the anti-war movement. The counterculture was trying to change everything. Going to the demonstration was the best party ever. It was drugs, sex, radical politics and rock and roll all mixed into one giant Happening.

Being in the military part time with all this social upheaval going on left me wondering which side I was really on. I tried to explain to Danny, "During my sophomore year, two of my friends blew themselves up while burning down the ROTC building at DePauw. They threw gasoline all over the place and then stood right next to it while they lit the match. They survived the explosion but not without horrible injuries. One guy is still in a wheelchair. People thought I was involved, but I wasn't. At that point I was still trying to change the system from within. But part of me admired what they were trying to do, even though they didn't accomplish a thing in the end."

Danny kept listening. I was trying to sort things out in my mind.

"The worst part of being in ROTC during that time was having to keep your hair trimmed short. After the Beatles and the Rolling Stones, long hair became the ultimate badge of hipness. For four long years, except for my semester abroad, I had to abide by short hair regulations. Now here I am, a long hair at last, on extended leave from having to explain how I can be in the Air Force and still be against the war. The last thing I need is you bringing me back down to the ugly reality of my situation. Unless I do something drastic, I'll soon be dropping bombs on people I don't even know for reasons I totally reject."

Danny waited for me to continue. Suddenly, I felt a glimmer of hope rising from deep within me. It was an epiphany rolled up in a revelation. It was the perfect way to untie my inner knots. I looked at her and said, "I'm not going to do it. I'm not dropping bombs for anybody. The war is wrong. It's genocide. I won't be a part of it anymore. I'm quitting!"

It felt good to say it. It was cathartic. It was like walking out of prison after years of confinement. How many times had I defended my Air Force involvement while secretly wondering if I believed in what I was saying? How many times had I told my hippie friends that the Cold War was a sad reality and even if Vietnam was wrong, we still needed a strong military? Now all that could be over. I could finally take the high moral ground. I could do and say what I believed in instead of living like other people wanted me to live. I felt a rush of goodwill in my bloodstream.

Danny hugged me as if she'd orchestrated my escape from Alcatraz. "You can't do what you don't believe in."

My sense of triumph did not last long. I'd had these moments of decision before. They had an insidious way of unraveling into indecision. How could I forget marching into the captain's office after my summer motorcycle journey and announcing I was quitting the military? That decision lasted about forty-eight hours. My firm resolve melted when they issued me a flight suit.

Firm resolve is a fat man declaring war on ice cream.

The next day Danny finally agreed to let me drive. She could defer to an officer and a gentleman. It was good for her to give up control. She had been exhausting herself, trying to make things go her way.

We rolled into Spain and the long beaches of Torremolinos. In between naps, Danny was making good progress reading *The Drifters*.

Even so, she seemed to be slipping back into an angry, self-centered depression.

"You know, this book is nothing like reality," she commented that night in the hotel room she'd rented. "This town is a giant tourist trap. The book makes it sound like a quaint fishing village. This place is nothing but a bunch of high-rise buildings and expensive shops. Nobody meets anybody here. They all just spend their money."

She was right. All the romance James Michener poured into Torremolinos was long gone by the time Danny and I got there. Likewise, the romance between the two of us was fading fast. We'd been together less than a week, but we were quarreling like a couple that had been married too long. Each of us was getting in the way of the other's need for alone time.

When I suggested we simply sleep on the beach, she responded nastily, "We can't do that, you idiot. They'll kick us off and arrest us."

That did it. Getting called an idiot was more than I was willing to tolerate. Even so, the anger brought things into perspective. *Maybe I am using her. Maybe it's time to get back on the road by myself.*

"Danny," I said sternly. "We can't go on like this. It's time for me to go."

She looked at me like she thought I couldn't mean what I was saying.

"All I'm asking is one last favor." I tried to sound conciliatory. "Take me to the edge of town and drop me off somewhere I can camp for the night."

Danny watched in stunned silence as I packed up in less than two minutes. Neither one of us said a word as we got in the car and rode through the jangle of the downtown carnival and into the darkness of a road winding up a mountain. The Renault was a funeral procession of one. We kept turning onto smaller and smaller roads until we reached a vast, open field that looked like it stretched out forever. The road had turned to gravel several miles earlier. We passed through two sets of tall, metal gates that appeared to be open for no good reason. I began to wonder why there was no development in such a large, empty region so close to the city.

Danny stopped the car and turned it off. We both got out. She was crying as she opened the trunk. "I'm not going to beg you to stay with me," she said. "But something's not right about this place. There are no signs or lights anywhere around."

I pulled my pack out of the car and looked around. She was right. The place was spooky quiet and dark. There wasn't even an insect to be heard. I thought I saw movement out of the corner of my right eye. I turned my head quickly but saw nothing. My eyes had not quite adjusted to the darkness.

"Maybe I should turn the car on," Danny said.

"Don't be silly," I said, shouldering my pack. "You know, Danny ..." I started to say when we both heard a twig snap like something quite large had just stepped on it.

"There's people out there," Danny said as she moved to get back in the car.

Before she could open the door, soldiers in full combat gear materialized out of the darkness and surrounded us, shouting Spanish commands and pointing their automatic weapons at us. We had been much too busy with our tearful goodbye to notice their stealthy maneuvering.

I instinctively put my hands in the air and began shouting the only Spanish I thought would help: "*Amigos, amigos!*" Danny followed suit and raised her arms in surrender. Our hearts were pounding. It felt like our bodies were about to be riddled with bullets in a thunderous barrage.

"*Touristas!*" I almost begged as the circle tightened around us. A camouflaged commando of obvious rank broke through the ring of soldiers and approached us in exhilarated exasperation. He ordered the men to shoulder their weapons and said something in Spanish that made them laugh. I realized how foolish Danny and I must have looked to them. The officer ordered me to take off my pack and demanded to see our passports. We produced them with shaking hands. I began to think we might make it out alive, even if we had to do some jail time. We had obviously stumbled into some sort of military installation.

The commando looked us over carefully with his flashlight. He knew enough English to communicate we were in the middle of an artillery range. By morning I would have been target practice. He saw the tears in Danny's eyes. He must have thought she was terrified and that we were simply looking for a romantic hideaway. He made another comment about me that made the men laugh again. He was making fun of my pack. Or maybe the fact that he had an American hippie standing at full, military attention.

I could see that he was ready to have some fun with us. Then his radio went off, and he was apparently being ordered to move his men on to where they were supposed to be. Amazingly, he simply ordered us to get back in the car and leave the premises.

We left in a hurry and tried to retrace our route back to town.

It was Danny who spoke first. "Did that just happen?"

I pounded the passenger side dashboard with both hands.

"Man, I thought it was all over!" We both began to laugh in nervous relief. Then Danny stated the obvious, "The gods aren't quite finished with us."

Back at Danny's hotel room it was too late in the evening and too late in the relationship for make-up sex. We did cuddle up in the same bed, grateful that our relationship had been saved by military intervention.

The next morning, we backtracked west a bit to the smaller town of Fuengirola, which, although well on its way to becoming another Torremolinas, still had a little of its original flavor left. The beach was less littered, fewer empty Coke bottles floating in the water and on the sand. We found a place called The Sugar Shack with lots of young people from all over the world, the latest rock music, and beer for fifteen cents a mug. An Italian guy with a tan and some great hashish started hitting on Danny. She flirted back and made sure I noticed.

The party raged on most of the day and into the night at an old villa in the mountains. The place was so jammed we had to park a quarter mile away and walk. Everyone was ragingly high, smoking and drinking. There was probably cocaine and heroin around somewhere, but I wasn't really looking to find it. French girls and Swedish girls and girls from who knows where were stripping down to dance on the veranda. The night was hot. It didn't matter where you were from, anyone under thirty was welcome. Rich Brits jammed on guitars with vagabonds from South America. Young kids in beads and leather partied with decorator-dressed people who looked like they just stepped out of fashion magazines. World peace had arrived, and we were right in the middle of it.

Expatriates from North America and Europe had lots of advice for us regarding Spain. Mostly, it was to stay away from the large coastal cities and watch out for the Guardia Civil, the powerful Spanish police that seemed to be everywhere. They were everywhere but at certain parties on the beaches and in the mountains. Somebody had to be getting paid off.

Several men told me to forget about hitchhiking in Spain. It was impossible to get a ride because it was illegal. Arrests were common. I resolved then and there to continue my journey through Spain by train.

It was after 3 a.m. when Danny managed to drive us back down the mountain. I had her drop me off at a cheap campsite and she went off to find a hotel room. By now, we both realized we had opposite traveling styles.

I woke up around noon, incredibly lonely. Being alone can make you feel invisible. People walking on the beach seem to look right through you. For a day and a half, I wandered and wondered why I missed her so much. It was a little bit of a shock, being alone again after such an intense romance.

Then, I found a note with her new address clipped to my tent. I broke camp and decided to pay her a visit before walking out of town. Danny had rented a fancy beach house for a month and let me know she'd already met an interesting man. We talked awkwardly for half an hour and thanked each other for everything, managing to laugh a little. At least those soldiers on the artillery range had kept us from parting on angry terms. Finally, I hugged her and said goodbye and walked away. I thought I'd never see her again.

Over my shoulder I heard her say, "Good luck," like she knew I was going to need it.

I felt like turning around to tell her she was the one who would be needing the luck. But I kept walking. I was still in shock from the spontaneous combustion of our romance. I couldn't shake the nagging notion that she had taught me a valuable lesson. The only thing I knew for sure was it felt good to be on my own again.

CHAPTER TWO

Malaga to Vienna

LESS THAN AN HOUR AFTER I left Danny, a blond American woman in a red convertible picked me up. I wasn't even trying to hitch a ride. I was walking along the side of the road, feeling sad and lonely, when she pulled up beside me and motioned for me to jump in the car. Without thinking about what I might be getting into this time, I threw my pack in the back and slid into the passenger seat.

"Hey," she said loudly enough to be heard over the noises of the street, "you look like you could use a ride. Where you headed?"

"The train station," I shouted as she pulled out into traffic with a squeal of her tires while shaking my hand firmly at the same time.

"I'm Anna," she shouted. "Who are you?"

I introduced myself and, after a few more questions from her, told her I was headed east to Hungary.

My mind was so dead set on my destination I decided to tell her about it right away. This singleness of purpose, combined with my unusual itinerary, seemed to get her attention and pique her curiosity. It didn't take her long to size me up and decide I was worthy of her time and talents. She was looking for a party. I told her I had a train to catch.

Undaunted, she offered to take me to the train station. "It's a beautiful day for a drive," she gushed. "The best train station is in Malaga, about twenty kilometers from here. I'll take you all the way." Her crazy driving made me wonder if we'd make it that far. We sped up the Spanish coast with the wind blowing in our hair, feeling just a little bit like movie stars.

Anna proceeded to give me a guided tour of the coast all the way to the train station, which would have taken me days to find on my own with no transportation. She was quite knowledgeable about the area and obviously more of a resident than a tourist. I didn't ask her much about herself. I didn't want to know. I was still processing how quickly Danny was shrinking in my rearview mirror. The ten days I'd spent with her had changed me in ways I did not yet understand. It was hard to believe she was gone. It was even harder to believe that a new woman could be taking her place. I wasn't ready for another lover, but I was grateful for the amazing ride.

When we got out of the car at the train station, I could see Anna was almost six feet tall and weighed at least 150 pounds. She wasn't fat; she was a large, attractive woman in her mid-thirties. She wasn't about to drop me off and say goodbye. This woman was prepared to be much more than helpful.

Fortunately, she was fluent in Spanish and only too happy to help me purchase the cheapest train ticket available to Genoa. I thanked her profusely.

Since I had two hours before the train departed, she took me to a nearby bistro where she ordered an expensive bottle of red wine. She was on hiatus between what sounded like high-level marketing jobs and seemed intrigued by my plans to travel by hitchhiking and camping.

"You know," she said halfway through the bottle. "You don't have to be off in such a hurry. I've got a marvelous place on the beach. It's just a girlfriend and me. We could play for a couple days and then you could go."

We looked in each other's eyes for a deep moment. She was delightful, not a wicked bone in her body. Who could blame her for wanting to have a little fun? Only a fool would turn her down.

"I can't stay," I said as she wet her lips with the wine. "I've got two weeks to be in Debrecen. That's in Hungary and that's a long way from here. I've got no idea how long it will take me to get there. After this train ride, I'll be hitchhiking the rest of the way. I can't afford trains."

"You don't have to worry about money," she said coyly. "I can help if you want."

"No, you've already done more than enough for me," I said, determined not to get involved. It was beginning to occur to me that women were becoming much more forward these days, particularly in tourist areas.

In the early days of Women's Liberation, every day was Sadie Hawkins Day for some women. It wasn't just me getting picked up by strange women. Every man was fair game.

"So, what about Hungary?" she asked, unwilling to take no for an answer. "Why are you in such a hurry to get to Hungary? Isn't that country on the wrong side of the Cold War?"

Her direct approach was hard not to like. We ended up talking about how profoundly Hungary had changed my worldview when I'd studied there as 1970 turned into 1971. "It was my first time out of the USA and, suddenly, I was partying and talking politics with the brightest students in Budapest. By day I was reading Hegel and Feuerbach and Karl Marx and Vladimir Lenin's book, *Imperialism: The Highest Stage of Capitalism.* By night I was arguing that democracy was working in the US and that the anti-war movement would soon end the Vietnam War.

"But the big thing I learned in Hungary," I concluded, "was that communists are not the enemy at all. They're just crazy kids like me trying to figure out their place in the world."

Anna nodded and ordered another bottle of wine. She had an

MBA from Yale University, so she eagerly kept up when we talked about society's economic evolution, according to Karl Marx, from feudalism to capitalism to socialism to communism.

"So, you're a communist?" she asked dreamily, taking my hand in hers. She was shameless. We were both getting a little drunk. I thought about having her drive me all the way to Austria but quickly dismissed the notion. I didn't need another thrill ride.

"No, I'm not a communist," I said, "but I don't think people should be so afraid of a word they don't understand. Communism is about the state owning the means of production instead of private capitalists having all the power."

"That's right," she said. "The United States left capitalism behind when they passed the legislation to stop the monopolies of the robber barons like Vanderbilt in railroads and Roosevelt in oil and Carnegie in steel. Those guys treated workers like slaves."

"And when you consider the New Deal and Social Security and how many jobs come from government," I reasoned, "the United States is already evolving into socialism."

"Don't say that too loud." She laughed, moving in to kiss me. Her only purpose with this conversation was to get next to me.

I took her hand off mine and told her it was time to go. She kissed me anyway, warmly and wetly on the lips. "You know, you can still change your mind about coming home with me."

She tasted delicious as I backed out of her embrace. "I know we'd have a blast, but I really do have to keep moving."

I never told her I was an Air Force officer, wandering and wondering what to do about my military obligation. That would have fired up the conversation to the point of no return. Instead, I picked up my pack, thanked her with a hug, and trudged off for the train. She looked like a fisherwoman who had just lost her fish. I felt like that same fish, just off the hook.

I knew there would be many lonely days ahead when I would deeply regret this moment of purposeful self-discipline.

The train ride to Genoa was a gruesome two-day ordeal. The train zigzagged to stop in every single town, picking up more passengers at every station. I soon found out that one of the reasons my ticket had been so inexpensive was that I had no assigned or reserved seat. There were lots of longhaired backpackers on board and most of us were crammed into the aisle outside the more expensive private compartments. At first, morale was high. We were all off to see the world, and the Spanish landscape was rolling by like a never-ending movie. Then it got dark and there was no place to sleep or eat or drink. A sign in the tiny restroom had a drinking cup with a line through it, which obviously meant "Don't drink the water."

Around 10 p.m. the first night, I was leaning out the window to watch the stars when a young American woman came crashing out of her cabin door and grabbed my arm with a wild look in her eyes. "You've got to come to our cabin and help. You've got to come right now! He's going to rape my friend and me. He wouldn't let me go!" I saw a man duck his head back in the compartment from which the frightened woman had fled. I let her push me into the cabin ahead of her.

Inside I found not one but two men sitting on a bench seat and looking guilty. They lowered their heads and wouldn't look at me. Across from them was a second American woman pulling her shirt back on and pointing her finger accusingly at the offenders. She was shaking all over and sobbing hard without making a sound.

"Out!" I screamed at the men as I grabbed one by his coat collar and lifted him off the seat. The Spanish men were much smaller than me but there were two of them. Neither seemed ready or willing to fight. They looked like evil twins. Each had greasy hair, a rumpled suit, and a thin mustache under a large nose. They were intoxicated and wide-eyed, terrified to be confronted so suddenly by a large, crazy man with wild hair and a booming voice. I started yelling for the police as they scrambled for their bags and fled the cabin.

The two women, who turned out to be college students from Illinois, started crying in relief and hugging me in gratitude. Neither one of them was twenty-one yet. They looked like women, but they were really still children. Deborah and Julie told the story of how the men started drinking some kind of alcohol from a metal flask and became progressively more forward with them until their behavior became nothing short of criminal. Julie had torn clothing and scratch marks on her skin to prove it. Without warning or any time to think about my instinctive action, I had become their hero. I quickly resolved not to take unfair advantage of my newfound status, but it was impossible not to bask in glory, deserved or not.

Once we all settled down from the shock of the confrontation, I grabbed my pack and moved into their cabin. Deborah made me promise to spend the night with them in case the drunken Spaniards returned. *What unbelievable luck.* I had enough of a seat to stretch out and sleep. The women had food and bottled water.

"Don't worry," I assured them, "those guys won't be back."

"How can you be so sure?" they asked in unison.

"They're probably six cars away by now and ready to get off at the next station," I reasoned. "They think they're being chased by the police. They know what they did was wrong."

Julie was not convinced. "But they're drunk, and they paid for their seats."

I grabbed her by the shoulders and looked her in the eye. "Did you see the look in their eyes when they ran away? Those guys aren't coming back. And if they do, they'll be sorry they did."

Deborah noticed the machete strapped to my tent by the fold-over top of my pack and gasped. "What's that for?"

I pulled it from the pack and unsheathed it. "Oh, it's just a deterrent. I've never had to use it."

Julie took the machete from me by the handle. "But you would use it if you had to."

I squinted hard and stuck out my chin. "Absolutely." I'd never stabbed anybody with anything, but I needed to project confidence. These two were still pretty shaken up.

We talked into the night as they fed me well and even produced a bottle of wine as they felt more comfortable. It had become brutally apparent to them that it was foolish for women to travel unaccompanied by a man in southern Spain, or probably anywhere in Europe. Even before the incident, they had decided to cut their summer vacation short and fly home early.

Strange, how the Women's Liberation movement is getting ahead of itself, I thought. *Liberated women from North America are marching themselves into harm's way in Europe like Napoleon marched too far into the Russian winter.*

"Chauvinistic men from Spain and Italy think American women are easy," Deborah said. "Most of what they know about the USA comes straight out of *Playboy* magazine. Their macho come-ons are absolutely ruthless. We can't even say hello without causing ourselves a lot of trouble."

Suddenly, there was a loud knocking. Deborah and Julie grabbed each other in fear as I got up to answer the door. *Could it be the drunks returning to claim their seats? Maybe they've forgotten something? Maybe they have reinforcements? Maybe they have a gun?* I thought about grabbing my machete, but instead opened the door a crack to see who it was.

It was a uniformed conductor. He pushed his way into the cabin, not at all amused by the cozy little party we were having. "Tickets," he demanded.

Julie tried to explain how I had saved her from sexual assault and deserved to stay in the compartment since the men had fled. The conductor wasn't having any of it. It was late and his English was as poor as our Spanish. Not only did he kick me out, he promised to throw all three of us off the train if he caught me trying to sneak back into the private compartment.

I departed as graciously as possible and went out into the aisle to stumble over bodies to the back of the car. There was no place left to sit. At the end of each car, between the outside of the car and the coupling to the next car was a small metal floor with a railing around it to keep one from plunging to the tracks below and certain death. It was noisy and cold and no place to take a nap, but there was room enough for two or three people. Quite a comedown from my previous co-ed digs. I kept thinking about sneaking back in with the Illinois women but decided not to jeopardize their ride.

For the rest of the night, fellow passengers occasionally joined me on my dangerous perch. They were looking to escape the smoke-filled stench of the crowded train. I talked to a schoolteacher from Des Moines, Iowa; an artist from Scarsdale, New York; and people speaking languages I couldn't identify. Everybody wanted to chat the sleepless night away. The topic was always about how slow and awful the train was. One guy kept working on a saying. "The train in Spain stays mainly in the pain," he began. Not bad. Needed some work. Finally, we came up with "The train in Spain is painful on the brain."

By morning the train was getting less crowded. I found a spot on the floor inside the car near the restroom and dozed off. It must have been almost noon when I woke up to the smell of vomit and diarrhea. I had to move down the aisle to keep from getting sick myself. I knocked on the cabin door for the Illinois women, hoping to score some breakfast. No one answered. I opened the door and peeked in.

Deborah and Julie were gone. I felt betrayed. *They forgot me. Maybe they looked for me to say goodbye and couldn't find me.*

The conductor entered the car. I shut the door and took my place in the aisle. He glared at me as he squeezed by. He didn't need to check my ticket. He knew who I was. He locked the cabin door and the train rolled on. It didn't seem right, me on the floor with an empty cabin so near.

My indignation didn't last long. Hunger and thirst began to take over. How could they have no food or beverages on a train? Probably no one was traveling as far as Italy. It was mainly short hops. Not for me. I was in it for the long haul and I was going to have to do something to stave off basic starvation. After a couple hours, I developed a plan and put it to the test shortly thereafter.

Since the train was remaining at each town for nearly ten minutes, I eventually jumped off when it stopped and bought a loaf of bread, some cheese, and a couple bottles of water. I'd left my pack on the train in the restroom. It was still there when I jumped back on the train as it was pulling away from the station. I'd been watching closely as I waited in the short line at the food stand. I wasn't going to let it get away. My whole life was in that backpack, most importantly my passport and what little money I had left, $210 USD.

After an incredibly long stop-and-go day, I changed trains in Barcelona. There were sixty-four backpackers in the station. I counted each of them. We were like an invading army, tired and dirty and in various stages of missing the comforts of home.

The second night was not much better than the first, although the train was quite a bit cleaner. The hypnotic effect of the rattling tracks was mind numbing. I kept nodding off, and it seemed we were stopping less frequently. We made much better time through France, but it didn't matter. I felt like a rat in a trap. At several stops, I almost left the train but kept deciding to ride out my fare. Finally, arriving in Genoa much the worse for wear, I got off and determined to never again pay for a ride or step foot on another train. I should have known better.

I walked through the historic trading port, marveling at the ancient Roman, Baroque, and Gothic architecture of the city's many incarnations. It was early afternoon and I was starting to feel lost and lonely. I had a deep feeling in my bowels like needing to go, but not having to go. I began to get short of breath and panicky. I found the best way to fight it was to breathe deep and sing a little. Then it went away.

Genoa felt like a maze with no way out. I knew I wanted to head for Milan, but there were no signs to direct me. I sat down to gather my thoughts and courage when I remembered that Genoa's favorite son is Christopher Columbus. Now, there was an explorer to inspire any weary traveler. *He always looks so confident and courageous. I'll bet he had his moments of doubt and shame. I'm sure he felt totally lost on many an occasion. If he could discover the new world, I guess I can find the road to Milan.* No matter that at his death Columbus remained convinced his many voyages had ended in Asia. He was still at the top of my all-time adventurers list.

I walked on with renewed vigor and determination. The narrow streets of Genoa were jammed with crazy drivers and nobody was stopping to pick up a hitchhiker. I kept walking north and away from the lure of the Italian Riviera until I found a road sign for Milan.

I had walked at least five kilometers to get to the outskirts of the city when the road narrowed to pass through a small tunnel in the side of a mountain. There was no way to walk through it. If a wide truck came along when I was in the tunnel, I would be squashed. I sat down on a massive boulder to contemplate this tactical problem and play some harmonica. Nothing beats the lonesome wail of a harmonica when life starts feeling like the end of the road. Not that I was any good on the harp at that point. I was just learning. Waiting for a ride gave me plenty of time to suck and blow. It's just the kind of deep breathing you need to keep your courage up. The road was teaching me how to play. The spirit of John Lennon was on my side.

After more than an hour, a motorcycle screeched to a skidding halt at the tunnel's entrance. Actually, it was a little Italian scooter. The driver had realized my predicament and stopped to help. Traffic was fast approaching so I didn't hesitate when he pointed to the back half of his leopard-skin seat. Pack on my back, I jumped on the bike and off we buzz-roared through the tunnel.

His helmet was red, white, and blue with a coon tail hanging from the back, kind of a cross between *Easy Rider* and Daniel Boone. We didn't have to speak for me to know he was both a fan and a victim of American cinema. No wonder he would stop to help a hitchhiker. He shouted something over his shoulder, and I shouted back, but neither one of us understood the other.

There were no foot pegs on the scooter for a passenger, so I had to hold my legs out in front of me and hang on tight. The wind whistling through my hair felt wild and wonderful. My first ride in Italy! The mountainous countryside sprawled into spectacular vistas of purple and green and blue. The villages we passed were snuggled into the foot of the mountains like little toy towns. Distant mountain peaks towered over the valleys like ancient palaces of the gods.

Despite the breathtaking scenery, it didn't take long for my legs to start getting tired and weak. I shifted position and hung in there as best I could.

The driver had the unnerving habit of passing vehicles in front of us even when traffic was coming the other way. The scooter with the two of us aboard wasn't very fast unless we were going downhill, at which point the driver became an absolute Kamikaze pilot. We were nearly flying down one steep incline when we started zooming in on an old fruit lorry riding his brakes in front of us. I could see cars coming up toward us but there was no way we could stop or even slow down. We were going to shoot the gap between the lorry and oncoming traffic. Nothing I could do but pull my legs in, shut my eyes, and pray this crazy Italian had a guardian angel.

It must have been apples I smelled as we barely missed the left rear corner of the truck. Horns were honking and I think the scooter driver and I might have been screaming as we threaded the needle and sped off down the road. The adrenaline rush made me forget my sore legs and back for a short while, but soon I couldn't take it anymore.

I had hung on for nearly sixty kilometers when I finally had to motion for the driver to stop. My thigh muscles were cramping up. He pulled over and I got off and collapsed in the grass to stretch. He seemed ready to wait for me to get my legs back, but I waved goodbye and flashed him the peace sign. He signed me back as he sped off with his coonskin tail flying in the wind. Not a word had been spoken between us, but I knew he got a big kick out of scaring the crap out of me. After all, I had to admit I always had fun scaring people on the back of my motorcycle.

I waited about an hour before a well-dressed Italian man in an Alfa Romeo Spider picked me up. He made the scooter driver look tame. His roadster was fast and took corners with astounding agility. Neither of us spoke the other's language, but we shouted and laughed a lot as he raced to Milan. He stopped to buy us sandwiches and beer at a gas station. We used sign language to communicate fairly effectively. Italy was turning out to be downright friendly, if a little on the dangerous side. When he dropped me off in the center of Milan, it was getting dark. He thought he was doing me a favor, but the center of a city is the last place a hitchhiker wants to be. Nobody picks you up in the city.

So, I had to walk out of Milan to get to the road I hoped would take me to Vienna, which would put me in position to try to get through the Iron Curtain to Budapest. But since Milan is in the center of roads in concentric circles, I walked several miles only to find myself pretty much back where I started. Tired and hungry, I decided to spring for a meal in a restaurant.

Walking into the cheapest looking eatery I could find, I was greeted by two rugged men at a table near the door who seemed to be making fun of me in Italian. Rather than take offense, I walked over to them, smiled, shook their hands and said, *"Ich ben Mark. Sprechen sie Deutsch?"*

This friendly gesture took them totally by surprise and melted any animosity they might have felt toward the backpacking hippie. They'd seen plenty of us hitchhiking on the side of the road but never had a chance to actually talk to any of us. Somewhat embarrassed by their yokel attitude, they invited me to join their table and ended up buying me dinner and wine and several shots of Schnapps. My German ran out about as fast as theirs did, so we were left with sign language. I stretched my arms out to show them I was tired and rubbed my fingers together and shook my head to show them I had no money and stuck my right index finger through a circle made by my left thumb and index figure to show them I was ready to get laid. We laughed a lot and communicated much better the more we drank. They started singing songs and nearby diners joined in. Before long, the whole place was having a party. The waitresses spoke a little English and joined in the fun, becoming more flirtatious as they joined in the drinking and grandiose toasting.

Once the festivities had laughed themselves out, I found out my two hosts were truck drivers on their way to Vienna.

This was too good to be true. My heart jumped into my throat. Probably their trucking company prohibited hitchhikers, but I let them know I needed a ride to Vienna by standing up and sticking my thumb out. I was so excited I was jumping up and down. The whole restaurant was watching and laughing as the truckers agreed to take me along. We toasted each other and Italy and the United States and Vienna and women and anything else we could think of until the last of the wine was gone. Next thing I knew I was strapping my pack onto the top of their canvas-covered trailer and on my way to Vienna, some 1,000 kilometers away. What was happening to me? It was like Italy herself had invited me to ride on her back.

The truck cab was a sleeper, so I rode shotgun while one man drove and the other was soon snoring in the bed behind me. The driver tuned in to a rock station and turned it up loud. Even that noise and the rumble of the engine couldn't drown out the smell of the sleeper's socks. Actually, all three of us were in desperate need of soap and water.

It started raining as we barreled down the road. I kept nodding off, but the driver must have needed company because he kept punching me awake and cracking jokes in Italian. Every time he woke me up, we were splashing walls of water through narrow streets in tiny, darkened towns. When we stopped for gas, I jumped out to check and make sure my pack was still strapped down tight.

We got some coffee and continued on into the rain-drenched night. The driver offered me a cigarette, and like a fool, I took it and smoked it. I'd quit smoking for most of my senior year in college and had been a sarcastic critic of smokers ever since. Why I chose that moment, or that moment chose me, to start smoking again, I can't say for sure. It was a way to communicate with the driver and express my deep gratitude for his hospitality. Maybe it was the late-night coffee. As I inhaled that first cigarette in nearly a year and watched the exhale blow out the crack in the window, I became dizzy with an emotion I seemed to be feeling and realizing for the first time. All of a sudden, I understood at a visceral level that personal decisions are never final and that my beliefs and ideals would continue changing as long as I lived. I kept smoking and wondering how long my life might last and what, exactly, I wanted to do with it. At that moment, quitting the Air Force and suffering the inevitable consequences felt like a long truck ride in the rain I didn't want to take.

I was jolted out of my reverie and back into reality by a dull thud that shook the truck from its undercarriage. The driver pulled over immediately and the three of us got out to get wet and inspect the damage. It was 2:30 a.m., and a road sign said we were 150 kilometers from Udine, wherever that was.

The two truckers got under their vehicle for a short time, and then rolled back out, shaking their heads. From what I could understand, the axle had broken. The truck would be going nowhere for a long time. They helped me get my pack down, and then climbed into their cab, holding their hands up as if to suggest I find another ride. Three people couldn't sleep in the cab. They apologized. I thanked them. We shook hands. The driver handed me his half pack of cigarettes and some matches as if to say, "Sorry it has to end like this."

I walked on down the road, stunned by the sudden turn of events. The road dropped steeply on the right and there was nothing but a rock wall on the left. I was in the mountains. There was no place to make camp and nothing to do but keep walking. Waves of loneliness and self-pity washed over me. My head was spinning in confusion and disbelief. Nothing changes faster than the fortunes of a hitchhiker. One minute you're in a cabin with two girls and a bottle of wine, the next you're riding the rail. One minute you're riding in a warm dry truck, the next you're walking in the rain.

I had to laugh at my frightening predicament. The road disappeared ahead and behind. There were no roadside markers to guide the way, only a faded centerline, mostly hidden by the rain. I started singing "Strawberry Fields Forever" by the Beatles and felt a little better. The voice of John Lennon in my mind soothed me but did not stop the rain. I was wet and exhausted.

A grand total of three cars passed by slowly as I walked a couple kilometers. At least their headlights illuminated the highway. It didn't take long for their taillights to disappear. The road was winding.

Then there were lights up ahead and along the highway. It turned out to be a small town that had closed for the night, hours earlier.

Mercifully, the rain had slowed to a drizzle, but I was still soaking wet and shivering from the cold. I took shelter under a storefront awning that had a two-foot wide slab of dry concrete in front of it. I unrolled my tent for a tarp, took off my wet clothes, and got into my sleeping bag.

What an incredible day it had been! It had taken me halfway through Italy. There'd been a month's worth of ups and downs. I felt achingly alive. I thought of my parents and three sisters at home in Fort Wayne, Indiana. The concrete started getting softer and softer. I drifted off into a deep sleep.

I got back on the highway the next morning and found myself surrounded by the towering majesty of the Italian Alps. The mountains looked like pillars of heaven as they disappeared into the clouds. *How had I not appreciated their massive presence last night even in the darkness and rain?*

Everyone seemed extremely friendly as I got picked up for one short ride after another. Several drivers pulled into roadside restaurants to buy food and drink, which they were only too happy to share. The road was narrow and winding. Progress was slow. Near the end of the day, I arrived in Tarvisio, a ski resort near the Austrian and Yugoslavian borders. Even in summer, the place was bustling with tourists. I pitched my tent in a lot next to a commercial chalet and bought a dinner of cold meat, cheese, dark bread, water, and wine from an inexpensive grocer nearby. The sun peeked through the clouds as it was going down and turned the snow-covered rock peaks red and gold with alpenglow. I would have had the perfect picnic if there'd been someone to share it.

Despite the loneliness, there was a certain exhilarating romance in the knowledge that no one in the world had any idea where I was. I felt a rush of pride fill my head as I realized how far I had come. For the first time since California it felt like I would actually make it, at least to the Hungarian border. Hitchhiking through the Iron Curtain still felt like a bit of a stretch.

I thought about going to a tavern but decided to watch the stars as they dazzled and dangled low like shimmering, frozen ornaments in the darkening sky. There was definitely something out there, or up there, that was a lot bigger and more important than me. What I did or didn't do with my little life wouldn't matter one bit in the larger scheme of things. So why was I so consumed with this sense of impending doom about my military commitment? *Why can't I lose myself in the stars?*

It occurred to me that I couldn't lose myself because I was thinking about myself too much, sitting on a tiny pity pot. The Air Force dream had turned into a nightmare the last several years. It had become a preoccupation. It had become living a lie. I took comfort in the fact that the road was beginning to show me the truth.

Clouds gradually blackened the night as if to say, "Answers aren't to be found in the stars." It started raining. I crawled into my $59 two-man mountain tent with the double roof and went to sleep, grateful I'd set it up earlier.

It rained hard most of the night and didn't stop raining for the next three days. The first day was relaxing. I finished *The Drifters* and left it on the bar at a tavern. No point carrying the extra weight. Besides, the book romanticized traveling to the point where nobody ever got tired or dirty, and I was both. The rain did give me time to write in my journal and mail off a couple articles to my hometown newspaper, *The Fort Wayne Journal-Gazette.*

I wanted to keep moving, but it's never a good idea to hitchhike in the rain. Mud puddles get splashed all over you and nobody wants to pick up a wet mess. I decided to wait out the rain and began to feel a little like the crowd at the Woodstock Music Festival chanting, "No rain. No rain. No rain." There can be no greater exercise in futility than trying to stop the rain.

I walked around the town and marveled at its Tyrolean architecture—stone foundations, wood-paneled porches with large ornamental eaves and flower boxes. The churches were marvelous, even in the rain. They rose up straight from the mountain slants like beacons of hope, their gold crosses wet and shiny.

By the second day the tent began to feel like Chinese water torture. I took refuge in a small tavern that had a jukebox with around twenty rock and roll selections and a ton of polka music. People were buying each other strong beer from the tap and generally trying to beat the relentless negativity of the rain. Nobody could climb or bike or hike or work in their gardens.

One Swiss woman who spoke good English sat down and wanted to talk about Vietnam once she confirmed I was an American. "We are all confused," she began. "We see the horrible jungle war and the napalm bombings on the news and then we see the American people marching in the streets to stop the war. How can this be? If the United States is for the people and the people are not for the war, how can the war keep going on so very, very long?"

"Unfortunately," I began carefully, "not all American people are against the war. Many think we have to fight in Vietnam to stop the spread of communism. They call it the Domino Theory, which means once one country falls it makes the neighboring country fall next. It's like the game of dominoes. Do you know the game?"

The woman waved her right hand dismissively. "Yes, of course. We play it. But it's a child's game, not a way to govern international relations."

"I couldn't have said it better." I laughed. She didn't.

The woman began bearing down on her point. "You know people in Switzerland and France and all over Europe think the United

States has gone military mad ever since it took over the world after World War II?"

I hung my head in sadness. "I'm afraid I have to agree with that assessment. But you have to understand the United States is almost in a civil war over Vietnam. It's really a clash of the generations. The anti-war movement is growing stronger every day among young people and even among older folks who have become disillusioned with the war. It won't take much longer for the youth movement to stop the war."

She lowered her face and raised her eyebrows. "You sound so confident."

"I wish I was" was all I could say.

We talked for a long time. I asked her if she'd like to take a walk, but she said she had to go home. She acted like I was trying to pick her up, but I was just looking for some company. I went back to my lonely Chinese water torture. The rain came down so hard it felt like the tent would collapse. Then it slowed to an unnerving drip, drip, drip, followed by more thunder and sheets of driving rain. I had plenty of time to think about how crazy I was to think I could hitchhike through the Iron Curtain as an officer in the US Air Force.

After three nights and two days of continuous rain, the sun finally came out. I happily packed my gear and hit the road, a little better prepared than previously. I had food and water in my pack and a sign that said "*Wien*," which is the proper, Austrian name for Vienna. I had to walk by many disgruntled hitchhikers on the outskirts of town who had obviously been out too long in the rain. I kept walking all the way through the Italian-Austrian border. Nobody picks up hitchhikers at border crossings.

The sun poured its pleasure onto forests of pine and spruce and bounced wildly off rushing streams of melted snow coming down from the rugged rock peaks. I felt strong and happy and grateful for the beautiful day. About a kilometer inside Austria, I found a large boulder and took a seat to practice the harmonica. At my level of expertise, it was best to practice when no one was nearby. Even so, I was beginning to think I might actually get the hang of the instrument one day.

I waved in a friendly gesture as cars passed by. I had learned it pays to be friendly when being passed because many people don't decide to stop until after they've seen the goodbye wave. Anyone can be nice when he's asking for something. Being nice after being passed by is the true measure of good nature.

Sure enough, after one such wave, a Volkswagen squealed to a halt. The driver's name was Gerhardt, and he took me all the way to Wien, a 370-kilometer ride. He was a family man, and from what I could understand with my limited German, he was quite happy to be married and raising children. He also liked to drink the full-bodied Austrian beer *Gosser*. He stopped frequently to buy us freshly chilled bottles. At one point he stopped at a shop to show me a six-foot-tall beer mug he promised to buy himself one day. The man loved his beer. I, for one, was delighted he had decided to let me into his life.

We drove all day through the unparalleled beauty of southern Austria's fairy-tale countryside. I half expected Hansel and Gretel to go skipping across the road. From a distance, the chalets seemed made of gingerbread. Every mountain had gentle, sloping fields at the bottom with livestock grazing contentedly. Perhaps it was the beer we drank that gave everything such a rosy glow. Every little town had a roundabout and every roundabout had a monument erected in memory of a plague or an aristocrat or a composer. Gerhardt pointed them all out and explained them enthusiastically and in much more detail than I could translate.

Eventually, the road became a major highway and Wien appeared as a bubble of illumination in the night. Gerhardt offered me a place to stay at his house since his wife and children were away on holiday. He would be joining them the following day.

His third-floor apartment was cozy but well-appointed. The best thing about it by far was the shower. I hadn't bathed properly in nearly a week. He seemed to know that as he handed me shampoo and soap and a towel. The water was hot, and the shampoo smelled delicious. *The longer the wait, the better the shower.*

The kindness of strangers had always amazed me in my hitchhiking career, which had begun at the tender age of fifteen around the lakes of northern Indiana. I got my very first ride from a drunk at 9:30 p.m. on a Friday night in June 1965. His driving was impaired to the point of being dangerous, but I didn't care. It was my entrance into the club of thumb—no initiation, no dues, and no pledges. From that point on, much of my life had been dedicated to the thrill of the free ride.

Gerhardt's hospitality was truly overwhelming. He invited a younger couple over that night to meet me, his new American friend. We ate sausage and cheese and drank beer and Italian champagne until two in the morning. The woman spoke pretty good English, so she became the center of conversation. She was anxious for news of the Women's Liberation Movement. Amazingly, we had each recently read Kate Millet's manifesto, *Sexual Politics.*

"Austria," she assured me, "is way behind the United States. The patriarchy is alive and well here. Our men are still very much in control."

I pointed both index fingers at her. "Or so they think."

She laughed out loud and then translated for the two men. They tried to be polite and laugh, but I could tell they didn't think this line of thinking one bit funny. Shortly thereafter, Gerhardt yawned and announced he had to be up at 6 a.m. We said goodnight, and I went off to sleep in one of the children's beds. It was surprisingly comfortable after so many nights on train floors and concrete and cold ground. As my head hit the pillow it occurred to me how fast the world was changing. Civil rights and women's rights and rock-and-roll sexuality and televised war and international peace movements and the drug culture and a man on the moon were all gathering into one giant tidal wave of social upheaval.

I was beginning to realize that people saw hitchhikers as social surfers. That was one reason they were so willing to talk to me. They were eager for news from the front lines of the social and sexual revolution. Many people who had settled for lives of relative security yearned for the freedom they saw in the modern vagabond. As a hitchhiker, I was only too happy to let them ride with me on my surfboard of adventure.

I took the Strassenbahn to the Volksgarten in the center of Wien. The leaves of castanea trees formed an arch over my head as I lay down on a comfortable, green park bench. Small patches of blue sky slipped through my shady roof to complement the colors of the artistically planted rainbow of roses that caught the corner of my eye. The fountains of the park hadn't been turned on yet, but many people were lounging on benches before going to work.

A pigeon landed with a flutter on the end of my bench. I closed my eyes then opened them when I heard the bird flying away. In the bird's place, staring at me with the same curious look the pigeon had been giving me, was an elderly woman. Something in the way she appeared to me as if out of a dream made me realize she had something to teach me. She pointed at my pack and smiled and asked me in German where I was going. She lit up when I told her I was headed for Budapest.

It didn't take long for her to realize her English was much better than my German. She took me to an outdoor café in the park and ordered us a big breakfast. "You must be hungry." She beamed.

"Ich habe grosse hunger," I said.

She laughed and continued in English, "I am from Budapest. I grew up there. You know it is actually two cities, Buda and Pest."

"Yes, I know. It's beautiful. I've been there."

"It used to be beautiful," she said with a frown, "until the Russians took over. It's terrible what they've done. My husband and I had to flee in the night after the Russian tanks crushed the 1956 Revolution. They were going to kill him for being a doctor. They said he was part of the uprising. Rest his soul. He's gone now. He died a free man here in Wien.

"We had to leave our car near the border and wade through water and crawl through the woods to make it out. I'll never forget that horrible night. One of the men who helped us was killed days later by the Soviets. Our daughter came with us, but our son stayed behind with his wife and two young children. I haven't seen my own grandchildren in sixteen years." She fought back the tears as she told her story.

Our food arrived. She gathered her emotions like a cloth napkin into her lap and asked, "What makes you think they will let you into the country?"

"I have a visa. It gives me the right to enter from July 22 to July 23. It also says I can stay for thirty days."

"Don't believe a word they say or even a word they put on paper," she said angrily. "They can't be trusted. They never could be trusted. They promise one thing and do another. You must be very careful at the border. They kill people at the border, you know."

"Yes, I know, but I'm going to a youth work-study camp in Debrecen. My friend did it last year. I'm sure I'll be all right."

She took the last sip from her coffee cup. "How did your friend get into the country?"

"He flew into Budapest."

She set the cup down in full cross-examination mode. "And how will you get in?"

"I'm going to hitchhike from Wien to Budapest."

She poured herself another cup of coffee and sighed deeply. "No one, to my knowledge, has ever done that. They might shoot you before you have a chance to show them your papers. You don't know what you're dealing with. This isn't some peace march in the United States. These are Soviet troops. They don't fire warning shots. I should know. My nephew was killed trying to cross the same border you're talking about."

She stared hard at me. I met her gaze, not unkindly. "I'm going to do it," I said after a long pause.

"I know you are." She softened. "I know you are. And I hope you succeed, and I hope that someday there will be no border. It's going to take people like you to allow me to see my grandchildren before I die. So, I wish you Godspeed. Here, have another cup of coffee. We'll drink to it."

She kissed me on both cheeks and paid for the check, despite my mild protest. We walked arm in arm for a little way in the park and then she said goodbye. "Good luck, Mark. I'll be praying for you."

I watched her walk away and wondered if I should pay attention to her warning. *No, this isn't 1956. Times have changed. The blue jean invasion has already penetrated the Soviet Bloc. Besides, I can't afford an airplane ticket.*

So, there I was, alone in Wien, city of my junior year abroad, capital of the Austro-Hapsburg Empire, home of The Opera, The Rathaus, Grinzing, the Ringstrasse, and Schoenbrun Palace. The home of Lipizzaner Stallions, Strauss, Mozart, and Freud.

Despite being surrounded by immeasurable culture, it felt like I was walking through a ghost town. Nothing had changed, but everything was different. Without the friends who had previously accompanied me, Wien was just another lonely city. I walked through the park and remembered the wild LSD trip we had taken two years earlier that had turned the place into a shimmering maze of magic.

I was with Monty and David, fellow students. We had scored six hits of acid in a funky bar near the *Pension Neuer Markt.* "Wild World" by Cat Stevens was playing on the jukebox. Little did we know how wild our world was about to become.

We decided to take two hits each since our previous drug scores in Wien had been less than satisfactory. We didn't know that each of the hits we had just scored was a three-way dose, meaning we'd each taken enough for six people. And it was quality stuff. By the time we walked to the Volksgarten, sidewalks were melting, cars were turning into bright trails of piercing light, and trees along the pathway seemed to be waving angrily. Our body rushes were breathtaking. We huddled together, realizing no one could help us regain our sanity. Our only hope and comfort was to stay close together and help each other out as best we could. We were beginning to fear we would never return to three-dimensional reality. I kept reminding Monty and David that we would come back down in time.

I'd become quite the psychedelic ranger my first two years in college. When Professor Timothy Leary said in 1966, "Turn on, tune in, and drop out," I'd been paying close attention. The drug culture hadn't been a very good fit with my officer training program. Still, I'd taken enough trips to know that this one would eventually end.

Somehow, we found our way out of the Volksgarten and back to our rooms at the pension. Taking the rickety metal elevator up to our floor felt like we were launching into outer space. We were so disoriented by the LSD that even lighting a cigarette was a challenging task of muscle memory.

By dawn we were floating down to consciousness levels approaching sanity. Our conversation became quite personal. Monty was urging me to follow his lead and become a conscientious objector. His CO status had been confirmed a year earlier.

"Look at yourself," Monty said. "You just went to heaven and hell and back. You're a drug-crazed hippie. There's no way you can be a pilot and go kill people in Vietnam. I know you know it's wrong, so why would you do it? It can't be for the money. You can make more money on your own than you can working for Uncle Sam."

"Yeah," David chimed in. "All a pilot is anyway is a truck driver in the sky. Why would you want to be a truck driver? Especially if it means being a baby killer."

Oh, how I hated that term "baby killer." It was popular in the anti-war movement, but it never seemed fair, especially when used to taunt troops returning home from tours of duty in Southeast Asia.

I was in no mood to argue. I knew they were both right.

That wild LSD trip was the first night I had seriously considered dropping out of the Air Force. Now, it all came back in living color as I wandered alone through the Volksgarten. *What had kept me from following my heart all this time? Was it the desire to please my parents with the scholarship? Was it my childhood dream to become a pilot? Was it all those war movies growing up? Was it my refusal to admit I'd made a mistake by joining up in the first place? Was it not knowing what I'd do if I changed life directions?*

It was all of the above.

I wandered around the city for a few hours until I found some fellow backpackers who turned me on to a bed in a youth hostel. I'd read about these places in magazines and in Frommer's *Europe on Five Dollars a Day*. I decided to try one out even though my budget was more like "Europe on One Dollar a Day."

The place was huge: beds for nearly one hundred persons, male and female dorms with clean hot showers. The main rule of the hostel was you had to be in by 10 p.m. to keep your bed. That evening I was involved in a Frisbee game that involved at least twenty-five travelers from more than a dozen countries.

Many of the Americans I met at the hostel and along the road had become disillusioned by the backpacking experience. It wasn't as glamorous as the travel articles portrayed it. Traveling is a rough life, a constant search for food, rides, a place to sleep, and money exchanges. Plus, there was a rising tide of anti-Americanism sweeping through Europe. The war in Vietnam had turned the United States into an international enemy of the people. Several Americans I met had sewn Canadian flags on their packs to avoid the "Ugly American" stigma.

I spent two more days wandering around Wien, mainly hanging out at fountains with fellow backpackers. I had to wait because my visa only allowed entry into Hungary during a two-day time period. Everyone who heard my travel plan thought I was crazy to try to walk into Hungary, visa or not. I got so tired of hearing the warnings that I stopped talking about it. Besides, I wasn't as paranoid as most about entering a communist country. I'd been there before.

On July 22, I set off to hitchhike through The Iron Curtain.

CHAPTER THREE

The Iron Curtain

THE NO-MAN'S LAND BETWEEN the borders of Austria and Hungary was flat and desolate. Miles and miles of haunting, vacant nothingness. No houses, no fields, no fences, not so much as a tree or even a telephone pole to break the bleak horizon.

There were no cows grazing along the road, no chickens trying to cross it. No sign of life except for the occasional bird. Birds that flew high and never seemed to land, as if they understood the evil below. The two-lane, blacktop highway slithered through the man-made desert like a poisonous snake in search of prey.

This was the twilight zone of the Cold War, the scorched-earth scar of an ideological collision that had been threatening for decades to plunge the planet into nuclear holocaust. It looked like the bombs had already been dropped. This was the saddest, most lonely highway in the world.

There was no chance to hitchhike. There were no cars. My last ride had done me a favor and driven me all the way to the Austrian border. He wished me well with a look of profound sympathy in his eyes. I watched his car disappear back into the west, then turned myself around and started walking toward Budapest.

How odd for this land to be deserted. This had been the battlefield crossroad of the Austro-Hapsburg Empire. This was once some of the most valuable real estate in the world. Invaders from Genghis Khan and the great Mongol Empire had been proud to conquer it. The Romans declared it part of their empire. How much blood had this turf soaked up since humans turned their tools into weapons?

The sun was high and shining hot as I trudged into the void of the terrible truce. The nuclear bi-polar balance of power had turned the land into a vast and vacant lot. What folly to think Wien and Budapest could be cut off from each other by some man-made barricade called the Iron Curtain. The Danube River had connected the cities to each other even before they became cities.

The more I walked and thought about where I was, the angrier I became. *I had nightmares of mushroom clouds and nuclear immolation back when I was still wearing pajamas with footies. We had drills in elementary school on what to do in case of nuclear attack. Even as children, we knew getting under our desk wouldn't do much to protect us. Families built bomb shelters and stocked them with canned goods. Anybody with a television knew the whole world was about to bomb itself back to the Stone Age.*

Now, here I was, personally confronted with the insanity of the doomsday scenario. I kept walking. The pack was getting heavy. I was sweating. My anger began turning to fear as it slowly dawned on me that I was walking right into the gates of man's inhumanity to man.

Perhaps I haven't passed the point of no return?

NO. There will be no turning back.

My boots kept putting one foot in front of the other. Left, left, left, right, left. I could almost hear the Army Airborne drill sergeant calling cadence during my time at Fort Benning, Georgia. He'd taught us how to keep walking even when we thought we were too tired to walk. He'd also singled me out one morning in a troop formation of 300 men.

"Smith!" he screamed, three inches from my face, spitting on me inadvertently. "Look at you. Some fancy ROTC boy down here from college. Look at your little mustache. Look at your sideburns. And look at the no shine on them boots. Boy, you violatin' just about every regulation I can think of. What you tryin' to be? Some kind of Mr. Different?"

At the time, I distinctly remember thinking, *Why yes, I am. That's exactly what I'm trying to be. Some kind of Mr. Different.*

All I said was, "No sir!"

"Oh, if he could only see me now," I mumbled to myself. "He'd see some kind of Mr. Different, all right. He'd probably say he was looking at some kind of Mr. Stupid."

I started singing a cadence we'd all learned in jump school. "C-130 going down the line. Airborne Daddy gonna take a little ride. If my chute don't open wide, I'll be in for one helluva ride."

Singing that little song helped pass the time and fight the fear as I kept walking.

I was beginning to feel a lot like when I was standing in the door of the C-130 Hercules transport plane, waiting to jump out into the sky with a parachute on my back. I was more than afraid. A strange tingling that originated in my gut sent electrical signals of apprehension up my spinal column that ended up as a distant ringing in my ears.

And then I jumped into the thin air, feet first and held together, chin tucked down to the reserve chute strapped to my chest. The wind feels like death itself is carrying you away. And then the chute opens, and you feel relief and gratitude like you never thought possible.

Now, as I walked toward the Iron Curtain, I wondered if it would turn out as well as parachuting had. I hoped I would land on my feet.

Walking directly into what was bound to be trouble gave me plenty of time and reason to contemplate my life so far. For some reason, I focused on my time at Fort Benning in January of 1972. Running in formation at dawn on ailing feet that became more painful every morning was only part of the experience. Living in the bachelor officer's quarters with Army officers who had done tours of duty in Vietnam was the real eye-opener.

These were the macho guys who loved to tell stories about their own combat heroics. The tales often ended in vivid images of slain enemy combatants. "Yeah, I blew his head off with a rocket," one captain bragged. "His body kept walking for a couple steps like it didn't even miss the head. Blood gushed out like a geyser from his neck hole until he finally fell in the swamp. The blood looked brown in the green water. We looked for his head but all we found were some brains in the branches."

Everybody at the table laughed at that story. I laughed too but wondered inside if these were people I really wanted to befriend. Their bravado seemed a cover-up for something I couldn't quite articulate. Something so horribly sad they could only make fun of it.

I kept walking toward the Iron Curtain. Searching the horizon with squinting eyes, I thought I could see some kind of fencing in the distance, but then the road dipped slightly, and I lost sight of whatever it was. My fear was beginning to melt into fatigue. My mind started wondering how much farther to the border. It occurred to me that even prisoners on death row probably get to the point of "Let's just get on with it."

I heard a vehicle approaching from the rear. I turned around in surprise. Yes! It was an automobile, a fellow human being. I took my pack off with a groan and stuck my thumb out even though the vehicle was too far away to appreciate the gesture. *What luck! Maybe I'm not on the moon after all.* I waved as what looked to be a Volvo sedan approached. It wasn't military. The male driver was the only person in the car. At close range I could see he was wearing a tie. I smiled and showed him the thumb.

He wouldn't even look at me. He stared straight ahead and actually sped up slightly as he passed by. Even at 55 miles per hour, I could feel his fear. His hands were on the steering wheel at the absolutely correct position of ten and two. His posture was erect. This guy didn't like where he was going any better than I did. I waved appreciatively as I caught him looking at me in his rear-view mirror.

Who could blame him for not picking me up? Anyone walking through this forbidden zone had to be nothing but trouble. If our roles were reversed, I might not pick him up. It's hard to say what you'd do in someone else's shoes. Maybe he wouldn't accept a ride from me. I had plenty of time to speculate on the stranger's identity and motivation as I watched his car disappear over the slight hill ahead.

Something about the way he wouldn't look at me made me want to check my papers. I sat down on the road. *Yes, my Hungarian visa is in the little black, plastic folder that holds my passport. But, yes, my orders for the United States Air Force are also there. That won't do.* I rolled them up and stuffed them into the bottom of my sleeping bag. *Why hadn't I thought of that way before now? Why do I feel the need to bring those orders along anyway? Appropriate to put them in the sleeping bag. They really are like a security blanket to me, something to show a jailor before he locks me up in some town whose name I can't pronounce.*

I thought about burning the orders. I had matches. *No one will see what little smoke that small fire would generate. They're only two pages, letter size. One quick little blaze and the problem is solved.*

I had good reason to burn those orders. Any thorough search at the border would easily reveal the contents of the sleeping bag. If the border guards found out I was an officer in the US Air Force, the visa wouldn't do me one bit of good. They'd throw me in jail, or worse. *Why do I need the orders anyway if I'm going to resign my commission?*

I searched the sky in the frustration of moral confusion. High above, a lonely bird soared in a lazy circle, looking for all the world like an American eagle. It made me feel proud and guilty at the same time. Proud because I loved my country, guilty because I hated what we were doing in Vietnam and around the world.

How corny can you get? That's no eagle. That's just some vulture wait-
ing for you to die on this never-ending road.

I took a long drink from my bottle of water and had some bread
and cheese. By now, I was sitting down and using the pack as a back-
rest. It felt good to take a load off. I played a little harmonica and marveled at how soulful the sound was becoming. I was actually getting
the hang of bending notes by changing the shape of my mouth and
tongue.

It takes a long hard road for a white boy to find the blues.

The asphalt was too hot to lounge on for long. I got up, shouldered
the pack, and resumed my eastward trek. I had decided not to burn
my orders. I just couldn't do it. My mind wasn't really made up on the
military issue. Besides, I knew the best approach would be to just relax
and let the visa work its magic.

I was no stranger to difficulties at borders. One foggy night in early June, I had walked across the Blue Water Bridge from Port Huron,
Michigan, to Canada. It was nine at night and I was tired and wet
when the border guard asked what I planned to do in Canada. When
I said I would be looking for work on a freighter, he asked to see my
work visa. When I couldn't produce one, he sent me packing back
across the bridge. That was a long, depressing walk.

Once I got to the wrong side of the bridge, I had a flash of inspiration that would certainly help me get into Canada. It dawned on
me that the night guard wouldn't be working tomorrow morning and
the day shift would have no way of knowing I'd been turned away the
night before. *All I have to do is sleep under the bridge and walk back over*
the next day.

I found a soft, cozy spot under the bridge and got a good night's
sleep. There was nobody else there except for a few rats that kept their
distance. It must have been close to noon when I made it back across
the bridge to the border station. The guard asked what I planned to do
in Canada, and I said, "Just travel around and be a tourist."

Without searching me, except to check my identification, the guard waved me into Canada. I had never felt so elated in my life. It was a complete victory, a triumph of the individual over his oppressive government. It was also a great lesson in how to deal with the bureaucracy.

If you can't get what you want, wait for a shift change and try again.

Unfortunately, there would be no second chances at the Iron Curtain. This was going to be a one-shot deal. I would be careful not to say anything foolish enough to keep me from gaining entry. I would let the visa do the talking for me.

I kept walking to the crest of a gradual hill and shielded my eyes to take a long look. Sure enough, there it was in the distance, at least two miles away: the Iron Curtain.

It wasn't a curtain at all and it wasn't made of iron. You could see right through it. It was towers at regular intervals, fifty yards between them. At first, the towers looked tiny, but as I got closer, I could tell they were about three stories tall. There was an armed guard atop each one. I couldn't hear the guards, but I could see them pointing at me and gesturing excitedly to each other. I resolved to keep my approach steady, not too fast and definitely no stopping.

No one was pointing a weapon at me, but I could see they were all taking their rifles off their shoulders and checking to make sure they were ready to fire. They were wearing brown uniforms with cloth caps, no helmets. The towers were makeshift; each had a slightly different lean. They were made of what appeared to be wood, painted battleship gray, and connected by a tall wire fence that seemed more and more impenetrable the closer I got.

I began singing softly to myself as I usually did when walking alone and feeling afraid. My song of the moment was "Revolution" by the Beatles. I was mainly humming the words. I didn't want anyone to see my lips moving. I kept seeing John Lennon flashing the peace sign during his bed-in with Yoko Ono. *I'll bet even Lennon wouldn't try to pull off an entrance like this.*

It was hard to remember being this scared. My mind hearkened back to my first solo flight in a Cessna 150 airplane. The Air Force had enrolled me in private pilot school at the beginning of my senior year in college. The lessons and the flight suit they issued kept me in the Air Force at that time, despite my growing misgivings. I put on that one-piece flight suit, jumped on my motorcycle, and sped to the airport three mornings a week. My instructor was a colorful guy named Tex. He always said he could hear me coming a mile away.

Tex was a civilian instructor, not military. Right from the beginning he had me flying the plane. I was a fast learner. It was great fun becoming comfortable with the rudder pedals and flap controls and steering wheel you could pull back on to go up or push in to go down. I loved flying as much as I always thought I would. Nothing could compare to that moment of lift off, when you felt yourself leaping into the sky. It was like being Superman. And the view got better the higher you flew. Tex got a kick out of introducing me to the thrill of flying.

One morning, barely eleven hours into our instruction, Tex said as we taxied onto the runway, "Well, looks like I'll get out now. You're ready to solo. Go ahead and take her up and land her. You'll do fine." With that, he exited the plane, leaving me alone with a propeller whirling and a runway staring me in the face.

"I'm not ready" was all I could say. Tex didn't hear me. He was already walking toward the office.

I decided not to hesitate and quickly began to accelerate for takeoff. I felt more than alone as the little plane got up to speed. There was no Tex by my side to save the day if I messed up. I became keenly aware that any major mistake could be my last.

And then I was flying solo for the first time. The fear turned to exhilaration as soon as I was in the air. I was free as a bird, earthbound no more. I waved the wings at Tex and climbed up to the right altitude to circle the field for landing. I flew around happily for a few minutes. That's when it hit me. I would be landing the plane all by myself for the first time. In my near panic before takeoff, I had forgotten that landing the plane is the hardest part.

Sweat was pouring from my brow as I went through the checklist for landing and made my final approach to the field. I slowed the airspeed and put the flaps down for extra lift. There was a pretty good crosswind from the east, so I had to point the plane in that direction to stay on a straight course with the runway. I eased her down and straightened out at the last moment to come down for a two-bounce landing. Again, the fear turned into exhilaration once it had been overcome with proper action.

Now, as I walked toward the dreaded communist border, I tried to remember that courage is not the absence of fear. Courage is continuing to function in the face of fear. I kept walking.

The soldiers were watching me through binoculars. I could see the lenses reflecting in the sun. They also scanned the horizon to make sure I was alone. What must they think of the lone approaching pedestrian with the fuzzy hair, the bright red backpack, and patches all over his jeans? I held my hands over my head and flashed them a double peace sign. Then I realized that looked too much like President Richard Nixon at a campaign stop so I lowered my left arm and moved my right-hand peace sign so it was centered over my head.

This is the craziest stunt you've ever pulled. It looks like you've gone too far at last. No one can save you now. One of these guys is gonna shoot you by accident if nothing else. You should have listened when everybody told you not to do it.

Just as I was berating myself for being a world-class fool, I saw one of the soldiers, a man younger than myself, flash me back a peace sign of his own. *Ah, a ray of hope.*

They were all just kids, twenty years old at the most, and they came scrambling down the towers as I got close enough to shout, "Hello, I come in peace. I have a visa!" I had my visa and passport folder out, and I waved it as cheerfully as possible. There were nearly twenty soldiers gathered at the ten-foot, pipe-metal gate, curious and amused by the crazy young man attempting to waltz into the Eastern Bloc. One soldier started to point his gun at me until the others scolded him to put it down.

Just before I reached the gate, their commander came out of his quarters atop the brick building next to the road. He wore a bright green uniform with plenty of decoration that seemed to have been recently straightened up for the confrontation. He appeared most displeased that his men had left their towers. They snapped to attention. He started to order them back to their posts but apparently thought better of it. He bellowed for the gate to be opened as he rubbed his hands together like an insect preparing to devour its dinner.

Oh, shit, I thought as he motioned me to step through the open gate. *This asshole's going to make an example out of me.*

My knees went weak as I started forward, bowing slightly to show respect. My heart was racing, and I was having trouble remembering to breathe. The commander pointed at me and made some taunting remarks that made his troops laugh a little. He was making fun of my appearance. I found this pretty amusing from a guy in a stiff green suit on a hot summer day. I did not smile back at him. Nor did I salute.

I stopped ten yards from the commander and held out my papers. He sized me up and down and made another comment that made his men laugh nervously. They had to respond to their commander's lame attempts at humor, but I could tell they weren't making fun of me. They were kids, mostly teenagers and mostly on my side. They weren't enemy robots trained to kill. They were pulling for me in silent concentration on the scene.

The commander motioned me to come to him with both arms like a traffic cop. He raised his nose and sniffed autocratically as I approached slowly and handed him the papers. He snatched them out of my hands like an angry schoolteacher about to read a private note to the entire class.

No one said a word or moved a muscle as he read the visa, holding it up to the sun, studying it carefully, turning it over and over.

Slowly, ever so slowly, he lowered the visa to belt level. I thought he was going to rip it up and throw it away. The troops watched anxiously as their commander scrutinized the document. All eyes were on that one piece of manila paper, which contained the proper language, stamp, and signature. There was a dramatic stillness.

The commander looked down at that visa for what seemed like a full minute. Then he raised his head and looked at me with what could almost be interpreted as a smile.

"Passport," he demanded in a much less threatening manner. I presented my khaki-green passport. He looked it over carefully and had one of his men come up and stamp it. Then he sighed heavily, returned my documents, and brought himself to a boot-heel clicking state of attention, barking almost musically, "All is in order, you may go."

He didn't salute. He didn't shake my hand. He made no further gesture. He ordered no one to search me. The people who ran the international work-study camp I would be attending must have had some high-ranking person sign that visa. The commander was clearly impressed by the document.

The troops remained silent as they parted ranks to make a path for me to pass. Everyone was stunned that the inquisition had ended before it had even gotten started. As I was walking by the last soldier, he wished me well. I turned around to see the commander wasn't objecting. The rest of the troops quickly joined into kind of a good luck cheer as I walked away. I wanted to flap my arms like a bird and make them laugh, but I kept walking, not wanting to jinx my startling good luck.

Forty yards down the road I turned around. The commander was barking at the young soldiers to return to their posts. They scrambled to obey orders. I flashed one final peace sign and never looked back. I was walking in a daze. The commander had not asked me a single question. He had conducted no search whatsoever. My visa was all he really needed to see. The entire process at the gate had taken less than five minutes. I wondered what might have happened on another day with a different man in charge.

Then again, these were Hungarians. No one here was much a fan of the Soviet Union and what it had done to their country since taking over after World War II. They were probably pleased to let a hippie with papers dance on into their country. I knew how those boys in uniform felt. They felt trapped. I understood too well how it felt to be trapped in a military uniform. All they wanted to do was be free enough to hit the road like me.

I kept walking, still trying to wrap my head around what had just happened. All that worry had been for nothing, as worry most often is. A tremendous weight had been lifted off my shoulders. My backpack felt light. I couldn't wait to tell my friends I had hitchhiked through the Iron Curtain. As far as I knew, no one else had ever done it. Unfortunately, all my friends and family were a half a world away. *Let's see. Does walking through count as hitchhiking through? Technically, yes, since walking is a big part of the hitchhiking experience.*

Feeling good about what I was doing eased into my consciousness as a psychological bonus. It reminded me of eating at a crowded diner in Washington, DC, during the 1969 Peace March. There were five of us at the table. Our waitress was about forty years old and extremely busy. When it came time to pay the bill, she started crying softly and said, "There is no bill for you today. It's the least I can do to support what you are doing. I'm a mother for peace. I lost my only son in Vietnam six months ago."

It was awful hearing that mother's tragedy. We did our best to console her. She wiped her tears away and hurried to the next table. All of us at the table felt a new sense of purpose after that episode.

Hitchhiking through the Iron Curtain also gave me a renewed sense of purpose. It made me feel good about what I was doing. It made me feel like I was making progress on my journey, even though progress was slow.

Walking continued to be my hitchhiking experience for the next two hours. The countryside gradually came back to life as I made it to the first little town inside the border. Dogs barked and people waved from their gardens. There were no "Welcome to Hungary" signs, but I knew from my previous visit that the Hungarian people are a warm and welcoming lot.

As the sun was going down, I was taking a break by the side of the road when a man, who turned out to be a professor of theatre from Amsterdam, picked me up and took me all the way to Budapest. He was on his way to co-direct Chekhov's play, *The Cherry Orchard*, with a Hungarian professor. We had a good time talking about the Russians and how we were the first wave of invaders to begin ending the Cold War.

"It will happen one day," he said in perfect English.

"In our lifetimes?"

"Yes, yes. Look at us now. It's happening right now. Two years ago, neither one of us would have made it through the border."

"By the way," I asked. "Did you have any trouble at the border?"

"Not really, although it took them almost an hour to search my car. They even took the seats apart. I thought they were going to slash my spare tire to have a look inside. How about you?"

"They didn't search me at all."

"You must be joking." He laughed. "You, I would search."

"I know. I thought I might not get through at all. It turns out I think my visa is signed by the prime minister himself. The commander looked it over and let me in with no questions asked. Did you see the guy in the green uniform?"

"No, no," he answered. "No green. Only brown uniforms. They were young and friendly enough, but they tore my car apart. You got lucky."

I leaned back in the comfortable passenger seat. "I guess they saw me coming."

The professor dropped me off on the outskirts of Budapest. It was already dark. I found a field and stowed my pack in some bushes where I figured I could hide out and sleep for the night. I pocketed my passport and visa. They could not be left behind. These were the papers that turned a hitchhiker into a diplomat.

I wandered into the city and stopped in a couple taverns for beer and a sandwich. The first bartender gladly turned my twenty-dollar bill into forints. The black market for currency was obviously still big business. I was in such a celebratory mood I must have spent nearly three dollars, which is a lot at twenty-five cents a beer. English speaking patrons were eager to buy me shots of *Palinka*, Hungarian fruit brandy, once they found out I had hitchhiked into the country through the border. The women were more than friendly, but I eventually walked back to my campsite alone. I was a man on a mission, to get to Debrecen and the camp.

I had a little trouble relocating my camping hideout after all that drinking, but the stars and moon were shining bright. The night was warm and still. I drifted into the peaceful sleep of an innocent man who's had too much to drink. I couldn't believe I was in Hungary and all the drama of the Iron Curtain was behind me.

I woke up the next morning feeling guilty about my hangover. I'd spent too much money being a big shot and bragging about my hitchhiking accomplishments. Ordinarily, I could drink all night and not have any problems the next day. It was the brandy pounding my head. I walked through most of the city, eating pastries and drinking lots of water along the way. It took hours before I began to feel normal again. Three truck rides later I was in the capital city of Hungary.

My memories of Budapest were vivid: the glass-brick roofs of the Turkish baths, the red star on the hotel where we celebrated New Year's 1971 as students, the bullet holes in the buildings from the Revolution of 1956, the Danube view of Pest and the chain bridge from the hilltop in Buda, and all the late night bull sessions with young communists about the evils of capitalism.

Now, it felt much like Wien had felt, empty and lonely without the friends who had previously accompanied me. Deciding not to linger, I hitchhiked straight to Debrecen and the work-study camp. I knew something important, or someone important, was waiting for me there.

CHAPTER FOUR

Hanna

THE GROUNDS OF THE UNIVERSITY of Debrecen in eastern Hungary were stately. Concrete pathways wound around historic buildings of ivy-covered brick and stone beneath a canopy of giant trees. The architectural centerpiece was a palatial library reminiscent of Versailles, overlooking vast, polychromatic gardens. The focal point of this glorious landscape made me stop and stare. It was a fountain, spouting and pulsating, shimmering like a wonderful memory, so alive it made me realize the campus was deserted. The students were away on summer vacation, and I was evidently the first to arrive for the international work-study camp.

I watched the fountain spurting and splashing in the sun. Suddenly, it hit me. It had taken more than five weeks of tough travel to get to this point, but now, I could finally say, "I made it." This was my destination. I had arrived. The day was fresh and bright. I felt full of energy and a little lightheaded. Something told me that even though I had finally made it to the camp, my journey was just beginning.

I've been thinking for more than a year about getting here and how I was going to get here and whether or not I could make it here. Now, here I am. My worries are over, at least for a while. This is home for the next month.

I took off my pack and sat down with my back against the trunk of a tree. One thing about hitchhiking: it's hard work, but you always feel like you're getting somewhere.

Basking in the glory of my temporary triumph, I had to finally admit to myself how afraid I had been of undertaking this journey. Not only was I afraid of plane crashes and muggings and running out of money and not having any fun, I was afraid of what my life was going to become. I was starring in my own version of *The Graduate*. My entire life had been spent being educated on everybody else's terms and timetables. Now, I was fully graduated and finally on my own for the first time ever. I'd taken extended road trips before, but always knew when to return and what had to be done when I got there. Now, returning anywhere was not certain.

At many points along the way, I had deeply regretted heeding the call of the wild. Hitchhiking is hard and dirty work. Now, sitting in front of the fountain, I had an epiphany: the world was revealing itself to me in wonderful ways that would not have been possible had I remained at home, secure in my predictable surroundings.

If you want to live, *really* live, you can't play it safe. You've got to throw yourself out there on the seas of uncertainty to discover who you are and what you need to do.

I didn't realize it at that point, reveling in my moment, but the seeds of my faith were being planted in the fertile soil of life on the road. Fear can be a great gift, for by overcoming it we break out of the prison of self. Each of us has senses that make us feel like the center of the material world. No matter which way we look, or what we hear, the world is all around us. We are afraid not only of dying, but of not getting enough of what we think we need or not getting our own way when we want it. Fear is basically a lack of faith. By hitting the road, I had taken the leap of faith and faced my fears and become much more in tune with what was going on in the world.

It didn't take long for my thoughts to return to more mundane matters. I was getting ready to go search for a check-in station for the camp when two young women approached through the wooded walkway. We waved, excited to make what was undoubtedly our first acquaintance of the camp. They fairly ran to greet me.

"I'm Mary and this is my friend, Ann," she said in a heavy Irish accent. "We're from Ireland."

"I can tell." I laughed. "I'm Mark from the USA."

"We can tell." They giggled.

"Far out." I grinned, shaking their hands vigorously. They were pretty in a rosy-cheek way. They could have been sisters—early twenties, five foot five, a little on the chubby side, but obviously fit, carrying backpacks without camping gear. "You must be here for the camp."

"Oh, yes," Ann said. "I can't believe we're finally here. We've been on trains for the past four days!"

"Oh, trains," I moaned. "I did that in Spain and France. You have my sympathies."

Ann shook her arms out to her sides. "I hope they have good showers here. We haven't bathed properly since England."

The women knew where to go for check-in, so I followed them to a nearby administration building as we swapped road stories and shared expectations about the coming month. We agreed we were lucky that English would be the language of the camp.

A woman at the check-in desk who didn't speak much English greeted us warmly, noted our arrival, and directed us to a two-story, wood building that looked like a summer camp lodge in need of some repair. There were separate rooms for men and women. The Irish girls went off to their quarters. I surveyed the premises before choosing my room.

There were two bathrooms on each level of the building at opposite ends of long halls with plank floors that looked like they had once been painted green. Each bathroom had two open showers and four toilets with no doors on the stalls. Privacy was going to be an issue for the participants from around the globe.

There were four bunk beds in each large room, enough to sleep eight comfortably. I picked the middle room on the first floor and grabbed the bottom bunk by the window. The temperature was in the high 70s and there was obviously no air conditioning other than a slow-moving ceiling fan in the middle of the room. The building was old but spotlessly clean.

What a relief to stretch out on a bed I could call my own, if only for a month. The army surplus blanket was coarse, scratchy wool and the pillow was in a state of total collapse, but it was home for now. The thin mattress on the creaking wire-mesh frame didn't sag much in the middle. It had sheets that smelled fresh and clean. They reminded me how much I needed to bathe. I grabbed a towel from a stack near the door and my dopp kit and hit the shower. It took a while to warm up, but it was deliciously hot and soapy. My skin felt liberated as I washed off layers of road grime.

Feeling rejuvenated, I returned to the check-in building to see if anyone else had arrived. Sure enough, standing at the desk next to a large backpack was a petite, brown-haired beauty. She was five-feet-two with shoulder-length hair that framed her strong chin and flashing smile. Her legs seemed long even though she wasn't tall. She was unmistakably very full-breasted. One look in her wide hazel eyes told me I definitely needed to get to know this woman better.

"Hi," I said, deciding not to be shy. "Can I help you with that?"

"Are you from the camp?" she asked, obviously a little taken aback by my forwardness.

"Oh, yes," I said. "I'm sorry. I guess I should introduce myself. I'm Mark from the USA," I said, holding out my hand for a handshake.

"I'm Hanna." She smiled, relaxing considerably as she shook my hand. "I'm from Finland. And, yes, you could help me with this pack. It gets heavier every minute. It's already been a long day."

I walked Hanna back to the lodge and told her the Irish girls had already arrived. She seemed relieved to know I was taking her to meet other women. The more we walked and talked, the more comfortable we each became. By the time we parted company at the dorm, I knew she was a devout communist working on her master's degree in economics. She knew I was a reluctant capitalist, well on the road to socialism.

The rest of the group arrived throughout the day and into the evening: Gregory, Grace, and Irena, communists from Poland; Antonio and his wife Vivian, revolutionaries from Italy; Charles, English graduate of Oxford University; Louis, rich kid from Ecuador; Ustes, party animal from Holland; Klaus and Thomas, West German radicals; Remick from France; Hiroshi from Japan; Elin and Edvard from Sweden; Jonathon from Canada; Peesta, Leslie, Anna, and Mihaly from Hungary; Christian, the engineer from East Germany; Elina from Finland; and Maisa from Czechoslovakia. Not everybody's English was fluent.

Miklos Barabos, a gregarious Hungarian political science professor, was in charge of the camp. He was quite pleased at having brought together such an international cast of characters. He was in the dorm that first night, helping everyone get acquainted and settled into the accommodations.

It was great fun meeting kindred spirits from around the world and realizing how much we had in common. We all looked pretty much the same: long hair, jeans, leather pouches, baggy shirts, peace sign patches, sandals, tie-dyed skirts, beads, bracelets, and headbands. The Woodstock Nation had gone global. We were all in our early twenties and ready to turn the world into one big, happy family.

Vietnam became a major topic even as we were getting acquainted.

As the only American at the camp I had some serious explaining to do. Everyone wanted to know about the peace marches and the rock festivals and the communes and the free love and the LSD. They also wanted to know how a country with so many artistic souls could be waging such a cruel and senseless war in Southeast Asia.

I was quick to apologize for my country's unforgivable brutality but equally quick to assure everyone that the war was on its last legs in the States thanks to the anti-war movement.

I was thankful no one knew about my own military involvement. I couldn't tell a soul that information.

The presidential elections coming up in November were a hot topic. It came as no surprise to me that young people from all over the world loved to hate Richard Nixon. His secret escalations of the war had outraged the world. The fact that he would probably be re-elected was unthinkable. Everybody at the camp referred to him as "Tricky Dick." It sounded funny with a Polish accent, hilarious in French.

What surprised me was how much attention these young people had obviously been paying to American politics. Even more surprising was how different my country looked to me through their eyes. It wasn't a pretty picture. Yes, they were fascinated by the USA, but also bemused. Much of what they didn't find disgusting they found laughable. Television had brought the killing of Vietnam into their homes along with soap commercials and *I Love Lucy*. I resolved to paint them a more complete picture of my country, one that would include the purple mountains' majesty, amber waves of grain, and coast-to-coast interstate highways.

Miklos got us up early the next morning, and we assembled in the kitchen downstairs for breakfast. There was plenty of food, but it wasn't bacon and eggs. It was cheese and tomatoes and peppers and bread and sausage. No one complained. There had been no scheduled dinner the night before, so we were all hungry. Miklos gave us his first inspirational talk.

"First of all," he began loudly. "Let me officially welcome you all to the 1972 work-study camp at the University of Debrecen in Hungary. As you all know, I have handpicked each and every one of you to participate in this experiment in international living.

"You represent one of the best camps we've ever had here in Debrecen. Your month together will be a wonderful learning experience that none of you will ever forget. Hopefully, we will do our little part to promote peace and understanding in the world. As you may know, work camps started after World War II to help reconstruct war-torn countries. They continue today in many nations due to the increased mobility of the student world."

He spoke for only ten minutes and concluded with "What we are doing here is good for the planet." We cheered his positive approach.

"Immediately after breakfast," he continued, "we will board a bus and head out to a collective farm for our work. This farm is an apple orchard so we will be pruning trees and, perhaps, clearing land for new trees. Has anyone here ever worked on an orchard farm?"

No one raised a hand. There was a collective murmur at our lack of experience.

"Fine," Miklos shouted gaily. "Neither have I." We laughed. "That means we will all learn together. The people at the farm will be happy to help. They are eager to meet you. I've told them you are the finest young minds from around the world."

"Will they have work gloves?" Ustes asked. "Our hands are as fine as our minds."

We laughed again. "They will have everything we need, including water and lunch at noon," Miklos concluded. "Now, let's get ready to go. The bus leaves in fifteen minutes."

Spirits were high as we rode on the old bus through the rolling Hungarian farmland in the morning fog. We were all a little nervous about our first day on the job.

The collective farm turned out to be apple orchards as far as the eye could see. We unloaded in the dirt-circle center of a dozen massive barns and equipment buildings. Miklos interpreted for the farm leader who quickly divided us into teams of four and assigned one of his workers to each team to show us what to do. These workers spoke no English, but they provided us with gloves and pruning shears, large and small, and quickly showed us how to cut dead branches off the trees and stack them in rows for pick up.

The work was easy at first, but by 10:30 a.m. most of us were overheated and scratched from head to toe. Our team approach proved impractical, so we began to take the one- or two-person approach to tree trimming. I managed to pair up with Hanna. I cut and she stacked. We kept it slow and steady and got to know each other.

"It's so hot," she said, wiping the sweat from her neck. "We have some hot summer days in Finland, but I never really worked outside in the heat like this."

I handed her a few cut branches. "Where did you work?"

"Mostly in the kitchen. Even as a little girl I remember washing pots and pans in a big kitchen. I hated it. Every time I almost finished, they would bring me more dirty cooking pots to scrub."

"I used to love working in the kitchen at school," I said. "We got out of class early to get lunch ready and we got extra food for working in the cafeteria. Then I became the kid who poured the glasses of milk as everyone passed through the line. That was fun. I used to tell jokes and catch up on all the gossip around school."

Hanna took more branches from me. "I'll bet you had a regular show going on every day."

"We always had fun at lunch. It's still my favorite part of the day. People get together and talk about their day while they're still in the middle of it. By dinner, everybody's tired and ready to drink."

She placed the branches on the pickup pile. "What about the 'three-martini lunch' you capitalists are so famous for?"

"You capitalists?" I came out from under the tree and stood in front of her with my hands on my knees, sweat pouring off my forehead. "What do you think? Americans are all big, fat, cigar-smoking railroad barons? Don't lump me into that little cartoon."

She laughed, pleased to see she had touched a sensitive nerve. "You don't like being called a capitalist? I thought you Americans were so proud of your capitalist system."

"Wait a minute. You're the economics major. You know that capitalism is about economics, not politics. You know that capitalism is about private ownership of the means of production."

"Ooh," she mocked, "so you know about economic theory?"

"I can tell you the United States stopped being a capitalistic economy about the time Teddy Roosevelt busted the monopolies. And then, the federal government bailed the country out of the Great Depression. More than a third of our jobs now are in the public sector. That's some public ownership of the means of production. That makes us socialists at least."

Hanna put her hands on her hips. "I always thought World War II bailed you out of the Depression."

I pointed at her with a cut branch. "Or maybe it was us who bailed you out of World War II?"

We looked each other in the eyes for a long, sweaty moment. I smiled first, and then she joined in, an unspoken truce declared. Our connection had been made. "Let's go get some water and get out of this sun." She grabbed my arm and off we went. "You are already changing my thinking about the United States."

The camp turned out to be much more than working in the orchards. Miklos had a full schedule planned. We only worked until 12:30 p.m. most days and some days we didn't work at all. Then it was off to visit a factory or another collective farm or attend lectures at the university from ranking members of government. We had regularly scheduled times to visit the huge public pool in Debrecen and took field trips to parks and points of historic interest. We got to know each other well. By the end of the first week we felt like one big international family.

It was in the wine cellars of Eger, an historic city north of Debrecen where they make Bull's Blood Wine, that Hanna and I became more than friends. We were about ten days into the camp.

The ceilings were low in the damp rooms of the cellar. The long drinking and dining tables were made of wood, but everything else was stone: the floors, the arches, the walls, even the dividers between the tables. Above every table were round wooden casks of wine with rubber hoses that hung down with spigots on the end to provide anyone with a never-ending glass of wine. Dinner included all the wine you could drink, so we all set out to see just how much wine we could actually consume. We'd had a tough day touring old castles. After the first few fortresses, they all started to look the same. We were ready to let off a little steam.

Ustes was the first to start singing, entertaining us as he waltzed around the room with an imaginary woman, singing a dramatic love song no one could understand. The entire cellar cheered wildly. Then Klaus and Thomas sang a German drinking song and the Polish students sang one of their own. The wine kept flowing. Those who didn't want to sing made eloquent toasts to their newfound friends in the camp and to life in general. We lost Hiroshi about five glasses into the party. He started turning green and had to leave rather suddenly. Of course, we all thought this uproariously funny.

Amazing, I thought. *Here I am in Hungary with people from all over the world and the party feels like it could be happening at a bar in Indiana. Alcohol is a potent equalizer.*

Hanna was sitting next to me, getting closer with each glass of wine until her left arm was resting on my right leg and she was squeezing my knee. She was melting into me. We fit together perfectly, like the last two pieces of a puzzle.

Just as I was about to turn to kiss her, a guitar was brought into the cellar. Gregory handed it to me like he thought anyone from the States could surely play a song or two on the guitar.

Actually, that's exactly what I could play, a song or two. Ordinarily, I would have been too self-conscious to play, but I had just the right buzz on to give it my best. Mercifully, the thing was in fair tune. I launched into "Ruby" by Kenny Rogers and heard myself singing and performing like I never believed I could. By the time I hit the bridge of the song, my new friends and everybody in the cellar were cheering me on, pounding the tables and roaring their approval.

What an incredible feeling! In that moment, everything changed for me. I was doing something I thought I could never do. I was no longer the kid who got kicked out of Mr. Broom's fifth grade song flute class, banned for life from the music room. I was playing music for people and they loved it. I could feel John Lennon laughing encouragingly on my shoulder. I strummed the C chord to catch my breath and lowered the volume for dramatic effect. The cellar quieted for the last verse.

Our group cheered madly as I finished. People were trying to touch me. It was a faith-healing moment. My audience wanted more. I handed back the guitar, determined to quit while I was ahead. Hanna threw her arms around me and squeezed me tight. She made me feel like a rock star.

It took a while for everyone to settle back down. Then someone handed me a glass of Bull's Blood, and we all went back to getting seriously drunk and applauding each other's every comment.

Eventually, the place closed and our group stumbled up the time-worn steps and out of the cellar. Hanna and I sat in the right corner of the bench seat in the back of the bus. The moon was shining through the glass window, dazzling her eyes. We put our foreheads together and kissed, softly at first, then deep and passionate. That first kiss seemed to last the entire ride back to Debrecen. The back of the bus was nice and private. Her inhibitions were stripped as she let me unbutton her. The bus floated through the night.

Once we arrived at the university, I grabbed a blanket and we took a walk. There was a slight chill in the air, but we hardly noticed. We found a perfect place to lie down in the middle of three large evergreen trees. Our kisses were trembling with breathtaking anticipation. I moved my mouth to her ear and down her neck. She moaned gratefully as I undid her again. I took off my shirt and slowly stroked her with my chest. Moon shadows from the trees danced. I kissed her lips softly then moved my mouth down her neck slowly to her breasts. She groaned. I moved my mouth down to her navel and began to unsnap her pants. Suddenly, she stiffened.

"No," she said, trying to sit up. "Don't. I can't."

"What are you talking about? I won't hurt you. I promise."

Hanna sat up with a determined frown. "I'm sorry. You know I want to, but I can't."

I looked at her closely. "Why not?"

She lowered her face. I waited for her to speak, totally confused by the sudden turn of events. Eventually, she looked up and explained herself. "You don't have protection. You must have protection. I don't want to be pregnant. It happened to my sister. I don't want a baby yet. I'm not on the pill. I'm not like an American girl."

She started to get up. I kept talking, "It'll be okay. I'll be careful. I won't come."

With that, she jumped up and ran away. Evidently, she'd heard that line before. I ran after her and caught her at the door to the dorm. "I'm sorry, Hanna. I thought everything was the way you wanted. I didn't mean to push you."

She was crying. "No, I don't think that. I understand. You're a man. It was my fault. I shouldn't have let it go that far. I had too much wine."

With that, she kissed me quickly on the cheek and went inside without me. For the first time in my life, I felt cheapened by being called a "man."

The next few days Hanna kept her distance, hanging out with the women, although she let me know with her smile she wasn't angry. The truth of the matter was she had fallen for me pretty hard and didn't want to admit it, even to herself, for fear that I would be like other men she had known.

Actually, I *had* fallen in love with the little Marxist, not totally in love but infatuated in love. She was on the same road as me, off to find her true self no matter how far it took her away from home. Talking with her was continually an adventure. She was well educated and quite a student of current events. We had the same sense of humor. I loved making her laugh.

The main thing I was learning is that people all around the world are pretty much the same. We all want to love and to be loved, and we're all afraid of loving because of the risks involved, mainly that our love won't be returned or that it will be lost. We all want to find a purpose and a meaning in life even though none of us has an existential clue what we're doing on this place we call a planet. We all tend to run from pain even though "growing pains" must be faced in order to make spiritual or even material progress.

Meanwhile, I was enjoying getting to know Gregory, a twenty-four-year-old linguistics student at Marie Curie-Sklodowska University in Lublin, Poland. Originally, he had wanted to study political science but realized he would be forced to defend the Communist Party doctrine, with which he often disagreed.

We were riding the bus to the apple orchards when Gregory first told me his doubts about what the Russians called communism. "The

Party wants to create citizens who would merely cooperate with the State, instead of individuals who would contribute to the government by challenging it with new ideas."

"You sound like someone who believes in democracy," I said.

Gregory looked over his shoulder before continuing in a whisper. "In 1968, I was part of the student movement. We were fed up with the dogma of the State. We started an independent newspaper, but before even our first publication the police came in and shut us down. We were forced to collaborate with the police or be expelled from the university. I am ashamed to say it, but I betrayed my comrades. I think you call this a snitch. I didn't think I would, but they scared us so much we all did.

"About fifteen of the leaders were jailed for three to four years. The philosophy departments in Polish universities were closed down. I didn't even participate in the workers' uprising in 1970. More than two hundred people were killed by the police for demonstrating against the party leadership's price-raising actions."

I waited for him to continue, but he stopped talking and looked to me for a reaction.

"It's odd you should talk about that time. I was in Poland in early December of 1970. Our student group took a trip from Wien to Krakow. The place was as gloomy and depressing as the rainy winter. I'll never forget it. We got off the train early one morning. We'd been partying most of the night, so we were being pretty silly on the train platform. Then the train pulled away and we were face to face, across the tracks, with the saddest looking bunch of people I ever saw. They looked like prisoners of war waiting for the train to take them to the death camp. It sobered us up in a hurry. We picked up our bags and scurried into the station. The people were actually scary. They looked like zombies."

"Yes, 1970 was a terrible time for Poland," Gregory said. "Since 1970, though, and the expulsion of the Gomulka regime, many positive changes have occurred in Poland. The National Health Service has improved, and agricultural reforms are helping to restore people's faith in the government." He looked over his shoulder again and then back at me. "One day, Poland will be free again."

"Free from what?"

"The Russians. You call it the Soviet Union. We call it the Russians. They are imperialists, the same as your country."

"We're not imperialistic," I joked. "The USA is fighting in Vietnam to stop the spread of communism."

"Hah." Gregory sensed my sarcasm. "Communism is only an economic idea. Ideas don't need armies to spread. Besides, Russia isn't communistic. It's fascist. Stalin murdered twenty million of his countrymen to stay in power. How many has your country killed in Korea and Vietnam? The USA and Russia won World War II and they've been fighting over the spoils ever since. That much we can all understand.

"What I really don't understand about your country is how wealthy Americans can allow the depraved conditions of black life in the ghettos to continue and how your government can pay farmers for not growing food when so much of the world is starving."

I pointed out the historic nature of the problems created by slavery and how much progress the Civil Rights Movement was making. It was impossible to explain away the racism. I shifted topics and mentioned the tremendous amount of foreign aid provided the world by the USA.

Gregory acknowledged these arguments but insisted that America was a sick country because the capitalistic system demanded ruthless competition, which made its citizens self-centered and indifferent to the needs of others. "I admire the open-minded attitudes of young people in America," he said, "but they'll probably lose all that once they are forced to compete for their livelihood."

"I'm amazed you can be so opposed to the USA when you tell me how they shut down your publication in Poland. We have freedom of the press and freedom of speech," I argued.

"You may have some political freedom," he countered. "But there is no economic freedom in the US. What good is political freedom when there is no economic freedom? What good is freedom of speech when the rich won't listen to the poor?"

I tried to tell him that the American dream was all about people from poor backgrounds working hard and earning themselves better lifestyles. He wasn't hearing it. As far as his education had taught him, America was not the land of opportunity. It was the land of privately owned big business exploiting the working class.

Gregory wasn't alone in his feelings toward the United States of America. The anti-Americanism at the camp was pervasive. It came to a head one night when we built a campfire behind the dorm and started drinking copious amounts of red wine and vodka. Klaus decided to get down on the US.

"You Americans are nothing," he blurted out of nowhere. "You smoke marijuana and have rock and roll festivals. But you do nothing. The war goes on while you have your parties. People die while you make movies about motorcycle men. You think you are so different, but you change nothing. You are nothing. No, you are worse than nothing. You are criminals of war!"

He paused, running out of breath, surprised by his own vehemence, scanning faces illuminated by the flames for reaction. He looked at everyone but me, watching them wait in shocked silence for my response.

For once, I was at a loss for words. In fact, I found it hard to disagree with most of what he said. I stared into the blaze, deciding not to fight fire with fire. Ustes came to my rescue.

"You must be shocked, Klaus," he said. "You must be horrified. I'm sure nobody in Germany could imagine killing innocent people. Oh, no, not in Germany. Not the German people. Oh, no. The German people are so much more civilized than the Americans. You wouldn't slaughter five million Jews, now, would you? Oh, no, you are the master race. You are superior. Maybe that's why you sell so many Mercedes in the US."

The faces around the fire shifted from me to Klaus. It was his turn now to respond to hateful comment. He looked as if he'd been jolted by a bad connection in an electrical circuit. It's always shocking to hear your own criticism coming back in your face. After all, we criticize most in others what we least like in ourselves.

Klaus couldn't handle it. He said nothing, glaring angrily at Ustes. Then he glared at the rest of us, one by one, turning his reddening forehead around the circle. Finally, he returned his glare to Ustes.

"What do you know about anything, you Dutch disease?"

Everyone groaned in disapproval. The international peace theme of the camp was obviously being put to the test. Klaus picked up a small log in a menacing manner. Ustes wasn't about to back down. In fact, he laughed at Klaus. Not the smartest thing to do to a pissed off German drunk with a weapon in his hand.

The confrontation seemed certain to escalate into physical violence until Gregory and Anthony stepped between the two to keep the peace. Ann jumped in as well and started lecturing both of them.

"Look at you two. Just look at you." She shook her finger in their faces. "It's shameful. You are forgetting why we are here. We're here to get along. That's what this is all about. If we can't be peaceful, how can we expect the world to survive? You disgust me. Like all men. Stupid, stupid men. My sister was killed in Belfast by men like you." Her voice started to crack and falter. "Men who fight for no reason. Men who kill for nothing but pride. It's always the men. Little men trying to be big men. Why is it always the men?" She began sobbing.

Klaus looked at her as if he'd been shot. Then he stalked off into the darkness. Antonio and Vivian followed after him. Ann stumbled off with Grace and Mary comforting her. Nobody stayed much longer than that. Soon Hanna and I were the only ones left at the fire.

"Why did you say nothing to Klaus?" she asked softly, moving to sit next to me on the large log. I didn't answer.

She rubbed my back gently. It felt good. "Why did you not defend yourself?" she asked again. "I mean, I'm proud of you for not fighting and for not getting down to his level, but it does not seem like you to not put him in his place."

"Hanna." I sighed deeply. "There's something I need to tell you before we go any further in this relationship. I'm not just the wandering, anti-war hippie you think you know. I'm actually an officer in the United States Air Force. I'm on leave now but when I go back, I'm scheduled to learn how to fly jet planes so I can drop bombs on Vietnam."

Hanna pulled away, almost involuntarily. "You're not going to do it, are you?"

I hung my head. "No, I've decided I can't do it. But I don't know what I can do to get out of it."

Wheels were spinning inside her head. I could feel her coming quickly to a conclusion. I should have seen it coming, but I didn't.

"You can come with me to Finland!" she squealed triumphantly. "You will be a hero there. We will have a wonderful life. I have many friends. Friends who can get you political asylum. Friends in the Party who would love to work with an American. Oh, my family will love you. My mother will love you. I will love you. I do love you!"

She threw her arms around my neck and kissed me hard. I kissed her and let her know how good it felt to be back in her romantic good graces. She took a deep breath. "Oh, no, I'm going too fast, no?"

I nodded my head yes and smiled. It felt good to tell her about my predicament even if I knew instinctively that her solution would never work for me.

We talked for hours that night, mainly about how I could never turn my back on my family and my country. I found myself explaining how I'd gotten into the Air Force in the first place.

"My father was a combat veteran of World War II and the Korean War," I told her. "He was in the Army. Everybody was in the Army or the Navy or the Marines during the war. I used to love hearing my father's war stories. My favorite was the one about how he stepped on a German trip grenade behind enemy lines at night and, somehow, no one on his patrol was hit.

"Going into the military and wearing a uniform was something every American boy assumed he would do. As a child, I played with toy soldiers all the time in my room alone. We played guns in the neighborhood, sneaking around and killing each other with imaginary weapons. War was glorified in the movies and on television. I used to daydream in school about how I would defend the place against enemy attack. The brainwash was thorough and complete."

Hanna took me by both hands and encouraged me to continue with her vulnerable eyes wide open. "So how did you decide to become a pilot in the Air Force?"

I lowered my head to kiss her fingers, then looked up and into her eyes to try to explain what I didn't understand myself. "My father served in two wars. He was an enlisted man in World War II on the front lines in France. After the war he became an officer in the Army Reserves. His reserve unit was called up to active duty for the war in Korea. He always impressed on me how much better life was as an officer than as an enlisted man. For him, it wasn't a question of whether or not to go to war. Everybody was going to war. The question was how would you go to war, carrying a rifle through the mud or flying a plane in the sky?

"He was extremely impressed with pilots. He had wanted to fly but he was colorblind. So, I guess I got the pilot bug from my father. Plus, I fell in love with the notion of flying the first time I ever saw a plane."

Hanna waited for me to continue and then encouraged me with a question. "What about your mother?"

"My mother always let me know it was something I didn't have to do. She used to ask if I was sure I wanted to join the military. She understood the dark side of war. She lived through my father's nightmares her entire married life."

"What did your father say about the nightmares?"

"He let me know the terrible side of combat—the fear, the grief, even the insanity. But for him, like everyone else, it was a reality. Everybody went to war. Better to go as a pilot than an infantryman. And I always wanted to fly. From the time I was a young boy, I wanted to be a fighter pilot. It looked so wild and free and courageous and heroic."

Hanna let go of my hands and stood up. "You don't have to go to war. No one does. War is a power game played by the ruling class, paid for by the blood of the working class. Even a child can see how wrong and foolish it has always been."

I remained seated and looked up at her in amazement. "I guess that's the problem. There has always been war. The history of mankind is written in blood."

Hanna stepped back and turned to address the fading fire. "Yes. That's the problem. Mankind is the problem. What the world needs now is womankind. It's time for women to take over and bring an end to war."

I stood up. "I don't think you need to be a woman to want to bring an end to war."

Our conversation continued until the fire was nothing but smoke and glowing embers. Hanna told me about growing up happily in Finland and how her father had encouraged her and her sister and brother to join the Communist Party at an early age. She was an idealist. She was exactly what I needed. Someone to encourage me to do what I knew was right. I was perfect for her as well. She could save me from myself and fight the evil forces of capitalism at the same time.

I was learning that being an American wasn't always something to brag about.

Neither of us spoke as we held hands and strolled slowly to the sanctuary of the three pine trees. We were ready for each other. Our love was gentle and free. Our passion was complete. She wrapped her legs around me and took me deeply inside her. We went wild on each other.

It took a while for the Hungarian night to chill our afterglow. The first signs of sunrise were beginning to shine when we dressed quickly and walked back to the dorm. We kissed tenderly and parted without saying a word. There was nothing more to be said.

CHAPTER FIVE

The Fountain

O NE NIGHT, ABOUT THREE weeks into the camp, Hanna and I took a walk through the university gardens. We strolled arm in arm for nearly an hour before settling on the grass near the main fountain. Lights on the dancing water changed color every few minutes from red to green to blue. The fountain misted us occasionally with a gentle shower when the wind changed to blow in our direction.

A group of five Asian students joined us. We got up to greet them in the spirit of friendliness and international cordiality that pervaded the university and its many foreign-studies programs.

Only one of the students spoke English. They were exchange students from North Vietnam.

I could feel them shudder when Hanna introduced me through their interpreter as an American. We shook hands all around. They tried to hide their feelings toward me but did not succeed. I could see a steely glint of instinctive fear and hatred phase through their eyes. The fountain lights changed from blue to red. I didn't waste any time.

"Please tell them," I urged the interpreter, "how truly sorry I am for what my country has done to your country."

She looked surprised by my apology but translated it directly to her companions. This led to a commotion of conversation in Vietnamese, most of which sounded fairly friendly. When they finally quieted, she turned back to me and said, "We don't blame you personally for the war. We know many American people are trying to stop the war. We see the newsreels. But we are surprised to see an American here in Hungary. Are you a communist?"

Hanna grabbed my arm and said before I could answer, "He's learning." Everybody laughed even before the interpreter could translate.

"You must know," I addressed the interpreter, "most young people in America are not in favor of the war. I'm not in favor of it at all. I've marched in Washington, DC, against the war. I've been tear gassed by the police. So have many students at my university and around the country. You must understand the United States is on the brink of civil war over Vietnam."

The interpreter listened to what I had to say and then launched into a translation five times as long as my statement. She was obviously embellishing. When she finished, there was more excited talking amongst the North Vietnamese. Then she turned to me and said grimly, "We see your jet planes dropping bombs by the ton every day on Hanoi and throughout North Vietnam."

She waited for her words to sink in. They all waited. They could see the statement had taken me by surprise. I was not aware of the scope of American bombing in North Vietnam at that time. The American public had been kept in the dark as to the terrible scope of supersonic slaughter we had been raining down on these poor people in Southeast Asia. Operation Rolling Thunder had been in the news, but it had been suspended in 1968, having failed to intimidate North Vietnam. President Richard Nixon began his "secret bombing" campaign in 1969 and devastated Laos, Cambodia, and North Vietnam for the next five years without a single press release.

"Wait a minute," I began slowly. "Are you telling me you live in Hanoi and bombs are being dropped on you all the time?"

Once the interpreter communicated my naiveté, they all began talking to me directly in high-pitched voices, animated by the untold truth finally being told. The horror in their faces bore witness to atrocities that defied interpretation. I felt the agony of their nation for the first time, deep in the marrow of my bones. It made me nauseous. These were heartfelt testimonials, eyewitness accounts of inhuman crime.

It made me dizzy. The grief was overpowering, the communication complete. In a very short time, these five students from North Vietnam poured generations of suffering and injustice into my soul. I didn't understand a word they were saying. I didn't need to. Their truth was obvious and undeniable. They gave me a blood transfusion of sorrow and empathy. My worldview shifted during that sudden and unexpected confrontation.

Finally, the interpreter called for quiet as she positioned her body between theirs and mine. They fell silent. I stared at them in wide-eyed disbelief. They stared back as if to say, "You better believe it."

"Listen to just one story," the interpreter said as she brought forward one of the young men, who was obviously quite reluctant to be singled out. It took some time for him to begin, but once he did, he told a powerful and unforgettable account of how his fiancée had been killed in a US airstrike on Hanoi. She died while working as a nurse in a civilian hospital.

The man began crying halfway through his narrative. He made wild, hand-waving gestures describing the terror and panic of being attacked by the screaming thunder of jet planes. He sobbed as he demonstrated digging through hospital rubble to find his girlfriend mangled and mauled by the unthinkable power of a missile attack. His sobs turned to shrieks as he imitated the nightmarish sounds of the jets and their rain of death.

One of the women tried to comfort him but he pushed her away. He jumped to his feet and stood in front of me, clenching his fists and wailing at the sky. Hanna clung to me as I positioned myself for a possible attack. The interpreter rose to grab her grief-raging comrade by the shoulders. Instead of pushing her away, the grieving man collapsed in a pile of sorrow at my feet, his head touching my knee.

The wind shifted and the fountain blasted us with a spray. We were all in such shock nobody noticed a drop. The Vietnamese student raised his head to look at me. His face was a portrait of pain I could never forget. Tears ran down his cheeks, snot ran out his nose, a pathetic moan trembled his lips, and his eyes begged for compassion if not understanding. He was sobbing and shaking his head in futile denial.

He could see my tears welling as I helped him up by the shoulders and hugged him without saying a word. He held me so tightly I could feel his anguish. His thin arms shook as he squeezed me as hard as he could, not in anger but in pain. As he sobbed into my chest, I looked around the group. The fountain changed from red to green. Sorrowful faces changed color with the light on the water.

I buried my face on his shoulder and cried softly, "Oh, God, oh, God. I am so sorry."

Hanna hugged me from behind and the others followed suit until the seven of us were weeping together in a mournful huddle. It took some time for us to untangle. Nobody said anything. We were emotionally drained. We bid adieu with individual embraces. I took Hanna's hand and we walked away. Looking over my shoulder, the fountain seemed to be weeping. Weeping for those who had lost their loved ones. Weeping for the world.

The water changed from green to blue.

We walked back to the dorm in silence. I kept seeing Air Force training films in my mind. They always started with dramatic shots of jets in flight, the sun glinting off their wings. The shot rolled as a jet peeled out of formation for an attack run. Then an inside shot of the cockpit with all its dials and levers. And finally, an aerial view of the deadly explosions and napalm fireballs turning the jungle into scorched earth. I replayed these films in my head, scanning them for content. Thinking back through it, I had never seen a film of a jet attack on a city in Vietnam. It was always the jungle being destroyed. The films were completely impersonal. They focused on the technology, not the pitiful souls on the wrong end of an F-105 fighter jet or a B-52 jet bomber. The officer showing the film usually narrated it by saying something like, "Gentlemen, this is incredibly effective ordnance you're seeing."

Now, I wasn't watching training films anymore. I had seen my country's insanity through the eyes of its victims. I was shaken and stunned. My previous outlook on the war and my role in it suddenly seemed selfish. I had been wrapped up in what would happen to me if I declared myself a conscientious objector and quit the Air Force. Now, I had to think about what would happen to "them," the untold people I would kill and maim anonymously from the sky, if I didn't declare peace on the United States.

I had met "the enemy," communists in the Eastern Bloc, and found them to be no enemy at all. Meeting "the enemy" from North Vietnam confirmed my theory that the United States was making up enemies out of innocent people in order to consolidate and advance geo-political power. It was a sickening thought to know that my country was committing crimes of war all over the world.

Hanna sensed my angst and finally broke the silence. "That was unbelievable. Those poor people. That poor man."

I couldn't speak. We sat down for a moment. She kissed me. Her sweetness brought me back. "That was so heavy" was all I could say.

"It definitely takes things to a new level," Hanna observed. "I mean, I've been radically against the war for years, and I never felt anything like that. You handled it well, I must say. Those people felt your pain too."

"My pain is nothing compared to what they've been going through."

"So, what are you going to do?"

"I don't know what I'm going to do, but I know what I'm not going to do."

She hugged me. We walked to the dorm and kissed goodnight. It was definitely not a night for romance. It was a night to attempt to comprehend and process what had just happened.

When I walked into my room there was still a bull session going on. Ustes was lecturing Louis on the danger of national stereotyping. "Holland is much more than wooden shoes, tulips, and windmills," he said, barely acknowledging my arrival. "Come visit and you will see."

I was in shock. I could still see the faces of the North Vietnamese as I lay down on my bunk and closed my eyes. I couldn't talk to my roommates about the situation because I wasn't about to confess my military status. They were busy with each other anyway. The last thing I heard as I drifted off to sleep was Charles lamenting the fact that many English people refer to the Irish as "bogtrotters."

As much alike as we all were, our cultural differences continued to emerge as our month together progressed.

The camp became less and less about working on the collective farm. Miklos didn't seem to mind that we had all lost interest in the apple orchards. There was a lot going on at the university. One day, he scheduled a soccer match between our group and a team from Ethiopia. No one questioned what a soccer team from Ethiopia was doing in Debrecen. Our camp was only one of many international projects going on that summer.

We put a team together to compete. Our European players were excellent. None of the women in our camp had played enough organized soccer to even think about competing for our side. I was selected to play goalie even though I'd never played soccer before, not even once.

The game was exciting and attracted quite a crowd despite the heat. I blocked the first few shots on goal since they were in the air. I had good hands from growing up with basketball. Then they took a shot that stayed on the ground. It went through my legs for a score. It became apparent to everyone on the field I had no feet or legs for the game. Klaus pulled me out and took over the position himself. It didn't matter. The Ethiopians were in much better condition and seemed to handle the heat well. We called the game when they went ahead ten to two.

My pride was wounded. Miklos consoled me good-naturedly. He was absolutely amazed to find out soccer was not a popular sport in the United States. "How can this be?" he asked incredulously.

"We play football, basketball, and baseball in school. That's about it," I explained.

"One day your schools will play soccer," he predicted.

I turned my head toward him in surprise. "Maybe. But not for a while. We're pretty wrapped up in what we have. We mainly play sports that were invented in the US."

Miklos laughed. "Your country thinks it invented the world." I had to laugh with him. The camp was making it apparent to me that I had been brainwashed as a child into thinking the US was the fountain of all things creative and good. Now, I was beginning to see the US as only one part of the big, beautiful world.

No one can really see his own country until he looks at it from the outside.

On another evening, Miklos invited a group of students from the Soviet Union, Estonia, to have dinner with us at the Pioneer Hall. Besides the fact that the men's hair was quite a bit shorter than ours, they looked pretty much the same as us, even some bell-bottom jeans amongst them. Only a few of them spoke English so things were a little quiet over dinner. The party picked up in a hurry after dinner once we started drinking wine and brandy.

Hanna got involved with some of the Finnish-speaking women. I wondered why women from Estonia would speak Finnish. I had forgotten, or perhaps I never knew, that Estonia is right across the Gulf of Finland from Helsinki.

Ustes, Klaus, Charles, and I started drinking shots with the boys from the Soviet Union. At one point I made the mistake of saying, "You Russians sure know how to party. I don't see why we have to keep this Cold War going. Who needs it?"

The Estonian men met my remarks with dead silence. This took me aback since I thought I was striking a harmonious chord with my little plea for peace. "What?" I asked, still trying to be jovial. "Did I say something wrong?"

Klaus stepped in to explain, "They don't like being called Russians, Mark."

"Oh, oh." I slapped my head. "My mistake. I take it back. Here, let me pour us another shot. Please, forgive me. Let us drink to Estonia."

They chuckled mercifully at my clumsy apology and we soon got back to drinking. *Man, everybody's touchy about the Russian thing.*

Grace from Poland heard my Russian faux pas, and after we were all back on track took me aside to offer her explanation. "You must understand, Mark, the Russians have killed so many of the Estonian people. Not only in the name of the Soviet Union, but also for hundreds of years. We in Poland feel the same way about the Russians. Not just because they took over our country after World War II. It goes back much further than that. But in World War II the Russians killed many of my family. They blamed it on the Germans, but it was the Russians who massacred the Polish officer corps in the forest at Katyn, 22,000 of our finest men! Two of them were my father's older brothers!"

I threw my arms out and took two steps back. "Oh, that is so terrible. Your father's brothers? Your uncles? Good Lord! That's not something you get over in time."

Grace frowned and lowered her head. "No, it is not."

I stepped forward to comfort her with a hug. "You know, Grace, in my country we think of Russia and the Eastern Bloc and all communists in general as one entity. In fact, most people in my country think of communism as a beast trying to take over the world, something we need to fight to preserve our freedom."

Grace leaned back, looked up at me, and managed a tight smile. "The communists can't keep themselves together, let alone take over the world. Look what the Russians have done to Poland. Food prices are higher than wages. Our markets have nothing to sell. Our people can't get health care. The Soviet Union has done nothing for us. The Soviet Union is nothing but imperialistic Russia, greedy and brutal as ever. We hate the Russians, just like the Estonians and the East Germans and everybody who's not a Russian hate the Russians.

"So, when you Americans say you're fighting in Southeast Asia to stop the spread of communism, the whole world laughs at you, even China. How do you think China gets along with Russia?"

We laughed together and had another glass of wine. Grace could see she had me to herself for a moment, so she raised a topic we had discussed before. "Mark, you know I want very much to come to your country." I nodded. "And you know I need a letter from a US citizen to sponsor me." I nodded again. "And I was wondering if you would be that person for me?" She looked at me with eyes that said she would do anything for me to be her sponsor.

I answered without hesitation. "Sure, I'll do it. I'll write the letter right now."

Grace shook her head. "No, the letter has to come from inside the United States. When are you going home?"

I looked at her for a long time, realizing I had no answer to that question. "You know, Grace, it could be a long time before I make it back home."

She stuck out her lower lip and moved a little closer to me. Just then, Hanna was there to whisk me away. "Come with me." She stepped between me and Grace. "I've got some people for you to meet."

Grace and I didn't speak much until we were saying goodbye at the end of camp. She gave me her address and I promised to write the letter when and if I made it back home to Indiana.

The camp concluded with a four-day vacation to Lake Balaton, a 77-kilometer, inland lake, and the scenic and historic resort center for much of the Eastern Bloc. We stayed in a massive historic hotel with a hilltop view of the lake. It had all the luxury appointments of Western European hotels, as well as gypsy musicians wandering and playing in the well-manicured courtyards. Hanna and I had a room to ourselves. We were in the blissful stage of early romance— every touch a tingle, every breath an exciting taste of each other. Our previous political and economic discussions on such things as "the dictatorship of the proletariat" had been replaced by concerns over what would happen to us once the camp ended.

One morning, we woke up before dawn to walk down to the lake and watch the sunrise awaken the world with color. We had to climb a fence to get to the beach. The morning air was cold. "I'll bet the water will be warm compared to the air," I challenged her. "Let's go skinny dipping."

Hanna laughed as I pulled off my shirt and unbuckled my jeans. She pulled her peasant blouse over her head. She wasn't wearing a bra. My pants were halfway down my legs. I almost fell over from staring at her naked breasts. They were round and full and not sagging one bit. She shook herself at me and laughed as I stumbled out of my jeans. She slipped out of her panties in one fluid motion and then raised her

arms to the sky. In an instant, she looked like the most impossibly perfect sculpture ever carved. Her young body was silhouetted against the
shadowy mist of the low mountains rising with the sun in the east. I
took a snapshot of her in my mind. My chest resonated with gratitude.
A symphony of classical music swelled in my head.

I lifted her up, and she wrapped her legs around my waist. We
kissed madly to warm each other up as I waded into the water. The
first rays of sunrise slipped through the trees on the other side of the
lake. Hanna squealed in delighted anticipation of getting wet as I kept
walking in, deeper and deeper. She arched her back and raised herself
up by my shoulders as she felt the water on her feet. It was very cold,
but I was already getting used to it.

"Take me in," she yelled as I jumped up and into the water with
her legs still wrapped around me. With a big splash, our embrace went
underwater. We held our breath and kissed for a long time before
coming up for air. We gasped together as we surfaced and the sudden
chill sunk in. She brushed wet hair out of her eyes. She was beautiful
and young and more alive than she had ever been. I felt completely
fortunate to be with her at that perfect moment.

We swam into the rising sun together. The lake began its shining dance of morning as our bodies became comfortable in the water.
When we finally stopped to tread water and look back, we were a
hundred yards offshore. Hanna kissed me softly and then dunked me
when I was off guard. Instead of coming right back up, I dove deeper
and came up behind her. She screamed playfully when I tapped her on
the shoulder from behind and dove under again.

We played in the deep water for a short time, and then agreed to
swim back while we still had enough strength. The air was cold when
we waded out. Neither one of us had thought to bring a towel. We
dried off with our hands and dressed quickly. The sun was shining
bright. There were signs of life at the hotel. We held hands and walked
back up for breakfast.

"We have only two more days together and the camp will be over," Hanna said over our third cup of coffee. She waited for my response. I'd told her many times I would not be coming to Finland with her. Now, I was wondering what I would do. The month had gone by so quickly. Everybody was saying goodbye and talking about where they were headed and what they would do. I had absolutely no plans or itinerary. I'd thought about Africa or maybe the Middle East. I had about $185 left. At a dollar a day, that would last six months.

"Why don't we travel together for a while?" I offered on impulse.

Hanna grabbed both of my hands across the table and smiled in delight and relief. "That would be my dream. You are my dream. Where will we go?"

"I have absolutely no idea."

She scrunched up her nose so I quickly added, "It doesn't matter as long as I'm with you." That made her smile. We got up to go to our room and I said, "How about we head west to Austria?"

Hanna bounced on her toes. "That would be perfect! I've always wanted to go there."

She hugged me hard. I hugged her back. The woman trusted me more than I trusted myself. Yes, I had fallen for her and, yes, I would take good care of her on the road. But I knew there would come a time in the not-too-distant future when we would be saying goodbye. It was inevitable. I thought Hanna was looking for a husband. I was wrong.

We made love the rest of the morning like there would be no afternoon.

We took a nap and she awakened to find me brooding. Everything had seemed so clear that night at the fountain with the North Vietnamese students. Now, with nothing but uncertainty in my near future, a selfish yearning for security kept creeping into my mind. For the one thousandth time, I was rethinking my Air Force decision.

Hanna already knew me so well she could pierce my thoughts. "I thought you made up your mind?" she challenged. "Why go back and worry through it again and again. There is no other choice to make and you know it. Your eyes shine with power when you talk about standing up for what you believe. They fog over and you become distant when you doubt yourself. I love the man with courage. I can't even talk to the man who thinks of himself as a victim."

She was up and pacing the room, getting carried away by her own rhetoric. Her beach thongs made loud slapping sounds against the soles of her feet as she stormed into the bathroom. Hanna would not put up with indecision.

I got out of bed and off my pity pot, put on my bathing suit, and knocked on the bathroom door. "Come on out. You're absolutely right. Don't worry. I'm over it. Come on, let's hit the beach."

CHAPTER SIX

The Torch

HANNA AND I SET OFF ON FOOT from Debrecen headed for Austria. We had agreed to hitchhike the rural roads instead of taking the main highway through Budapest. We were ready to truly experience Hungary, not just watch it speeding by in a 70-mph blur.

The camp had put us both in an adventurous mood. We were feeling invincible, like unarmed soldiers in an international peace crusade. The last month had convinced us that people from all over the world could get along quite well with each other despite cultural and hereditary differences. Our time together had been meaningful and a lot of fun. What little interpersonal drama that developed had dissolved into well-wishing and the exchange of addresses once it was time to  say goodbye. We all came away from the experience realizing that our similarities vastly outweighed our differences. Most importantly, we had recommitted to the proposition that the people of the world want peace, not war.

"I can't believe it's over," Hanna said as we reached the outskirts of the city. "I looked forward to the camp for at least a year and then it happened, and it was even better than I thought it would be, and now it's over."

I took her by the hand. "I know what you mean. The month flew by like a weekend."

"It's sad in a way." She squeezed my hand. "We got so close. It was like we became one big family. We all came together only to have to say goodbye. We'll probably never see any of those people again."

"You never can tell," I said as I stopped and put down my pack to rest. She did the same and watched me carefully. She wasn't at all certain about this hitchhiking plan. She looked down the highway like she was waiting for a bus. She had never hitched a ride in her life.

"Looks like we're on the right road," I pronounced, laughing at her nervousness and knowing I had no idea where we were. All I knew was it was time to head west. "Time to start hitchhiking."

She held her hands out as if to say, "What now?"

I gave her a thumbs up sign with both hands. "It's time to stick out your thumb and get us a ride."

Hanna cocked her head slightly to the right and opened her mouth. "Why me? You're the great hitchhiker."

I couldn't help but chuckle at her reluctance. "One thing you learn hitchhiking is you always put your best foot forward. You, my dear, are definitely our best foot. So, turn around, stick out your thumb, and show those drivers you mean business."

She gave it a try. Cars were coming along about one every minute. She was on her toes for the first few, slumping slightly in disappointment after each passed her by.

"Don't take it personally," I coached. "You never know what's going on in their world. Just because they don't pick you up doesn't mean they don't like you. And wave as they pass so they don't think you're mad at them for not picking you up. Lots of times they don't decide to pick you up until after they've gone by and seen the wave. It makes all the difference. And don't be afraid to hold that thumb up high. Let them see it."

She followed my advice but still had no luck. We were having fun talking about going to Vienna, but I could tell she was getting frustrated. After about thirty cars had passed us by, I said, "Come on, girl, give it some attitude. Drop that shirt over your shoulder. Stick that hip out. Let them know who you are."

Hanna dropped her thumb and turned around to push me in mock anger. "You get out there and show them who *you* are."

I rolled up my sleeves. "All right then. I'll show you how it's done." I stepped up to the road and started waving at drivers as they passed by.

"See?" Hanna gloated. "It's not so easy, is it?"

"Hanna, Hanna, Hanna," I said. "You've got to learn the first rule of hitchhiking. Actually, it's the first rule of living in general."

Hanna waited for me to make my point then realized I would have to be asked before I would answer. "Okay," she grumbled. "I'll bite. What is the first rule of hitchhiking?"

I turned and leaned into her until our foreheads were almost touching. "The first rule of hitchhiking is to never get impatient."

The moment I uttered the words a young mother with two children in the backseat approached in a four-door sedan. I smiled and waved as she passed, then watched in amazement as she came to a skidding halt forty yards down the road.

"That's us!" I shouted as I grabbed my pack and trotted toward the waiting automobile. Hanna hurried to catch up. The driver was out of the car and opening the trunk when we arrived. We thanked her profusely for stopping, threw our packs in the trunk, and crowded into the front seat with Hanna in the middle.

"I can't believe you got so lucky," Hanna muttered as we got in the car.

"Luck is a state of mind." I laughed. "Look how lucky you are. This is your first ride! It doesn't get any better than this!" Hanna squeezed my arm in delight. The trip was already turning out to be as much fun as she had anticipated.

Our benefactor drove us sixty kilometers into the rolling farmland, chatting away the entire time. We nodded and laughed whenever she did, but we didn't understand one word of her Hungarian monologue. That didn't bother her. She was grateful to have adult company. The children in the back kept trying to climb into the front seat with us. Mother's driving was a little scary every time she turned around to lecture them about staying in their seats. Even so, she managed to be quite the tour guide, pointing out one landmark after another. We nodded and used what little Hungarian we had acquired to show our appreciation for her kind attempts to acquaint us with her homeland. We managed to communicate that we were going to Vienna. She told us we were on the wrong road, but we managed to convince her we were happy to be taking the back roads to our destination. Finally, she dropped us off in the middle of we-didn't-know-where and bid us a cheery farewell. When we retrieved our gear from her trunk, she pointed west to confirm the way to Wien. She then drove south to disappear into the countryside.

"What do you suppose she was talking about?" Hanna wondered as we stared down the deserted highway.

I looked both ways down the road and saw no vehicles of any kind, not even a farmer's tractor. "I think she might have been saying she was leaving us in a place where no one could ever get a ride to anywhere. She'll probably tell her husband tonight about the two foreigners who are going to spend the next three weeks walking to Austria."

Three hours later, exactly five vehicles had passed us by and one of them was going in the opposite direction. We had walked a good ten kilometers by then. Storm clouds were forming on the late afternoon horizon. Hanna turned to me and said, "I thought you said this would be easy. You said the Hungarian people are so friendly. I'm beginning to think no one will ever pick us up. I don't see how they can drive by and not help us out of this vast emptiness. Maybe we should think about taking a train."

It began to rain softly.

"Nonsense, my dear," I replied in full bravado. "There are no trains out here. Fear not. All things come to those who wait. Have faith. We're going to get lucky soon. I can feel it. It only takes one. You never know when that one person is going to come along and take us all the way to Wien. That's the beauty of hitchhiking. If you wait long enough, you know you're going to get lucky."

Hanna wiped the rain off her face. "I'm not feeling too lucky."

"Don't worry," I reassured. "You're with the luckiest man on the planet."

She looked at me warily. I grabbed her by both shoulders. "No, no. I can prove it."

She raised her eyebrow and waited for me to make my case. I backed up and held my arms up to the sky. "As the rain is my witness, I am the luckiest man on the planet because . . . I'm with the most wonderful woman in the world."

That made her laugh. She wrapped her arms around me and squeezed tight. "You make me happy even when you drag me out to nowhere in the rain." She pulled a parka out of her pack and put it on. The rain glistened on her hood. We trudged on. Dusk was just beginning to settle in when we came alongside a wooded area.

"Looks like time to make camp," I said. "This wood will be a perfect place."

Hanna stomped her feet on the puddling pavement. "A perfect place for what? A perfect place to sleep in the rain?"

"Now, now." I tried to sound soothing. "I've got a great tent. We'll be fine. Come on. You'll see. Follow me." We left the road and waded through tall, wet grass to reach the woods. Hanna didn't complain. She could be intrepid.

We selected a campsite in a relatively dry spot beneath a giant oak tree on high ground. The rain became steadier in the short time it took us to set up the tent. I threw the tarp down on the floor of the tent for added protection and stacked our packs inside, back to back. When I came out of the tent, Hanna was standing in the rain, asking, "How are we going to get dry?"

"We're going to get naked and hang our clothes on our packs to dry," I said, untying my shoes and removing my socks. "Then we're going to spread out our sleeping bags and kiss each other dry."

We laughed as we got naked and embraced. The raindrops felt delicious on our exposed skin. We kissed each other deeply. The weather was the last thing on our minds. We touched each other.

A drum roll of not-too-distant thunder brought me back to reality. A big storm was rolling in. The sky was darkening. We crawled into the dry and cozy tent and spread out our sleeping bags on top of each other to make a comfortable bed. We both still had droplets of water all over our bodies. I laid her down and quickly but gently sucked each and every drop off her grateful skin.

The rain began to pour, pounding on the double roof of the tent, increasing our excitement. We had each entered an altered state of heightened sensuality.

The thunder and lightning were upon us as we rolled with each other into a blissful exhaustion. Rain beat down on the tent. Hanna began what sounded like soft crying but turned into gentle laughter. We disentangled our limbs. The moisture on our bodies was no longer rain. We were sweating heavily as we clung to each other like survivors of a sinking ship. Humidity in the tent was one hundred percent. Neither of us said a word. We were out of breath. It was damp and dark and warm in the tent. We were babies together in a womb of satisfaction. We fell into a deep slumber.

The storm awakened us in the middle of the night as it became more violent. Lightning bolts were striking ground much too close for comfort. They illuminated the tent. We felt like insects trapped inside a flashing neon light. Hanna clung to me.

"I remember when I was a little girl," she whispered. "Storms like this always made me run into my parents' bedroom. They let me sleep with them when I was afraid. My mother liked to sing me this song." With that, Hanna hummed a beautiful Finnish folk song, soft and melodic.

"What does it say?" I asked dreamily after she finished.

"It's about a hunter who saves a princess from an evil queen."

I raised up on one elbow. "Wow, it sounds too mellow to be talking about all that."

She could only see me when the lightning flashed. "Most of the song is the hunter telling the princess everything will be all right."

"Do you need me to be your hunter?" I asked, playfully curling her hair.

Hanna breathed deeply and sat up. "I need you to feed me," she said as she flinched involuntarily when another blast of lightning struck.

We were well prepared for our expedition. There was even a candle to light. We laid out a feast of bread and cheese and sliced meat and carrots and apples. Hanna grinned as she pulled out a bottle of Bull's Blood wine. "Look what we forgot in all the excitement." Then she frowned. "Now, how are we going to open it?"

"Not to worry," I said, pulling out my Swiss Army knife. "This will definitely do the trick. Look, it's even got a corkscrew."

"You never cease to amaze," she said with her mouth full as we began stuffing our faces and washing it down with long gulps from the bottle of wine. Once we'd eaten everything in sight, I blew out the candle and we slipped under one sleeping bag. The storm raged on. We snuggled up, safe and warm and dry, sleeping soundly in our tent under the oak tree, somewhere in Hungary.

We slept in late. Neither of us had a watch. It didn't matter. We felt totally refreshed as we slipped into dry clothes and packed up the tent and our gear. The rain had stopped, although the sky was still overcast. Our clothes from the day before were still wet, so we draped them over our packs. We walked through the trees to the highway, avoiding the tall, wet grass.

There were no vehicles on the road for quite some time. We didn't mind. It felt good to be walking west. There were many blackbirds in the fields that cheered us on with their songs.

After walking more than five kilometers, we stopped when we heard a car approaching from the rear. I waved as the driver passed. He seemed to be pointing behind him at something.

"Did you see that guy pointing?" I asked.

"I thought I saw that," Hanna said. "What do you think he was saying?"

I watched his car as it faded in the distance. "I don't know. Maybe he had too much in his back seat to pick us up."

I looked down the highway, which stretched out as far as I could see. There was nothing on the road. And then there was something. A large shape stretching over the last hill on the horizon. At first, I thought it might be some kind of farm implement. Then it began to look like more than one vehicle.

I pointed at the distant hill. "Look, Hanna. Do you see that?"

She squinted and looked down the road. "Yes, I see something coming over that hill. It looks like ants in a column."

Whatever it was kept coming over the hill. Even as the first part was disappearing into a valley, the "ants" kept coming over the hill. They were still coming when the first part of the column came into view again atop the next hill closer to us. I couldn't make out what it was until it disappeared into the next valley and reappeared on the next hill. Now, it was getting close enough to identify. It looked like a flame dancing down the highway, followed by a long line of cars. As the procession got closer, I could see a runner was carrying the flame. The smaller vehicles around the runner were a motorcycle escort. The heat of all those internal combustion engines turned the humid horizon into animated waves of heat, dancing above the two-lane blacktop.

I knew I should understand what was approaching, but I couldn't wrap my mind around it. Hanna said, "Maybe we should get off the road. It looks like some kind of military thing."

Then it hit me. "It's the Olympic torch!" I howled. "It's the Olympic torch procession. They must be on their way from Athens to Munich. This is unbelievable. We're going to hitch a ride on the Olympic procession and they're going to take us all the way to Munich! See what I told you? It only takes one!"

"I don't know," Hanna said. "Do you really think it's the Olympic torch? They wouldn't come this way, would they?"

I turned around in circles with my arms outstretched like I was flying. "How could you doubt the master hitchhiker? It was I who tested you last night in the forest. It was I who set you up for this, the ultimate in hitchhiking adventure. It's the Olympic torch all right. We're on the road from Athens to Munich. Yea, only those who survive the thunderstorm of midnight will have the chance to ride with the gods in the morning!"

Hanna laughed at my crazy optimism and started getting excited with me as the procession drew near. It was formidable. The ground shook from the motorcycle thunder. I stepped to the edge of the road and stuck out my thumb with all the formality I could muster.

First came the police on motorcycles with blue lights spinning on their handlebars. I had to back up and off the shoulder of the road to make room for them. They were obviously prepared to run over anyone who remained in their path. They looked at us warily as I kept my thumb out. They didn't stop.

Next came the runner. His torch smelled like a kerosene heater. He laughed when I turned my hitchhiking thumb into a thumbs-up sign of approval. He was thin and showing no signs of fatigue. His tracksuit was white with something about the Munich Olympics emblazoned on his chest. He wasn't about to stop.

In fact, not one vehicle in the entourage stopped, although most of the drivers acknowledged my hitchhiking thumb with a thumbs-up sign. I realized no one could stop to pick us up, even if he or she wanted to. They had to keep moving as a unit.

I watched the last couple of black sedans disappear into the west. The silence was deafening. The entire procession twinkled off into nothingness over the next hill as if it had vanished into space. Hanna and I watched the empty road for quite a while before turning to each other in amazement over what we had just witnessed.

"Man, that's something to tell the folks back home," I said. "Just when you're least suspecting it, something comes along to show you how truly bizarre and beautiful the world really is. I mean, they run that torch from Athens all the way to Munich. What a statement for world peace. And we were here to watch it. We had our own private Olympic preview!"

Hanna put her hands on her hips. "But we didn't get a ride."

"Don't you realize what just happened?" I said, trying to reason with her. "You just witnessed a major sign in both of our lives. Think about it. That torch is a symbol of everything I'm starting to believe. We wouldn't have seen it if we'd taken the main highway. You've got to throw yourself out on the road to nowhere to find out where you're supposed to go. You taught me that. You're the one who said I should quit the Air Force without worrying about the consequences."

"I know what you're saying." Hanna hugged me. "I'm glad to be with you. The parade was fantastic." She sounded less than enthusiastic.

"I'll go you one further," I said. "That torch is the light of faith, the light of hope, the light of a meaningful existence in the darkness of self-doubt. That torch was a sign that there are better things to come for both of us. In fact, I predict that in less than an hour that torch will be followed by someone who will give us a ride, a ride unlike any ride before."

Hanna shook her head in mock wonder. She had fallen in love with a dreamer. "Should we wait here for the miracle, or should we walk while we wait?"

We started walking. The sun was trying to break through the clouds. Twenty minutes passed, then twenty more. Not a single vehicle appeared on the highway. I was beginning to doubt the accuracy of my prediction when a canvas-covered military truck lumbered up the road and slowed to a stop in front of us.

"See!" I exclaimed. "What did I tell you?"

An officer in a green uniform got out of the passenger side of the vehicle and greeted us warmly. We told him we were headed to Wien, and he nodded affirmatively. He seemed much more interested in Hanna than me as he escorted us to the back of the vehicle and threw open the canvas backing. As we climbed into the truck, we realized it was full of two squads of Russian soldiers in full combat regalia.

The soldiers were quiet at first, but as our eyes adjusted to the light, it was obvious they were all eyeing Hanna closely. We rolled on thirty kilometers or more. Two of the men across from Hanna and me began laughing in a way that let me know it was only a matter of time before they started having fun with the only woman on board. I could see fear in Hanna's eyes.

Sure enough, one of the men reached over and tried to stroke her hair. I pointed my finger in a way that brushed his arm aside and said, "No!" in a commanding voice.

The soldiers uttered a low moan of disapproval and impending doom. I held up my hands as if to say, "I come in peace." I knew we could be in grave danger. The truck was moving too fast for us to jump out. As much as we wanted a ride, this was not the ride we wanted.

The man across from us pointed at me and said, "No!" even more loudly than I had said it. The soldiers waited for my response. It was clearly not the time to get angry. *These guys could throw me out the back of the truck. What would happen to Hanna then?*

My days as a small kid on the playground came to the rescue. I tried being funny and went into my stoned hippie routine. "Come on, man. Don't be a bummer. It's all groovy. It's far out. Peace out, my brother." I flashed a double peace sign and rolled my head back.

The entire truck erupted in laughter at my desperate but successful attempt at humor. After all, they were all young men about my age. They were decent guys, trapped in the military. Comic relief saved the day. Even the soldier across from us nodded that a truce could indeed be had. One of the soldiers struck up a conversation in English once he realized I was from the USA. He was amazed that an American would be hitchhiking in Hungary. I was relieved to be talking our way out of what had seemed like an impossible situation.

In another thirty kilometers, the truck rumbled to a halt. The officer flung open the canvas and Hanna and I got out, squinting in the sudden light. The soldiers were silent as we disembarked. I saluted them and indicated to their commander that this was a fine group of gentlemen. They all waved and said goodbye in Russian and English. The commander shook my hand, bowed slightly to Hanna, got back in the truck, and drove away.

Once the truck was out of sight to the north, Hanna collapsed in my arms. "I thought I was going to be raped," she cried. "I really thought I was going to be raped. You saved me. You were so brave." She kissed me. "You were funny. You saved me."

"Man, I thought we were in serious trouble," I said, holding her tight. "Those guys are just like soldiers everywhere, though. They were just looking to have a little fun. Did you see them? They were just kids. Heavily armed kids, to be sure. They're out on maneuvers. No surprise to see Russian troops in Hungary. Maybe they've got something to do with the Olympic torch."

"Some of those men looked like hungry animals to me," Hanna said, beginning to get a grip on herself. "You didn't see the way they were looking at me. I know what those looks mean. Thank you for being so good."

"We got lucky," I said. "It might have been a different story if their officers hadn't been riding up front. Nothing beats the chain of command for preserving order."

Hanna looked at me longingly and said, "I feel safe with you, but you do get us into strange places."

We sat down on our packs. I kissed her forehead and cheeks and lips and said, "You know I love you, and I promise not to let anything bad happen to you."

She threw her arms around my neck and whispered in my ear, "I love you too. I'm so glad we found each other."

"This might be a good time for a hitchhiking story," I said as she sat back down.

She straightened her sagging shoulders. "Yes, it would be. I could use a story right about now."

I stood up to tell the tale like Hanna was a crowd of a hundred people. "Okay. Like I said, it's a road story. I was hitchhiking back from California. In fact, I got a criminal citation for illegal hitchhiking there. Never did go to court for that. There's probably a warrant for me by now. Anyway, I was trying to get home to Indiana. This is in June, two months ago. I made it to the middle of the desert in Nevada. It was so hot the asphalt on the side of the road was melting. There was no water or even any shade for miles. A thousand people must have passed me by that day. Nobody would pick me up. Nobody even slowed down. I don't know why, but I couldn't get a ride to save my life. The sun went down and there I was, still alone with no water, dying of thirst along the highway. It must have been close to midnight when I finally walked down off the road a little and rolled up in my tarp and went to sleep."

Hanna was in the palm of my hand. Her eyes widened. "Weren't you worried about snakes?"

I bent down and put my hands on my knees. "Odd you should mention that because I do have an unnatural fear of snakes. They terrify me. On this night, though, I was so tired and burned out from the sun that I fell asleep immediately. I didn't wake up until the sun got burning hot again the next morning. I started walking down the road. By now, thirst was such an issue I knew I had to get somewhere to find water. There was a road sign that said the next exit was thirty-five miles away. I figured I could make it on foot, but it was getting hard to believe no one would pick me up."

Hanna stood up as I straightened up. "Why couldn't you get a ride?"

I thought about her question for a short time. "Well, sometimes it just happens. You can't predict the road. It has a mind of its own. That's kind of the point of the story."

"I see."

"So, anyway, there I was about to give up hope when a Volkswagen bus comes to a dusty stop to give me a ride. I'm running up to it and I see a bumper sticker that says *Jesus liebt dich* and I think it's some German Jesus freak who's probably going to try and save my soul."

Hanna sat back down. "Oh, I hate those people."

I moved in closer to her. "No, this guy turns out to be pretty cool. He's American, for one thing. For another, he's got a big jug of ice water and he lets me drink most of it. He tells me his name is Grover, and we really hit it off, talking about everything from Vietnam to the Beatles."

"Did you tell him how you met John Lennon?"

I had to laugh out loud. "Of course I did. I tell that story to anyone who will listen, as you know. He didn't believe me at first, but then he realized I was telling the truth and that really took our conversation to the next level. We started talking about spirituality and realized we were each trying to escape the material world of our parents. He never mentioned Jesus until I brought it up and, even then, he wasn't pushy about it. He just said his life had gotten a lot better once he had something to believe in."

Hanna shook her finger at me. "Once he accepted Christ as his personal savior?"

I shook my head. "No, he wasn't 'holier than thou' about it. He was pretty down-to-earth. So, we keep talking and talking, and pretty soon he tells me his last name is Coors. Coors like the beer."

"What do you mean?"

"There's a beer called Coors. It comes from Colorado and kids from the Midwest drive to the mountains to bring it back and sell it to their friends."

Hanna raised her eyebrows. "Why do they do that?"

I shrugged my shoulders. "I don't know. It's got a light taste, brewed from mountain spring water, they say. It is good. They don't distribute it east of the Mississippi, so the only way to get it is to haul it back from the mountains in the trunk of your car. It's mainly just fun to have something you can't buy in your home state.

"But that's not the point. Once I became aware he's a member of the Coors family, I realize this ride could take me all the way to Golden, Colorado. That's the headquarters for Coors beer. And that's just what he did. He took me from dying of thirst in the desert to the beer capital of the United States in one ride!"

Hanna hung her head. "Oh, so this is a story to make me feel better about being stuck out here in the middle of nowhere?"

"Yes, but it's more than that. Grover took me to the family cabin and I had dinner with the entire Coors family. They turned out to be friendly and welcoming people. We had steak and salad and Coors for dinner. I thought I'd died and gone to heaven. They're a conservative family. Grover was obviously the hippie of the family. But they were kind and hospitable. They let me pitch my tent there for the night. They had just enough beds for the family. When I told them I was headed to Europe for the summer, they invited me to their hotel suite in Munich for the Olympics."

Hanna looked up expectantly. "Did you tell them you were in the Air Force?"

"Oh, yeah. Right away. Being a second lieutenant didn't hurt me at all with the Coors family."

Hanna laughed. "Does this mean we're going to Munich for the games so we can visit your beer family friends?"

I looked down the road again. "I don't know. We'll have to see. The first thing we've got to do is get a ride out of here."

"That was a good story," she said. "I'm feeling better already."

I sat down with her. "The real point of the story, though, is how the road leads you to places you would never find until you let yourself go. I mean, what are the chances of having dinner with the Coors family? It never would have happened if I'd stayed home. What are the chances of seeing the Olympic torch pass by in rural Hungary? And what are the chances of sitting here on the road with this beautiful woman from Finland?"

Hanna hugged me gratefully. She was trying to let herself go. She was learning to trust the road. A wave of well-being washed over us. At least the Russian soldiers episode had turned out well. Maybe everything else would too. Of course, I could tell from her questions that she still had her doubts, not only about the road, but also about where our relationship was heading.

Within an hour, a Volkswagen bus with three Americans from Chicago stopped to pick us up. Their names were Tom, Susan, and Joe. They were on their way back from Istanbul, nearing the end of a two-month journey.

"Chicago?" I asked incredulously. "I can't believe it. I'm from Fort Wayne, Indiana. What are you guys doing here?"

"We're just passing through," Susan said, introducing herself to Hanna and stowing our packs in the back of the bus. "What are you doing here?" She shook my hand. "And how long have you been waiting along this deserted highway?"

We explained ourselves. They were happy to meet a woman from Finland and happy to add some new people to their conversation. The van was a typical, live-in travel unit. It was a mess. In the back corner were piles of dirty clothing and unrolled sleeping bags. On the engine between two front seats were the remains of a fruit basket and several unfolded maps. The windows around the sides all had curtains rigged up haphazardly with string. The middle seat had been taken out. I sat on a tire and Hanna joined Tom on the back seat.

"You got any smoke?" Joe asked.

"Sorry, man," I said. "I haven't been stoned on anything but wine and brandy since Spain."

"Bummer, man," Tom said. "We had nothing but great hash in Turkey, but we had to ditch it because of all the borders."

"Man, Turkey sounds so cool," I said. "I'd love to get there. What's it like?"

"Istanbul is pretty crowded," Susan explained. "It sure is fun, though. Lots of discotheques like any big European city. If you get to the outskirts of town, you can still see the primitive culture and hear those weird priests wailing in the towers. It's really spooky."

"Where are you headed now?" Hanna asked.

"We're on our way to Amsterdam," Tom said. "We're going to sell the bus and fly back to the States. We're a little burnt out from driving so much if you want to know the truth. Every time we hit a border, they take one look at our long hair and tear the bus apart. The communist cops are the worst. They can get away with anything."

Hanna tried to bite her tongue but couldn't do it. "Communist cops?" she began sarcastically. "What about Chicago cops? The whole world saw what they did at your political convention in 1968. Europeans used to be afraid to go to Chicago because of the gangsters. Now, it's the police that really frighten us."

Tom realized he had unwittingly opened a political can of worms. Susan, Joe's wife, turned around to mediate. "Cops are the same everywhere. That's why we call them pigs."

Joe joined in. "Yeah, you won't catch us defending the Chicago police. We've all had unpleasant run-ins with them. It all starts with the mayor, Richard Daley. He runs the city with an iron fist. It's the mayor we've got to get rid of."

"We've got plenty of those party bosses ourselves," Hanna said in a conciliatory tone.

The conversation turned to the American presidential election. We all agreed that Richard Nixon was going to crush George McGovern no matter what happened with the anti-war movement. Too many Americans were still caught up in the Red Scare, the anti-communist rhetoric of the Cold War. Nixon was also doing a good job co-opting the peace movement by promising to bring the war to an honorable conclusion.

I told the Chicagoans about our experience with the North Vietnamese students in Debrecen and how the Nixon administration was secretly bombing civilians in North Vietnam. I also told them about my military status and how I was planning on declaring myself a conscientious objector. Hanna beamed as she saw me trying on my new identity. Susan, Joe, and Tom were surprised by the news that confirmed their suspicions about what was really going on with the war. They also expressed complete support for my decision to not participate in the madness.

From then on, the talk turned to Chicago and all the things they missed about the Windy City and the States in general. It occurred to me that these weary travelers were just plain homesick.

We made it through the Hungarian border without too much trouble. It was much easier getting out than it had been getting in. We arrived in Wien and began looking for smoke. It took less than an hour in the Volksgarten to score three grams of hashish from a stringy-haired, bleary-eyed street freak. Joe quickly crumbled a chunk of the hash into a joint with some tobacco and we all celebrated getting high for the first time in a long time. Everybody, that is, except Hanna. She clearly disapproved as the bus filled with intoxicating smoke. She also made it plain that she didn't like seeing the side of me that loved getting loaded. She wrapped her arms around her knees and didn't say a word for fifty miles. Despite her self-righteous indignation, she ended up getting a contact high and loosened up considerably.

We floated out of town like the Furry Freak Brothers on patrol as we drove on to find a smaller town with less expensive places to eat and sleep. We found a youth hostel about 9 p.m. in the next small town but it was completely full. The little old lady in charge gave us directions to a place she thought might have a vacancy. It was raining, so camping was not much of an option.

When we arrived at the address she had given us, it didn't look at all like a hotel. There were no signs out front. The door was unlocked, so we walked in and called out, "Is anybody home?"

A young American woman walked down a long corridor to meet us and looked surprised to see us in the hall. She quickly regained her sense of hospitality. "Welcome, come on in. I'll bet you're hungry."

We expressed gratitude as she walked us into a large dining area with four long tables and a serving counter. Another woman soon joined her. Despite the late hour, the two of them prepared us a quick meal of vegetable soup, milk, bread, and cheese. We only protested a little. The food tasted great. The women joined us at the table, and soon two men sat down as well. They introduced themselves as Ronald and James. They were quite friendly and unpretentious. We introduced ourselves all around.

"How many people live here?" Tom asked.

"People come and go a lot," James said. "Usually, there's about thirty of us. As you can tell from the outside of our building, we don't solicit guests, but we are always pleased when the Lord sends someone our way."

"Oh, wow, Jesus freaks in Austria!" Susan exclaimed.

Our hosts laughed heartily. Ronald explained, "I wouldn't exactly call us Jesus freaks. We're from the Children of God sect. Every one of us knows Jesus Christ personally. He lives in all of us and we live to serve him. But we're not freaks about it. We're a faith-based community. Our mission is to spread the gospel."

Hanna looked at me like she was ready to walk out then and there. I wasn't about to leave. These people were fascinating and not at all like my negative notions about missionary types. Several more members joined the table as we finished eating. There was an author and his wife, an ex-Ford Motor Company executive, a middle-aged couple who used to teach middle school in Pennsylvania, and several reformed members of the "drug culture," as they put it.

What impressed us most about these people was that they wouldn't accept money from us for food and lodging. As our conversations continued it became obvious we were invited to stay as long as we wanted and to become full members of the sect whenever we chose.

"How do you people get money to survive?" Joe asked.

"Put your faith in the Lord," one of the Christians replied, "and He will provide for you."

I leaned across the table with outstretched arms. "You've got to be kidding."

It was no joke to them. These people had been living on faith for more than two years. We listened to stories about financial support through the mail from people they had never heard of and gifts such as cars and refrigerators from perfect strangers. It was more than Hanna could take. As a Marxist, she had been trained that "religion is the opiate of the masses." She politely excused herself and went off to sleep on the hall floor. Sue, Joe, and Tom joined her. The women apologized for not having any extra beds, but they did provide some nice thick blankets for padding.

I was much too intrigued to go to sleep. We continued talking into the night. Their faith in Christ sounded exactly like the philosophy I had been developing. My faith was in The Road. I now knew I could walk down any road and be fine. In fact, I was coming to believe that surrendering myself to The Road was the only way to get wherever it was I was supposed to be going. "No maps, no money" was in the early stages of becoming my motto.

It was beginning to dawn on me that it doesn't matter whether you put your faith in Jesus Christ, or The Road, or The Buddha of All Enlightenment. The important thing is the leap of faith that gets you outside of yourself so you can connect with whatever it is that's out there. And every hitchhike is a leap of faith in the kindness of your fellow man.

As I lay under the blanket provided by the faithful, a universal truth came to me. *There are only two things you need to know about God or the Universe or whatever you want to call the great unknown. Number one, there is one; and, number two, it's not you.*

CHAPTER SEVEN

The Cabin

THE "KIDS" FROM CHICAGO dropped Hanna and me off on the highway overlooking Innsbruck. They weren't interested in getting tangled up in what they called the "Tyrolean tourist trap." We thanked them profusely for the ride and set off walking down the road. The jewel of a city sparkled in the sun as it nestled in the valley beneath massive snow-capped Alpine mountains. I took a deep breath and felt myself filling with excitement at having such a wonderful opportunity for exploration and discovery.

"You'd think they could have driven us to a hotel," Hanna complained.

"Those guys are burned out," I responded, trying not to let her negativity bring me down. "They're done with sightseeing. The road is no longer their friend. The only place they want to go is home. But who cares? This has to be one of the most beautiful walks in the world. Let's just stroll on down to Innsbruck for lunch."

Hanna stopped walking and pursed her lips into a full pout. "It's a lot farther away than it looks." After less than three days on the road, she had already realized that hitchhiking wasn't going to work for her. I kept walking. She had to hurry to catch up to me, grumbling all the way. "I don't like feeling dirty all the time and I don't like trying to sleep on the ground. I can't wait to get a nice hotel room and take a long, hot shower."

We had walked halfway to town when a small truck pulled over to give us a ride. We piled into the open back bed of the truck. It was half filled with piles of debris and smelled strongly of manure and gasoline. Hanna rolled her eyes and held her nose in disgust. This was not how she wanted to arrive in Innsbruck. She wanted a limousine, not a garbage truck. She was missing the point. It was a ride. It beat walking by a mile, or maybe by five miles.

It was becoming painfully obvious that Hanna was also missing one of the key ingredients to successful hitchhiking. She was not able to laugh at herself and the insanely silly situations hitchhikers must not only endure but also embrace. Without a keen sense of humor, the road can take you down pretty fast.

Despite the stench of the truck, we bounced into Innsbruck with eyes wide in appreciation of the gothic palaces and churches of the medieval old town. Green copper domes rose high above the wall of houses on the banks of the Inn River. Beyond the Hofburg Palace we could see ski lifts rising into the wall of mountains in the distance.

Hanna wasn't interested in the scenery. Once we stopped in the city center, she marched into the nearest hotel and booked a room like she didn't care if I followed her or not. I almost didn't.

She hadn't slept well on the floor of the Christian commune, and she hadn't appreciated the faith-based conversations I had found so challenging. She was tired and cranky. We didn't speak as she undressed quickly and slipped into the shower, which was a curtain on a hoop over a tub. I let her bathe alone and sat down to roll a hash joint. She took a long time in the bath and was obviously feeling much better when she emerged. "It's all yours," she said cheerfully before her mood darkened again. "Is that hashish I smell?"

"It sure is," I said in a stoned tone as I stripped for a shower. "I would have saved some for you, but I know you don't want any." Hanna did not respond. Hashish for her meant nothing but being put in danger of arrest.

We spent the rest of the day wine tasting our way through the city and carefully avoiding the issues we both knew would prevent us from continuing to travel together. At dinner, I finally said, "You know, I don't think I'm going on to Munich."

"I know," she said flatly and much to my surprise. "I'm not ready for Munich either. It's going to be crazy with the Olympics going on. I've been thinking it's time for me to get back home anyway. Where will you go?"

She asked the question so matter-of-factly that I didn't know how to respond. *Is she leaving me or am I leaving her?*

"Do you want me to go?" I asked.

Hanna took both my hands over the table and looked me in the eyes. "I don't want you to go, but I can see you have to go. You're still searching for yourself, and you can't do that with me tagging along. I can't help you find what you're looking for. I'll only be in the way. It's not that I don't love you. I do. Our time together in the camp was the best part of my life." She was starting to cry. So was I.

Hanna sniffled and blew her nose gently with a cloth napkin. "You're not ready for a woman in your life. You have no idea where you're going in this world. I know you will go all the way and I know you will succeed. But you really don't know what you're looking for. You know there's something out there somewhere you've got to find. I can't help you find it. And I can't travel like you. It's too hard. I don't want to live like a refugee."

I shifted uncomfortably in my chair. I wasn't sure if she was insulting me or encouraging me, but I knew one thing for sure. She was right. I was looking for adventure, off to see the world. In some ways, I had taken her with me from the camp as a companion to buffer the loneliness and uncertainty of traveling without having a destination. I needed the road to show me where to go and what to do about the Air

Force. I couldn't admit it to Hanna, but taking the easy way out and serving my time in the military remained an option in the back of my mind, especially when the road got rough.

It took a while for me to express myself, but I eventually managed to say gratefully, "I love you." I couldn't believe she wasn't making a scene or accusing me of using her and playing with her affections. In fact, I was disappointed she seemed so ready and willing to let me go.

"Let's go back to the room and make love," she said with an irresistible twinkle in her eyes. I smiled in surprise and came around the table to kiss her. *How can this intense romance be ending so abruptly? How can we give it up without a fight?*

That night we were tender and gentle with each other. There was no talk about politics or economics or the Air Force. There was no talk at all.

We rolled over and over in our sexual acrobatics. Hanna somehow managed to always come out on top. A streetlight through the window cast a luminous glow on her gorgeous glowing body. She was saying goodbye sexually. She wanted me to know she loved me even though she knew it was time to let me go. She kissed my face and neck and shoulders. Somewhere in the delicious warmth of her whispers, I fell asleep.

I found myself back on the highway looking down on Innsbruck, alone this time. Neither one of us had cried when we kissed and hugged goodbye. We exchanged addresses and promised to meet again. Now, I wondered how she was doing down there. She would be headed back to Finland soon.

It was August 24th. I had $172 to my name and I was thinking about heading for the Middle East or maybe even Africa. I knew I wasn't going to Munich. That would be one expensive world circus. The Coors family wouldn't miss me or probably even remember me.

Instead, I headed east for Leoben, Austria, to see my friend, Peter, and his wife, Helga. I'd been planning on going to see them after the camp. My trip with Hanna had taken me west of their home. Now, it was time to head back east to see them.

The hitchhike from Innsbruck back to Leoben was surprisingly easy. I kept thinking about Hanna and how wonderful our time together had been. And how suddenly it had ended. It was hard to believe she was gone; even harder to believe I left Innsbruck without so much as a gondola ride into the mountains. We could have stayed there together for a month. Instead, I ended up virtually fleeing the scene. I felt much the same as I'd felt leaving Danny in Spain. My heart was heavy but not broken.

Each of these women taught me an important lesson. Danny showed me the shame and fear I felt about my Air Force involvement. Hanna showed me the shame and fear I felt toward my country in general.

The seeds of an important thought had been planted in my sub-conscious mind and were beginning to sprout into a conscious notion. I was beginning to understand how the women in my life would shape my worldview. I didn't know it yet, but my encounters with women were more important spiritually than sexually. The women were my guides and teachers. They were mirrors for my soul.

My twenty-two-year-old hormones were at the helm of my ship. Even so, a small voice inside kept telling me to pay attention to the women on a deeper level. Each one was an important point of reference on my life journey. I wondered if I would ever connect the dots.

Peter and Helga were happy to see me. Peter had stayed with my family in 1969 as part of an international exchange program. He was nearly thirty years old now and beginning to take over his father's construction business. I hadn't realized how prominent his family was until I visited him in 1970 while studying in Wien. He'd taken me skiing, to a formal ball in Salzburg, and to his family's rustic cabin in the mountains. He and Helga had met as members of the same exchange program. They married after returning to Austria. They had no children yet and lived in a spacious apartment in Leoben. Their travels through North America had broadened their horizons considerably. Hippie vagabonds were nothing new to them.

"It looks like you are ready for anything." Peter laughed as he inspected my backpacking gear. "I hope you haven't had to use your sword on anybody."

I slapped the sheathed machete on my right thigh. "This is for peace of mind more than anything. My father brought it back from Costa Rica."

Helga grabbed me by the shoulders. "How long since you've talked to your parents?"

One look in her concerned eyes and I realized the import of her question. I lowered my eyes. "Almost two months."

Peter put both hands on his head and opened wide his eyes and mouth. "We must call them tonight. I'll bet they're worried sick about you."

I could see Helga moving for the telephone as I offered up a lame explanation. "No, I've written them letters. They know I'm coming to see you."

The telephone conversation with my parents was wonderful. They were vastly relieved to hear I was safe and sound with Peter and Helga. I became instantly homesick the moment I heard my mother's voice. My sisters, Terri, Amy, and Laura, each got on the phone and said how much they missed me. They were so sweet. Life on Sunset Drive was clearly going on quite well without me. My wonderful mother was worried and wondered where I was headed and when I was coming home. I was vague and told her I was going to bum around Europe for a while. No need to worry her with my plans to explore the Third World and resign my Air Force commission. My father told me he loved me and to be safe. I told him about the camp in Hungary and all the wonderful people I'd met. He laughed at the story about me playing goalie for a soccer team.

When we hung up, I thought about heading home immediately. I missed the security of my hometown. All I really wanted to do was go jumping around the golf course on my motorcycle.

I had no place to go and there was nothing I had to do. But there was a big wild world waiting to be explored, and I was feeling as though I had just scratched the surface of my own identity. Running for home would be giving up. I knew I had many miles to go before my decision to quit the Air Force would become settled in my mind. The road would show me where to go and what to do.

I spent nearly two weeks with Peter and Helga. They worked during the day while I explored the town and surrounding mountain trails. At night, we had dinner and extended conversations. Peter was alarmed at my plans to declare myself a conscientious objector.

"What will your father say?" he asked.

I took a big drink of beer and wiped my moth with a napkin before answering. "He's not going to like it much. He served in the army in both World War II and the Korean War. He's a veteran through and through. But he's not in favor of the Vietnam War. It took a while, but he finally came around to being anti-war."

Helga began clearing the dinner plates. "What will the Air Force say?"

I jumped up to help her. "That is the much tougher question. The Air Force will want to throw me in jail."

Peter waited to speak until I came back from the kitchen. "Will you go to Canada?"

I sat down, put my elbows on the table, and held my head in my hands. "I don't know what I'll do. All I know is what I won't do. I won't kill innocent people for no good reason."

They listened with interest as I told them about my experience with the North Vietnamese students at the fountain in Debrecen. I still had quite the vivid recollection of the North Vietnamese man's face as he sobbed through his story of the US bombs killing his fiancée. Peter and Helga shook their heads in sorrow as I recounted the scene. Although they were quite conservative, each of them was resolutely against the American action in Southeast Asia. They could understand my plans to quit the Air Force even if they thought it would lead to terrible consequences for me.

Peter was concerned about my plans to travel in the Third World with no money. The next day he bought me a pair of expensive Austrian hiking boots and gave me fifty dollars. "I know you don't think you need money, but believe me, this will come in handy."

Helga brought out an old white leather purse with a shoulder strap. "Here, you'll be needing this to carry your passport and money. It never has to leave your side. And it won't look feminine if you sling it on your hip."

I started using it right away and it became a personal attachment for the rest of my journey.

Near the end of my stay, a college friend of mine named David showed up in a 1958 battered blue Fiat truck with the roof raised two feet by a fiberglass top. Borneo, as I called David, had Peter's address and we had loosely agreed to meet up in late August. Much to my surprise he showed up. The truck's owner was Claines, a twenty-three-year-old business graduate from South Carolina. The two of them had teamed up in Amsterdam. Traveling with them was another Dave, a twenty-nine-year-old carpenter from Alaska. We took to calling him H.L.D., which stands for horny little dude, due to his short stature and keen interest in women of any age or body type.

Before they knew what hit them, Peter and Helga had a house full of longhaired, pot-smoking hippies. Rather than freak out about it, they took us all to their mountain cabin for the weekend. I had a feeling we were all going to learn a lot about ourselves and each other on this little expedition.

The cabin was nestled deep in an Alpine valley, next to a sparkling, gurgling stream, its only source of water. The setting bore witness to a culture left untouched by time. Dairy farmers still brought their cows with bells clanging around their necks down the mountain for the winter. Herders in lederhosen fed their deer hay and grain from well-stocked sheds at the end of wide foot trails and stone steps. During my visit in 1970 we had hidden under the hay in one of those sheds and watched as two ten-point bucks charged each other and crashed horns to fight for standing in the herd.

The cabin itself had only one large room with no running water or electricity. One brick stove was the only source of heat, and there was always plenty of wood outside for splitting with an axe. Water came in by the bucket from the stream. The toilet was an outhouse. Behind a large wooden table for dining was one bed as wide as the entire structure, which slept ten close friends.

"This is like something out of *The Hobbit!*" Claines exclaimed as we threw our packs into the cabin.

"I'll be Frodo," I called out.

"What do you mean when you say this place is like something out of *The Hobbit?*" Peter asked.

"Oh, it's a compliment for sure," Claines quickly clarified. "Actually, it's like something out of the Shire. That's the idyllic community where the hobbits live. The hobbits are little people with big, hairy feet who turn out to be the bravest of adventurers. Their houses are small but expertly crafted."

Peter and Helga looked at each other like they weren't sure they even wanted to try understanding hobbits.

H.L.D. sensed their discomfort and casually saved the moment by saying, "It's just books about the adventure of traveling. We can all relate. You can tell a lot about a person by which character he identifies with in the book."

I'd been thinking of myself as Frodo for some time. The evil ring of power I carried was my commission in the Air Force. I became invisible, even to myself, whenever I slipped it on my finger. It hung around my neck like a lead weight of guilt and shame. It shackled me like a slave. I hoped the journey I had undertaken would somehow lead me to a place, perhaps in my own mind, where I could throw my ring into the volcanic lava of Mount Doom and destroy it, once and for all.

Peter wisely changed the topic, "Why don't we take a hike up the mountain? We've still got a few hours before it starts getting dark."

With that, we packed a snack and some beer, wine, and water, and headed up the road to the hikers' trail, then up the hikers' trail to the deer paths; then up the deer paths until our shirts were soaked with sweat and our legs felt like rubber. We were above the trees and into the rocks looking down on clouds winding their way through the valley. We could see snow-covered mountain peaks all around us. The majesty of the Alps was breathtaking even though we were already out of breath from the steep, one-hour climb. Our peak was about three hundred yards above us when we started getting into snow.

Peter suggested we head back down since the rest of the climb was going to be quite difficult and dangerous. It was pretty much straight up to the top, but it looked doable to me. "Come on, Peter, let's go all the way to the top."

Peter shook his head and gave me a raised eyebrow warning. "It's more technical than it looks."

"It looks way too tough for me," Borneo said. Everybody but me agreed with his assessment. They settled down to watch as I took off for the top. As usual, I was showing off.

It didn't take long for me to get into some fairly serious trouble. I wormed my way up a crevice and came out to continue upward on the face of a cliff. There were good footholds at first, but I soon found myself spread-eagled on a nearly vertical rock. My fingertips and toes felt reasonably secure, but my body was beginning to shake. I felt shivers of fear quiver through my body. I knew a fall could be fatal.

I took a deep breath and attempted to assess my predicament. The way up looked impossible as the rock became smoother. The way back down looked much worse than it had coming up. I could see Peter waving at me to come down. Everybody was craning their necks and beginning to get a little worried. They could see I was in trouble. I began to panic. My shaking got worse.

Peter started up after me. I knew he couldn't help much even if he reached my location. I was the only person who could stretch back down to my last position. And I had to move quickly before I shook myself off the rock. I took another deep breath and stretched my leg down but couldn't quite reach what looked like a fair foothold.

"Keep coming down with your right foot," Peter shouted. He was only thirty yards beneath me. "You're only a few inches from the spot."

I stretched again and had to release my top handhold to find the foothold. It wasn't exactly a leap of faith. It was more like a stretch of desperation. If my foot didn't find its spot, I would fall more than eighty feet. I was sweating and hugging the mountain as my foot headed for the tiny ledge below, promising myself that if I actually made it off this rock, I would never again try another macho stunt.

Miraculously, my foot found its hold. I was talking to myself loudly enough so that everyone could hear. "Come on now, come on now, come on now. You can do this. You can do this." It took a while, but I eventually made it back to the crevice and down to the group. I tried to act like nothing serious had happened.

"We could see you shaking from here," Borneo teased.

"Are your pants brown?" H.L.D. chimed in.

"You had us all very frightened," Helga said. "You must have ropes for a climb like that."

Peter patted me on the back. "Nice work getting down. I was wondering what I would do if I made it up to you."

"You were great, Peter," I said, hugging him. "I needed your encouragement. You saved me."

Claines patted me on the back. "He saved you from yourself."

Later that night, as we had dinner around a lantern in the cabin, the camaraderie was relaxed. The grilled steaks were delicious, and the wine flowed freely. Eventually, the conversation shifted to the Vietnam War. Peter wanted to know how my friends had gotten out of the draft.

Borneo drained his wine glass. "We all had high numbers."

"What do you mean?" Peter asked.

"They had a birthday lottery draft," Claines said. "They put every day in a hopper and pulled them out one at a time. If your birthday got pulled out first, you were number one and the first to be drafted. My number is 243, so I'm good. It doesn't look like they'll get past 150 the way things are going. Hopefully, we'll end this crazy war soon, anyway."

"They did the lottery to be more fair," H.L.D. added. "Before the lottery it was only poor black kids going off to die for their country while the rich white kids all stayed home with college deferrals and the like."

"What was your number?" Helga asked H.L.D.

"I don't even know," he said. "I burned my draft card in 1968. The lottery wasn't until December of 1969. I suppose I could look up my number, but I've already decided not to even register. If they want me, they can come to Austria to get me. By the time they get here I'll be someplace else."

We all laughed. Each of us had basically dropped out of society to hit the road. The thought of the authorities trying to locate us at this point was, somehow, beyond absurd.

"What was your number, Mark?" Helga asked.

I groaned as I filled up a few wine glasses. "March 8 was number 213. I would have been too high a number to get drafted. I should have quit the Air Force right then."

Borneo was quick to respond, "Yeah, why didn't you? I told you that myself at least a hundred times. We all knew you weren't going to fit into the whole gung-ho military thing."

I stared at him, wondering how to respond. I decided to try and explain myself. "At that point, when the draft lottery happened, I still wanted to fly jet planes and keep my full-ride scholarship. I didn't really get into the Air Force to avoid the draft." They all waited for me to continue, so I did.

"I remember the night of the lottery quite well. We were all sitting around a television, watching with intense interest. We knew the college deferment wasn't going to last, so the lottery was a life-and-death kind of event. One of the guys was number four. He got up and walked out of the room in stunned silence and headed right down to the bar. We didn't hear from him for days."

H.L.D. said, "I know guys who take five hits of acid and go in for their physical so tripped out they get a psychological deferment."

"And there's lots of doctors," Claines said, "who write out physical deferments just because they're opposed to the war or because they want to help a friend keep his son out of the Army."

"All anybody has to do to get out," Borneo said, "is say he's gay. But no one will say that because it's nowhere near something you admit to even if it's true."

"I know lots of gay guys who got out that way," Claines said.

"Maybe guys in New York or San Francisco," Borneo said, "but no one in Indiana is ever going to admit to being gay. It's illegal. You can go to jail for being gay."

We all laughed again. Peter spoke up to defend Indiana. "I know Indiana well from staying with the Smiths. We found the people there to be quite friendly, didn't we, Helga?"

Helga stood up and stretched like she might be getting ready for bed. "Actually, we found people all over the United States to be so open and friendly. We have a hard time believing your country continues the Vietnam War when so many people like yourselves are so opposed to it."

"It's like this," Claines said. "Our parents' generation came out of World War II a little shell-shocked and paranoid. Then this whole atom bomb thing came along and that led to the Red Scare, and before you know it, we're fighting in some country we never heard of, halfway around the world, to stop the spread of communism."

"We needed a new enemy," H.L.D. said. "Once Hitler was gone, the Russians stepped up to the plate quite nicely with the Berlin Wall and Sputnik and bombs of their own."

"The people in charge want to stay in charge and the best way to do that is to create a common enemy and rally the troops," Borneo concluded. "We're not falling for that shit anymore. We're going to end the war and end it soon. We don't care what it takes."

"Richard Nixon is using the FBI to crack down on war protesters," Claines said. "Which is funny because he's probably going to jail because of his Watergate coverup. That guy is evil to the core. He's trying to get John Lennon deported."

The very mention of Lennon's name launched us all into an impromptu version of "Give Peace a Chance," the John Lennon song that replaced "We Shall Overcome" as the anthem of the anti-war movement. We sounded as drunk and stoned as the record.

Shortly after that high note, our little party went to bed, one by one, until we were all tucked into the one wide bed along the back wall of the cabin. Peter and Helga were under their covers. Claines, Borneo, H.L.D., and I were in our sleeping bags. The fire had burned down to glowing embers in the stone fireplace. All was well in our cozy little cabin, even though so much was wrong in the big bad world.

It was the early morning hours of September 5, 1972. Even as we drifted into a peaceful sleep, commandos from a shadowy Palestinian terror group known as Black September were beginning a massacre in Munich that would claim the lives of eleven Israeli Olympic athletes and coaches, five terrorists, and one West German police officer.

The world would never be the same. It never is.

CHAPTER EIGHT

Mykonos

THERE WAS A LARGE MILITARY BAND playing on the dock in Athens, Greece, in front of an oceangoing ship. One look at that massive boat and I knew it would take me where I needed to go. Deep down, I hoped it was a slow boat to China.

I was alone. After eighteen days of partying with my crazy friends in the Fiat van through Austria, Italy, and Greece, it was time to head out on my own again. I packed up one morning while my traveling companions were at the market and start-ed walking toward the saltwater smell of the Aegean Sea.

I sidestepped through the middle of the blaring band expecting someone to stop my forward progress at any moment. No one did, even though I was quite conspicuously out of place with my long hair, patched blue jeans, and large-frame backpack. The horn players followed me with their eyes as I slipped through the musical formation. The bass drum player grinned broadly as I passed. Two tuba players who were completely engulfed by their instruments acknowledged my presence with a slight bow of their flared bells.

Walking this gauntlet of uniformed musicians and officials gave me a chance to put one of my pet theories to the test. That is, you can go anywhere if you just act like you belong there and know what you're doing.

I kept walking through the formation until there was nothing but a long unattended gangplank between the ship and me. I turned around to see if anyone might try to prevent me from boarding the vessel. No one was paying any attention to the ship. Everyone on the dock was preoccupied with whatever ceremony I had just breached. They obviously were not christening the ship. It was old and rusted from years of salty brine.

I took a deep breath and started up the walkway. It felt like walking the plank. There were police and armed soldiers all over the dock. Certainly, someone would spot my unauthorized entry and drag me off to jail. I kept walking.

Halfway up, two sailors in civilian clothing appeared at the top and walked down toward me. *Here it comes. These guys are going to kick me off the boat for sure.*

They looked at me warily at first, then relaxed and greeted me warmly as they shuffled past on the boarding plank, completely unconcerned by my presence. I couldn't tell what language they spoke, but they were not Chinese. I walked up the rest of the gangplank and boarded the ship. No one was there to greet me. The ship was about as long as a football field. There were people working at the bow and stern but no one in the middle. I looked up at the bridge and radio rigging of the ship but saw no identifying flags.

This was the perfect solution for a young man who had no idea where he was going. *Let the winds of fate decide my destination,* I announced to myself with shaky courage.

With another deep breath, I entered the ship through a metal door and started walking down stairways. Two stories down, the stairs turned to ladders. Everything was metal. No one was onboard. *Is this some kind of ghost ship headed for a watery grave?*

I continued down until I got to the bottom of the ship. The engine in the rear was shaking the metal floor as I threw down my pack beneath the dull glow of a low-watt electric light bulb. For the first time in my life I was officially a stowaway, thrilled and frightened by the sudden danger I put myself in. I had enough food and water to last for a couple days. Questions raced through my mind. *How long until the ship takes off? Where is it going? What will they do when they discover me? How long can I stay in this metal hole?*

I had plenty of time to think in the bottom of that ship. My mind wandered through the past three weeks of travel in the Fiat Van. It had been a blur of red wine and hash. In the end, I hadn't even said goodbye to Borneo, Claines, H.L.D., and Liza, a junior from Sarah Lawrence College we picked up in Salzburg. I didn't even leave a note.

I thought back to how I'd wound up here without them. Things had been getting a little crowded in the Fiat. Claines had taken to complaining about me not contributing enough financially. It became apparent that my hitchhiker's welcome was wearing thin. Besides, traveling as a unit kept us fairly insulated from the locals and their culture. We were a self-contained party unit, getting so high so often it was impossible to figure out where we were going with our lives.

I figured they would understand my departure once they saw all my gear was gone. I had taken a long, wistful look at that old Fiat and reckoned it would be much easier to leave without having to explain why I was leaving. Now, in the bottom of the ship, I realized I should have bid them a proper farewell. Not saying goodbye had been a personal declaration of independence. I was afraid they'd talk me out of leaving if I hung around to explain myself.

We had traveled well together. Top speed in the Fiat was 50 mph. We didn't care. We were in no hurry. First and second gear got quite a workout on the steep mountain roads of Austria and northern Italy. We stayed off the main highways.

It took the world a while to get on with life after the terrorist attack in Munich. Once we left Peter and Helga's cabin in the Fiat, police seemed to be everywhere. We were stopped several times for no reason except to show our passports.

H.L.D. thought the stops were ridiculous. "What? If we have passports, we can't be killers? I'll bet all the killers at Munich had passports. Why don't they search us for weapons?"

"They're not checking for weapons," Liza explained. "They're searching for Arabs."

Borneo turned around from the front passenger seat. "Be glad they're not tearing this van apart for drugs."

For a short time, it felt like Europe was about to slip into martial law. The world went into shock as photos of the victims appeared on television. There was talk of shutting down the games. But as the Olympics continued without further violence, you could almost feel the Continent breathing a collective sigh of relief. It was as though the peaceful purpose of the games had overwhelmed the ugly violence of terrorism.

I wondered what Hanna was thinking about the attack. She would find a way to blame it on United States imperialism. I thought back to our encounter in Hungary with the ultimate peace parade, the Olympic torch procession. We had been so full of hope in that moment and so blissfully unaware that our time together would be so short.

I missed Hanna and her sweet but determined demeanor. She never would have made it in the Fiat van. The hash and wine consumption would have been a deal breaker. She would have called our behavior childish and without redeeming social merit.

We were more interested in emulating Ken Kesey and the Merry Pranksters than in taking life too seriously. We became Frisbee ambassadors everywhere we went. Our whirling plastic disks were crowd-pleasers from the town square in Salzburg to the volcanoes outside Naples. People of all ages were amazed to see us skipping Frisbees off the pavement and through fountains and catching them behind our backs and between our legs. Although the Frisbee had been around America since the late 1950s, it was still brand new to many

Europeans. We taught hundreds of kids how to play Frisbee on the beaches of Italy.

Since none of us had much money, we cut down to two meals a day. In the morning we bought fruit and pastries at local markets. In the evening we found open-air restaurants and feasted on pasta, fresh shrimp, and giant green salads. Of course, we always drank way too much *vino locale* before driving into an off-road field to camp for the night. Some nights we drove into the hills and made campfire stews. Most mornings, we started off with a hash joint, crumbled hash rolled into a joint with tobacco. Getting high was as important to the trip as getting gas.

Even as the party raged, I knew it couldn't last forever. I had too much on my mind.

As orderly as Austria was, Italy was chaotic. Small wonder in a country where the Roman Catholic Church, the largest Communist Party in Western Europe, the Mafia, and a semi-fascist government are expected to peacefully coexist.

We spent our first night in Italy on the streets of Venice. We ate pasta and drank red wine with American tourists who were curious and attracted to our vagabond existence. It was two o'clock in the morning and we were stupidly drunk when we realized Liza had wandered away and was nowhere to be found.

We knew she wouldn't be safe on the streets alone at that hour, so we began our frantic search. We split into two groups and made plans to meet in an hour at San Marco's Plaza. We stumbled off into the night to rescue our friend. The city was a maze of tall buildings and narrow streets. We didn't know which way to turn. We kept walking blindly into the night, listening for a cry for help.

About a half-hour later, H.L.D. and I got lucky. We caught sight of Liza, without her shoes or glasses, being led down an alley by three Italian men. They fled when we ran at them, shouting obscenities. Liza was deeply shaken as she dissolved, sobbing, into our hugs. "How did you find me? I thought I would never see you again."

She was still drunk but her clothes were intact. She had not been raped. By the time we rescued her and talked her down it was much too late to catch a canal boat back to the van. Claines and Borneo located us at the plaza. The five of us hugged each other, grateful to be together. Exhausted and feeling foolish, we sat Liza down between us and went to sleep in the dead end of a cobblestone street, too tired to notice the stink.

It was still much too early in the Women's Liberation Movement for a woman to be on her own at any hour of the day on the back streets of Italy.

After touring Italy from Venice to Brindisi, we took a boat across the Adriatic Sea to Corfu, a large island on the western coast of Greece. We erected our symbolic bamboo shack on the beach and became part of a colony of beachcombers from all over the world. Every day was a party in the sun and the population remained mostly naked. There was quite a turnover in the neighborhood as people left for other islands and were replaced by newcomers. We moved on to Athens when it started raining.

After my unannounced departure from the Fiat van group, I spent a night sleeping beneath the Acropolis until the park police kicked me out at dawn. They used billy clubs to wake me up. I tried to jump up but tripped in my sleeping bag and rolled twenty feet down the steep hill. The cops were laughing so hard I knew they weren't going to arrest me. It seemed ironic that my civil rights were being mocked in the shadow of democracy's birthplace.

All these memories whirred through my mind like a silent movie as I tried to get comfortable in the hold of my stowaway ship. It was September 27. I had $180 to my name. The first of my travel articles for the *Fort Wayne Journal Gazette* had been published August 13, but I didn't realize it at the time. The warm hospitality and good cheer of the collective farm and Peter and Helga's home seemed like distant memories. The terror at Munich had cast a wary gloom over the entire continent. I was homesick and tired of traveling. My rear end was tired of sitting on metal. I could hear activity on the ship above, but I remained in my hideout.

I laughed out loud at the absurdity of my situation. My laugh bounced off the metal hull and fell to the floor. The ship did not appreciate my whistling-by-the-graveyard sense of humor. No one was laughing but me and I wasn't laughing for long. The silence seemed to make a hissing sound, like someone was letting the air out of my tires. My thoughts began to wander into worry mode as they often did during times of emotional letdown. I had a distinct image of my father being cornered by his conservative law partners once news of my quitting the Air Force hit the papers. They wanted to know what he was going to do about his son committing career suicide. He would keep telling them he couldn't control my decisions, and they would argue that he had to talk some sense into me. I heard myself saying out loud, "Tell them I'm doing the right thing, dammit! Don't let them make you feel bad."

The sound of my own voice brought me out of the imaginary scene. There was no underestimating my father's influence. It was he who had schooled me on how to serve in the military: "If you're going to be an officer, you should be a pilot. That's the best job in the world. You don't get dirty and you get three hot meals a day. Plus, you get to fly planes! What could be more fun than that?"

I wished he were in the hold of that ship so we could talk. I needed to talk to him. I needed to tell him that what I was going to do was the only thing I could do. I needed to tell him about the road and the collective farm and the North Vietnamese. I needed him to understand. I needed him to tell me I was doing the right thing.

I knew my feelings of doubt and uncertainty would pass. I bid a fond but determined farewell to thoughts of my father and of my Fiat companions and settled down to try to take a nap. Before I could get to sleep, I felt the ship's engine cranking up and heard commotion on the upper decks. The ship was leaving port!

Departure was exciting but also frustrating. I couldn't see anything. All I felt was the sensation of floating motion. There was nothing but a metal hull between me and all the saltwater in the world. I could only imagine how exhilarating it would feel to be standing on deck, watching the dock fade away as we headed out to sea. *I should be up there*, I thought, *waving in the sun*.

I couldn't hear anything except the engines, which had gotten much louder once we were underway. What had been a comfortable hum in the hold now became a deafening thunder. Worse yet, it seemed to be getting hotter by the minute. I recalled the Biblical story of Jonah in the belly of the whale. Jonah ended up in the whale for not going to preach in Nineveh as God had directed. Inside the whale, Jonah repented, and God had the whale belch him out on dry land. As far as I could recall, I had never been given a directive by God, much less disobeyed one. So, I had nothing to repent and no way to convince God to come to the rescue.

Then it occurred to me. This was no whale. I didn't need God to come save me. I simply needed to change my plan and get up on deck in the sunshine where I belonged. That's one nice thing about putting your faith in the road. If it leaves you someplace bad, you can just get up and leave.

In the back of my mind, I was always trying to be like Jack Kerouac in *On the Road* and *The Dharma Bums*. It had always seemed so romantic to head off for destinations unknown and find out who you really were. But Kerouac always had a car. I had already hitchhiked many more miles than he ever did. As far as I knew, his longest hitch-hike was from New York City to Chicago. The fact that Kerouac died in 1969 at age forty-seven from alcoholism hadn't dented my enthu-siasm for alcohol and drugs; forty-seven was much older than I was ever going to be.

I shouldered my pack and started up the ladder. It was harder go-ing up than coming down. By the time the sun forced me to shield my eyes, I had been in the hold less than three hours. It seemed like three days. The sky was huge and gloriously blue. The salty breeze smelled like adventure. There were people sitting all over the deck on long benches that had been empty when I decided to hide below.

No one paid me any attention as I discreetly took a bench seat on the foredeck. I had just tilted my head back to enjoy the sun when a curt man in a uniform loomed over and demanded to see my ticket. He was taking everybody's ticket, and it became instantly apparent he was not about to make an exception in my case. I bought the cheap-est ticket possible for ten US dollars and learned I was on my way to Mykonos.

I sank with disappointment. Now I was just another paying cus-tomer on a tourist boat to a Greek island. It was quite a comedown from being a stowaway Marco Polo on an Asian voyage.

Rather than bemoan my circumstance and loss of nearly five per cent of my total funds, I decided to make the most of it. After all, this old boat was my destiny, wherever it might land. The Aegean Sea glistened and rolled in slow motion. I savored the freedom. My home-sickness evaporated.

After four hours on the turquoise-green sea, the island of Myko-nos came into view. Several of my fellow passengers pointed it out in the distance before it became recognizable. I watched as one of the jewels of the Aegean came into focus. Gradually, I could see the white stucco buildings connected to each other along the coast in a low-slung architectural labyrinth. The island is part of Greek mythology. It is supposedly the site of the great battle between Zeus and the Titans, and is named after the son of Apollo, Mykonos. The ancient history and the island itself loomed large as our boat began to dock.

I disembarked and quickly got lost in the narrow, winding streets that felt more like tunnels as they wound around in no apparent order, making mysterious connections for the sea-level society. Around one bend was a bar with a little red neon sign shining in a window with no glass. It looked like it had been a fisherman's hangout since the days of Homer's *Iliad*. I was beginning to feel like Odysseus as my travels kept landing me in situations of vague symbolic significance.

The bar smelled like old fish and stale beer. I paid for a beer and the bartender poured me a shot of Ouzo on the house. One quick swallow and I became an instant Ouzo aficionado. The anise-flavored aperitif tasted a little like black licorice, but it had quite a kick. I bought another shot and another beer as the bartender knew I would.

I left the bar with a gentle buzz and set out to find the ocean and settle in for a sunset.

That night I tried souvlaki for the first time from a little stand in the main square. It was as delightful and new a taste experience as the Ouzo had been. I'd been through most of Greece to get to Athens and had somehow missed these two treats. It occurred to me that someone was going to make a fortune serving these flavors back in the States.

I joined some fellow backpackers at their beach fire just outside the city lights. It felt good to have somebody to talk to. They had good hash and were happy to share it. We told each other where we were from and how long we had been on the road. The longer you'd been traveling, the more status attached. After four months, I was beginning to qualify as a road veteran.

A skinny man from Boston with six months on the road told me to get out of the town of Mykonos and over to the other side of the island to a place called Paradise Beach. "The tourists still wear swimsuits there but a little farther away there's a place called Super Paradise Beach. Nobody wears anything there. That's where you want to go."

I thanked him for the information and said that's where I'd be heading in the morning. "Oh, here, man," he said. "Take some of this hash with you. We're leaving in the morning, and we can't get this shit through Turkish customs."

I tucked the hash in my pants pocket. "What are the police like around here?"

"There are no pigs, man," said a woman in a long skirt. "This place is free as long as you stay out of the streets."

I slept on the beach alone that night under a star-studded sky, the moon a Turkish crescent. My thoughts drifted to the Air Force, as they did any time I had time to think. I tried to change the topic in my mind, but I couldn't. I was sick of thinking about the military. I was going to quit and that was that. I could hear my college roommate saying, "I told you so." I should have listened when he repeatedly argued against my military involvement. I could have quit back then with no problem. Now, I was going to have to face military justice and a court-martial.

In the morning, the sun awakened me with its heat. I took a quick swim in the saltwater and hit the market for supplies. After exploring the town until mid-afternoon, I noticed a dusty old public bus with Greek letters on the headsign above its windshield. I boarded and paid a few coins to the driver. I had no idea where the bus was headed. I didn't really care. It was all Greek to me.

I took a window seat near the back of the bus and watched as it filled up with local passengers and their shopping bags. Suddenly, there was a commotion up front as people made way for a giant man with a backpack. At six feet, seven inches tall, he had to bow to get through the door. As he stooped next to the driver to pay and survey the available seating, all boarding bustle immediately ceased. Conversations turned to silence like someone had flipped a switch. All eyes were on the big man as he paused, grabbed both aluminum aisle poles with oversized hands, and glared at his awestruck audience with all the poise of a Shakespearean actor taking center stage.

Size was only part of his presence. His looks were exciting to behold, thrilling as a pirate boarding a ship. His beard was long and red, but his bushy eyebrows and long hair were albino blond. His eyes couldn't help but scowl beneath his Cro-Magnon brow. His powerful wide nose and stern mouth looked like they would rather growl than breathe. He looked like an angry Viking, ready to pillage and plunder.

Then his fierce face collapsed into an impish grin as he began hunching slowly and self-consciously toward the open seats in the back.

Our eyes met as he politely excused himself around an elderly woman who stared up at him in frozen fright. There were several empty seats, but sure enough, he sat down next to me. He wedged himself in and put his pack on his lap with a groan of disapproval at the crowded confines.

He turned his head and shoulders to look at me. "Do you know where is this bus?"

I grinned and shrugged to let him know he wasn't the only one who boarded a bus without knowing where it was going. We shook hands, realizing we had each stumbled onto a kindred spirit. The notion of buying a ride to an unknown destination struck us simultaneously as hysterically funny. Our chuckles turned to genuine laughter. He threw his head back and really laughed, a deep booming guffaw that started in his stomach and gathered momentum as it erupted through his lungs and vocal cords and shook his broad shoulders before leaping out of his open mouth.

The driver leaned around to see if everything was okay. The rest of the bus stared at us with open mouths of astonishment. We waved them off and looked out the windows as the bus took off for points unknown.

We rolled through rocky hills for at least an hour and stopped frequently. People kept getting off, but we couldn't see any place for them to be heading. They just walked off into the hills.

By the time the driver motioned to us that we had reached the end of the line, we had gotten genuinely acquainted. His name was Peter, and his English was good enough to communicate that he was twenty-three years old, one year older than I, born and raised in Holland. He'd quit his job driving food products around Europe and had spent the past few months on a kibbutz in Israel. He said he was happy to be getting out of the Middle East in general. I told him about the camp in Hungary and hitchhiking through the Iron Curtain and the fact that I was from Indiana in the United States. He understood most of what I said.

"Where is Indiana?" he asked as most Europeans did.

I gave him my stock answer. "It's right next to Chicago."

"Oh." he nodded knowingly, pretending to be shooting a tommy gun. Everybody knew from newsreels and movies about Chicago and the gangsters during Prohibition. It was becoming more and more interesting for me to see my country through the eyes of the rest of the world. We were largely viewed as a savage, violent nation. Action movies had played their part in this perception, as had two world wars, Korea, and Vietnam.

Peter and I got off the bus in the middle of rolling and rocky grazing pastures accented and divided by low stone-pile fences that never seemed to end. The beat-up bus bounced back down the two-track dirt road, leaving us completely alone. The only possible sign of civilization was the distant blue of what had to be the sea. We looked at each other and shook our heads at the absurdity of our situation. Each of us was happy to not be alone. We hoisted our packs. Mine was red. Peter's was blue and gray.

"What kind of animals are here?" he asked, looking around the deserted countryside.

"Must be sheep," I guessed. "This is Greece. They're big on lamb meat in Greece. I don't see any sheep, but that must be what these fences are for."

"I ask question," Peter said. "You say 'lamb' and then you say 'sheep.' Are these two words in English the same?"

I looked up at the sky to ponder the question. "I think so. At least they are to me. But really, I'm not sure. Maybe a lamb is a baby sheep. I don't know."

Peter put his thumbs under the straps of his pack. "You don't know your language?"

I shrugged as best I could under the weight of my pack. "Most of it, but not all of it."

"My English must be better," Peter said, frowning in frustration. "I am watching the sea."

"No," I corrected. "You see the sea."

After I explained the difference between the verb and the noun to him, he shook his head and said, "This English is very not easy."

Most of my early conversations with Peter involved me giving him English lessons. He never tried to teach me Dutch or help me with my limited German. He could see that was probably a lost cause. He was trying to learn English.

We started walking through fields and over fences toward the water. There was no path. The sea was much farther away than it initially appeared. We lost sight of it several times in valleys between the hills. Neither of us said much. He was the strong and silent type. I was focused on picking our way through the rocks. Every now and then we stopped to drink from our water bottles. I wasn't used to having someone tower over me. At six feet, three inches tall and 185 pounds, I felt like a little guy next to Peter. He was a gentle giant. He let me lead the way. In a few miles, we'd gone from being total strangers to brothers-in-arms, marching to the sea.

"Are your feet okay?" I asked, pointing to his flimsy sandals.

"No problem," he grunted stoically even though the jagged terrain had to be hurting him. "Your feet are big." He pointed at my heavy Austrian hiking boots. "Good for the rocks, bad for the beach."

I stuck one boot out in front of me by its heel. "I'll take them off once we get to the beach. I just hope we find a beach and not some cliff. We need a good place to sleep, a place where we can jump in the water. How far do you think we have to go?"

Peter had taken over leading the way. He turned and said over his shoulder, "Not far. Not far."

The wind was wild, and the sun was beginning to paint the panoramic sky orange and red by the time we slid down the last steep slope to a wide sandy beach. We stripped and took a dip in the pounding surf. It was cold and rough at first, but quite swimmable once we got out past the breakers.

After the swim, we gathered up driftwood while still drying off, and built a fire in a small space surrounded by huge, toothy rocks. Waves exploded against the jagged stone jetty in front of our fire pit, making the sounds of crashing cymbals in a furious overture. We stayed dry, shielded by the rocks. The wind was blowing hard.

Peter was impressed with my two-man tent and how fast I set it up on the nearby beach. Before we could even get our packs inside, however, the wind blew the tent down and would have taken it away had we not been there to grab it. There was such a gale we decided to pack up the tent and return to our rock pit. The fire blazed merrily and evenly. Smoke rose lazily until it cleared the massive stones and then got blasted away like banshees in the growing darkness.

I pulled out my cook kit and we stewed a pot of potatoes and canned beef. It was delicious with bread and cheese and bottles of wine and water. Peter and I had learned how to be well prepared for the middle of nowhere. Until we met, I thought I was the only guy who boarded public transportation without knowing its destination.

Peter leaned back against a rock and talked about his time on the kibbutz and how it had been such an exciting adventure at first. "Then it seemed people were just telling you what to do all the time. What to eat and when to eat it. When to go to bed and who not to go to bed with. It got to be the opposite of freedom. I'm on the road to be free, not to be told what to do."

Peter was rolling one of his own cigarettes when I asked him if he'd like a little hashish to roll in with the tobacco.

"Ah, I knew I liked you." He grinned. "Yes, I'd love to get high. In fact, let me add a few more papers to this so we can have a spliff."

He proceeded to roll up a nine-paper joint, which totally impressed me as I crumbled at least a half gram of hash into the tobacco. "This is how we do it in Amsterdam," he announced proudly as he finished rolling a massive cone of a joint.

I thought I'd seen it all when it came to drugs. But I'd never seen anybody roll a spliff so large and perfect. He lit it and took a hit so large and long it made the cone glow like neon before he passed it to me. I did my best to take a huge hit but ended up coughing most of it out. Peter grinned but he didn't laugh. He was busy holding in his hit.

I took another big hit and held this one in, determined not to exhale until he did. Finally, he let out a plume of smoke that challenged the smoke from the fire and I quickly followed suit.

Peter leaned forward and opened his eyes wide. "This is some good shit. Don't tell me you brought it with you on the boat."

I handed the spliff back to him. "No, I got it on the beach in Mykynos. Some guy gave it to me because he was headed to Turkey."

Peter nodded his head and took another huge hit. He exhaled more quickly since he had something to say. "Oh, yeah, they throw people away for a long time in Turkey. Crazy motherfuckers in Turkey. I've been there. Well, I've been to Istanbul on my truck route. That was enough Turkey for me. Istanbul is one dangerous place to be."

I told him my story of stowing away on the boat. "You know, I could have had hash on me. Nobody searched anybody going out of Athens or coming into Mykynos."

Peter put a large piece of driftwood on the fire. "Nah, the Greeks don't care. They let the tourists do anything they want. All they care about is the money."

Peter and I talked and smoked the giant hash spliff as the stars began to shine. It was odd to have a clear sky on such a windy night. I was contemplating the weather in my stoned haze when Peter asked an abrupt question. "How did you get out of Vietnam?"

The question caught me off guard, even though it was a common query in those days. Every American male on the road had a story about dodging the draft or how he avoided military service. It wasn't that unusual to run into men who had done their time in Vietnam. Those guys were the haunted ones. You could see the pain and fear in their eyes no matter how much they tried to hide it. They got that thousand-yard stare every time Vietnam got mentioned.

I stood up to let the wind blast me in the face over top of the rocks. "To tell you the truth, Peter, I'm still in the military. Even as we sit here, I'm a second lieutenant in the United States Air Force, scheduled to report to jet school to become a pilot early next year."

Peter lowered his head and leaned toward me. He had not understood much of what I said. "Are you a deserter?"

"No," I responded carefully. "Right now, I'm technically on leave. At some point I'm going back to declare myself a conscientious objector."

Peter stood up with me. "What's that?"

I turned to look up at him. "That's a person who refuses to go to war based on religious and moral grounds."

"Can you get away with that?" Peter asked.

I sat down to hide from the wind. "I don't know, but that's what I'm going to do."

Peter sat down with me. "What happens when they throw you in jail?"

I picked up a stick and stirred the fire. "I go to jail, I guess."

"Man, that is so heavy." Peter sighed deeply. "Do you ever think about not going home at all?"

"No, I can't do that. I miss home too much already."

"Yes, I know what you mean," Peter agreed. "You know the whole world thinks the United States is out of control with this bullshit in Southeast Asia. How can your country be this insanity?"

I answered his question slowly and repeated myself when I saw he wasn't understanding. "Peter, I don't think we ever got out of World War II. We built up this incredible military machine and it just keeps rolling on and on. We conquered the world and now we want to keep what we got."

Peter seemed eager to hear an American explain his country. "How are two stories true? Half is hippies marching against the war and half is helicopters and soldiers killing in rice fields."

I nodded, hung my head and then raised it back up. "The only way I can explain it is to say that America is at war with itself. The children are at war with their parents. Everything is changing. So far, the parents are still in control and the war goes on. But every generation eventually wins as they take over from the old folks. That's what's going to happen. The young people are going to win and we're going to end this crazy war. That's why I know I'll go back. I've got to help stop the war."

Peter raised his eyebrows and opened his mouth. He held out his hands and shook his head. "How is you in jail going to stop the war?"

I pointed my finger at him to let him know I was serious. "I'm not going to jail without a legal fight. My father's a lawyer, like I told you, and if he can't help me, I'll find somebody who can. Lots of people are taking on the United States government in court about this stupid war and some of them are winning."

Peter thought about that for a minute and decided to change the topic. "Where are you headed next?"

I shook my head and looked at him. "I have absolutely no idea."

Peter's response was barely above a whisper. "Me too."

I took back the spliff as he handed it to me. "I guess nobody really knows where they're going in this world."

Peter couldn't help returning to the Vietnam issue. "Your parents are not happy about the Air Force?"

"You know, that's a tough one," I said. "My mother and father are pretty open-minded. The dinner table at our house was always a big debate. My friends came over a lot and they're all totally against the war. My father used to think we had to fight communism like his generation had to fight Hitler, but he's coming around."

"Coming around to what?"

"To thinking we've got no business interfering in another country's civil war."

Peter grabbed my arm in surprise. "Did you talk him out of supporting the war?"

"I think more than anything," I said, "it was all the American casualties with so little to show for it. A lot of kids we know never came back."

He let go of my arm and folded his hands in his lap like he was embarrassed to have touched me. "It's cool you can talk to your parents. My father hasn't said two words to me since I grew my hair long and told him I thought it was okay to smoke marijuana."

I put my hand on his shoulder. "What's with that? I thought everybody in Holland was a flaming liberal."

"Not in the rural areas. And not the older people." Peter took another hit. "It's good you will not bomb Vietnam."

I took back the spliff and inhaled a massive hit. "Making up my mind has been a long time coming." I was amazed at how certain I sounded when deep inside I didn't know for sure what I was going to do or when I was going to do it.

I still had some roadwork to do.

We were delighted to discover that the cinder block hut on the beach was open for breakfast with a few fruits and cheeses and even yogurt and honey. Beach campers materialized out of the hilly dunes and created an international social scene. Peter and I played chess for hours. He told me weeks later that after I'd beaten him several times, he decided maybe it wouldn't be so bad to travel with me and polish up his English, even if my harmonica playing needed some serious work.

We had arrived on Paradise Beach. After breakfast and lunch at the shack, we hiked on to Super Paradise Beach, made camp and took our clothes off like the other twenty campers there.

It amazed both Peter and me how soon the novelty of nudity wore off. When everybody's naked, nobody's nude anymore. In fact, at the end of our first day we both put on shorts. It was more comfortable. Besides, it felt a little strange hanging out with another guy with no clothes on.

Some of our fellow travelers were talking about the inexpensive boat that went from Mykonos to Izmir, Turkey, on an almost daily basis. Despite our initial misgivings about Turkey, it was clearly the best way to head east. Peter wasn't going back to the Middle East. If your passport got stamped in Israel, you couldn't go into any surrounding countries. The region was basically a war waiting to happen.

We were just deciding to team up and head for Turkey when the wind picked up again and blew down the tent in a sudden fury. A campfire was impossible, so we went to sleep in our sleeping bags early.

Then came the rain. The best we could do was drape the collapsed tent over ourselves for some shelter. It was a wet, uncomfortable night.

By morning, the rain had stopped. We aired out our wet sleeping bags and clothing and had an open-air breakfast. One thing about Peter—nothing fazed him. We shared an essential attitude that made hitchhiking attractive. We loved the adversity. The tougher things got, the better we liked it. After all, we were out to prove ourselves and discover who we were at the same time.

Later that afternoon, I was swimming when I saw what looked to be a beautiful naked woman walking on the beach from the wilderness part of the island. As she got closer, I could see she was athletic and buxom with no sag whatsoever to her breasts. She was a young white girl with brown, silver-dollar-sized nipples. She wore a thin belt with a small pouch to the side that did nothing to hide her perfect triangle.

Chest deep in the cold salty water, I massaged myself so as to make a more manly first impression. I waded out of the water and greeted her cheerfully. She responded with a wave and a smile. It's hard not to be friendly when you're naked.

"Where you coming from?" I asked as she came within hearing range.

She didn't answer right away. She kept walking toward me. *Oh my God, she's gorgeous.* Her hair was long, brown and thick and blowing in the wind. Her shoulders were square. She had a small pack on her back and a leather-bead ankle bracelet on her left foot. She was about five feet, six inches tall. Her legs were lean but muscular. The closer she got, the more her heavy eyebrows seemed the ideal set-off for her full lips. She walked like a dancer. She was innocence begging to be corrupted. She might as well have had the snake of temptation wrapped around her neck.

"I'm hungry," she cried playfully as we got close enough to speak.

"Hungry for what?" I asked hopefully.

"No, no. Don't get the wrong idea," she scolded as we came face to face and shook hands politely. "I mean I'm really, really hungry. Hungry for food. I've been on the Way Out Beach for two days, fasting and meditating, all by myself, with no food the last day. Do you have anything to eat?"

"Yeah, I've got an apple and a can of beans and a . . ."

"You've got an apple?" She didn't let me finish. "You've got an apple! Oh, my God! Can I have it? I mean, can I eat it with you?"

"I'll be Adam and you be Eve," I joked.

"No, I mean it. I'm really starving. Please don't laugh. If you've got an apple, let's go get it right now."

I walked her over to the tent, which was set up for drying. Peter jumped up like he'd seen a ghost. He was wearing shorts.

"Peter, I'd like to introduce you to . . . what did you say your name was?"

"It's Rebekah, with one 'k' and 'a, h' at the end," she said shaking Peter's hand firmly.

"By the way," I said as I retrieved a big red apple, "my name is Mark."

"Hello, Mark," she said, grabbing the apple greedily. "Nice to meet you and Peter." Her words crunched into the apple as she was already talking with her mouth full.

Peter widened his eyes at me as if to congratulate a fisherman on a fine catch.

After a couple ravenous bites, Rebekah caught herself and remembered her manners. "Here," she said, handing me the apple. "I shouldn't eat this whole thing too fast."

I took a symbolic bite of the apple, imagining it was Rebekah I was biting into. She was shivering from a slight chill in the air and her own exhaustion. We sat down and finished the apple. Peter threw his jacket over her shoulders.

"Thank you," she said. "I guess you could tell I'm cold," she said, glancing down at her fully erect nipples. Peter and I laughed nervously. Sitting so close to this incredibly sexual creature eating an apple was almost more than we could handle. I put on some shorts and a shirt. It was getting chilly.

"What else you got?" she asked with her mouth still full of the last bit of the apple core.

"How about some bread and cheese and wine?" Peter suggested.

She bounced up and down. "Oh, God, give me all of it. That sounds so good I can't stand it."

We talked as she ate and gave us a synopsis of her life. She was only seventeen years old and had left her California home a year earlier when she caught her boyfriend cheating with her mother. "My own mother, fucking my boyfriend. Can you dig how fucked up that is?"

She hitchhiked to New York City and ended up dancing in a strip club right away. "They never checked to see how old I was. What a bunch of chumps. I lived with my manager. He never pimped me. He paid me a ton of money, though, and I saved enough to go traveling, and here I am."

It was beginning to dawn on me that I wasn't going to get lucky with this exotic woman-child. Peter told her we were thinking about taking the boat to Turkey. "Oh, great," she said. "Maybe I'll see you guys there."

She stayed with us long enough for wine and cheese and then announced she had to go. I practically begged her to stay. "So why do you have to leave?"

She stood up in all her glory. "I've got to join up with a friend of mine."

"Who's that?" I pressed, thinking it was a man.

"No, no." She sensed my suspicions. "Her name is Adriana, and she is definitely not a man. She's a wonderful woman from Argentina, a little bit older than me, but we travel well together. I promised her

I'd be back before dark on this day, and if I don't make it back, she'll be worried."

I watched Rebekah walk away as gracefully and as beautifully as she had entered. Her ass was perfect, round, and suntanned. I turned to Peter and said, "Was she for real or did we just encounter a Greek goddess?"

"I can see why she made money dancing," Peter said. "Good she leaving. She is young for you." He was hardly ready to expand our new partnership into a three-way deal. We spent the next day on the beach, and then started walking along the sea and back to town.

Two mornings later, I awakened on the beach near the town of Mykonos. Peter and I were waiting to take the boat to Turkey. I raised myself up on one elbow and was startled to see the face of a beautiful woman sleeping not four feet away. She looked innocent and tough at the same time. Her nose was playful beneath golden-brown eyebrows that highlighted her face. Her chin was stubbornly set, even though her lips seemed to be kissing something. She was a little disheveled. There was sand in her hair and her sleeping bag had oil stains on it.

She opened her round brown eyes and the beach suddenly became much brighter. I pretended to be asleep, but I knew she had caught me staring. When I opened my eyes, she was watching me and smiling. "We sleep together last night, no?"

"No, I mean yes. I mean, good morning," I said as I sat up and saw she was with a man with a scraggly black beard and a ponytail in the sleeping bag next to hers. *Too bad.* It had been more than a month since Hanna and I split. And now, here was the second wonderful woman in two days who had magically appeared on the scene only to prove unavailable.

"Good morning," she said dreamily as she sat up and stretched her arms to the sea. She was wearing a peasant shirt that accented her full figure. "The water is so wonderful. All night long it sang its song to me. Oh, beautiful, beautiful sea, I love you!" She arched her back gracefully and shook the sand out of her shoulder-length chestnut hair.

I laid back down and closed my eyes. She was such a vision I found it impossible not to stare. I must have fallen asleep. When I awakened, the woman was gone.

I didn't know it at the time, but I had just met Adriana.

CHAPTER NINE

Turkey

PETER AND I WAITED all day for our ship to come in. Hippies from all over the world were on the beach in Mykonos, waiting for ferry rides. We shared what we had with each other, starting with hashish. Our attitude was that nothing beats getting good and stoned before you're really awake in the morning. It puts a whole new twist on the day.

After getting high, it never takes long to get down to eating. Peter had an apple. He took a big bite and passed it on. Each person took a bite. By the time it made its way back to us, it was nothing but an apple core.

Peter howled in delight. "Yes, this was once an apple. Now it is more than an apple. It is now an apple core! This apple I will never forget. This is the apple of the world." He stood up and threw the core into the sea with great ceremony. We all applauded and laughed. Everyone understood the message of sharing even though at least five languages were represented within the group.

Most of the day went that way. Every little thing turned into a joke of cosmic proportion. One Italian guy waded into the water with a Frisbee on his head until he was completely submerged, and the Frisbee was floating freely on the water. We all had to put our own spin on that trick. A Frenchman with a long beard crawled in on all fours with the Frisbee on his back. Two guys from Jersey piggybacked the Frisbee into the water. It was Beach Theater, fueled by hash pipes.

People went to the market and brought back fruit and vegetables. Peter and several others bought bottles of wine. We passed them around and drank them like communion until we had a pile of empties that a couple from Sweden turned into a sandcastle of bottles.

Ships sailed into port and gradually depleted our glassy-eyed crew as people went their separate ways. Nobody said goodbye, just, "See you next time." We all figured we'd see each other again, down the road.

Peter and I were among the last to leave the beach. By the time our boat to Turkey made port at Mykonos, three hours late, giant storm clouds were thundering across the horizon, blotting out the late afternoon sun and turning all blue to gray. It became difficult to see where the water ended and the sky began. The world was seamless and ominous, the sky furious. The sea began to heave mightily, as if angered at being awakened from a deep sleep.

The old Greek freighter we boarded by gangplank did not inspire confidence. It was about fifty yards long and all its paint had worn off long ago. The hull looked like it had been compromised by years of low maintenance, neglect, and constant pounding by the sea. The crew looked unkempt and wore no uniforms. There were no lifeboats anywhere to be seen. Even so, Peter and I never thought about not boarding the vessel for safety reasons. We'd been waiting too long and we were far too loaded for rational thought. Besides, we'd already paid for our tickets and it was the only boat going to Turkey.

"Rickety" was the best word to describe the boat. To make matters much worse, it was packed to the gills with peasant passengers and their pigs, goats, and livestock of all kinds. Peter and I were the only tourists aboard. Our tickets were cheap, which meant we'd be spending a long night in the hold of the ship with the entire cast of Noah's Ark if the approaching storm kept us off the main deck.

"Maybe we should have paid a little more for our tickets," Peter said.

"I don't know," I responded while assessing the situation by sight and smell. "It doesn't look like there are any good seats."

We stayed topside as the freighter took off, engines thundering, and diesel smoke belching into the air like full sails. The wind began reaching gale force as we made it out to the open sea. Our ship felt tiny and vulnerable. Giant waves were rolling the old boat like a drunk at the carnival. Saltwater began exploding over the deck.

Peter shouted over the crashing waves as as the brine burst in his beard. "I love the sea! I used to work on ocean vessels. I've been around the world on water. I've seen the wind break masts. Men swept overboard. Radios knocked out by rain that sprayed like a fire hose. I've seen it all. And let me tell you, we're in for one hell of a storm. Can you feel it? This is going to be a bad one. I can feel it in my eardrums. We're in a pressure system. Tonight, we will rock and roll!"

"Brave the mighty winds, lads, for tomorrow we die!" I shouted in jest as the world began to roar. So far, the storm was exactly what I had been looking for: high-sea adventure. I had no idea what I'd gotten myself into.

The full fury of the storm was upon us so quickly it started a panic among our fellow passengers as they fell over each other to get down the ladders and below deck. Waves the size of whales started breaking over the railings.

"Hang on tight!" Peter exhorted as a wall of water engulfed us. "Wrap your arms and your legs around the rail." I did as he told me.

One of the crew ordered us below as he descended a ladder from an upper deck. He looked alarmed. Another monster wave blasted us. It almost wrenched my hands and legs from the rail. An awning behind us ripped out of its sockets and blew off like a rocket. I looked at Peter. He nodded his head as if to say, "Time to get below."

A blinding flash struck the ship. The lightning made a cracking sound like a giant oak tree coming down. We bolted in a mad dash for the cargo door.

We made our way down to the hold, breathing hard and trembling. We were soaking wet. The steps were steep and slippery with animal waste. The lowest level of the ship was crowded beyond capacity. The pungent odor of goat shit had already taken over. Or maybe it was chicken shit. Or pig shit. Or all of the above. The animals were howling in terror. Bowel and bladder control was the last thing on their minds. I wondered how any four-legged creature could have done anything but fall down the stairs.

The seats in the belly of the ship were set up like a movie theater, facing not a screen but two one-stool restrooms, one for men and one for women. People turned to look as we staggered down a center aisle of the rolling ship and found two seats front-row and center, not ten feet from the lavatories. The wooden seats were uncomfortably small and attached in rows like an old public school auditorium. One bare bulb between the men and women toilets was the only light for the entire room. It was a stage set from an Ionesco play. It was Theatre of the Absurd.

"Let the show begin," I joked as we sat down. Peter found that quite funny and we both started laughing. No one else found any humor in our situation. I caught my breath and turned around to see most of the forty wide-eyed and frightened passengers staring at us like we were crazy and rude for making fun of their putrid and perilous situation.

I grabbed Peter by the arm. "Peter. Cool it. These people think we're laughing at them."

Peter turned around and saw what I was talking about. He tried to slouch down in his chair like a naughty schoolboy, but he was much too big to find any way to hide. He looked like the monster cowering before Dr. Frankenstein. The more we tried not to laugh the more we had to laugh.

Meanwhile, our fellow human passengers were becoming more seasick by the minute. One by one, they headed for the toilet. We could hear the sounds of violent retching coming from the bathrooms. One poor guy in a tunic waited outside the door, turning greener by the moment. He finally fell to his knees and puked just as the guy inside opened the door. The door hit the man on his knees in the head and the exiting man slipped and fell in the vomit. Peter and I tried to cover our faces in our hands, but we couldn't keep from laughing. This was high comedy. This was clown-tickling slapstick at its best.

Neither man noticed our laughter. The cacophony of human and animal sickness was much too loud. By now, the boat was rolling dangerously and most of the passengers were getting sick. Some made it to the toilets, others didn't try. The sounds of retching filled the hold like the night of the living flu. Horrible sounds. People sounded like they were dying. Some were guttural and evil sounding, like it was time to call the exorcist. Others were whiny and pathetic. There was some sobbing. One slender woman used a hand-woven shawl as a receptacle for her puke. Others weren't so careful. We could hear splattering on the floor.

Somehow, the macabre and fearful scene seemed funny to Peter and me. As veteran hitchhikers, we could take ourselves out of the scene and see it for the ridiculous mess it was. We were laughing too hard to get sick. In fact, we wondered aloud why we weren't throwing up like everybody else. Peter thought it might be the wine. I thought it was the hashish. We smoked a couple hits from Peter's small pipe. Nobody could smell the contraband.

Besides the human noises, there were at least fifty animals wailing their respective bleats and brays and grunts and honks. It sounded like the orchestra from hell, tuning up.

The place smelled like a ten-day-old corpse. We wrapped shirts around our mouths and noses. The putrid odor was complicated by the stench of fear. The old boards and metal of the boat were creaking and moaning like the sea could come crashing through at any moment. Water was seeping into the hold.

Peter and I began to sober up as the ship tilted wildly and seemed on the verge of capsizing. People screamed and began to panic. Women cried. Men prayed loudly. It sounded like a hurricane outside. Fear began to settle in on me like an unwelcome visitor. A wave hit the ship with such violence it felt like it could be breaking the old boat in two. The wood of the boat made terrible cracking noises.

Just when things looked like they couldn't get worse, the light blinked off as if an angry ghost had blown it out for spite. Blackness overtook the hold. Peter grabbed my arm to reassure me. I started feeling sick. It was a rumbling in my stomach at first and then a queasiness before nausea wrapped its arms around me and squeezed.

"This is not good," I moaned as I fell forward onto my knees and heaved my guts out into the darkness. Soon, Peter was on the floor next to me, doing the same thing. Neither of us was laughing anymore. Nothing was funny. The darkness intensified the fear and uncertainty. I began to think I might be meeting my maker in this putrid void. By the time I was able to take my seat, I had vomit of unknown origin all over my hands and knees. I could only hope it was my own.

We held on grimly to our seats as the storm tossed the ship up and down and side to side for what seemed like hours. People were falling out of their seats. Chickens were trying to fly. Goats were butting pigs. Donkeys were kicking. People tried in vain to restrain and protect their animals. One teenage boy fell on what sounded like a duck and crushed it to death. I thought the tumbling chaos would never end, or that it would end in disaster at sea. There were no lifejackets on board. Water kept seeping through the hull. We were ankle deep in saltwater vomit. If the ship went down, we were going down with it.

So much for high-sea adventure. Nobody will even know what happened. Damn! This is not how I wanted it to end.

A newsreel of my life highlights began playing in my mind's eye. I was at the family dinner table on Sunset Drive, kissing my high school sweetheart, then riding my motorcycle, flying solo in a small plane, and getting in a fistfight with the eighth-grade bully. My life wasn't "flashing" before my eyes. It was rolling by wistfully. After all, I wasn't actually dying. I just thought I was probably going to die. At the very least, I knew I was going to puke again soon.

Peter kept telling me we were going to make it through the storm. I did not believe him. "If she's taken us this far," he said, "she'll take us the rest of the way." I couldn't see his face in the darkness, but it sounded like he was still sick. It didn't take long before we were both on our knees again in the slime.

After what seemed like forever, we began to feel the storm subsiding. Gradually, the boat began to feel more stable. There must have been a pump or a drain in the hold because the water on the floor became shallower. I fell asleep to troubled dreams. I dreamed I was in a jet airplane, a fighter jet I didn't know how to fly. It kept spinning round and down as I waited for the emulsifying crash that would be the end. The crash never came. Instead, I realized I could open the cockpit canopy and simply climb down to ground-level safety.

Peter shook me awake. The ship wasn't rolling anymore. The stench was still overpowering but most of the passengers had lapsed into an exhausted sleep. A few rays of sunrise shone through cracks in the vessel's construction like laser beams. We climbed the crew ladder and crawled up on deck as if we were survivors of a nuclear holocaust. The sea shimmered brilliantly beneath a blue and cloudless sky.

"I feel like Jesus Christ after three days in the tomb!" Peter shouted triumphantly. "What do you call it when you come up from the grave? I want to say 'born again,' but I know that is not right."

"The word is 'resurrection'," I exclaimed with enough excitement to purge my lungs of the horrible air we'd been breathing. "We have died and gone to heaven. We have been resurrected! It's all gravy from here on out. A new life is dawning for us, Peter. A new life! Do you understand? This is our resurrection!"

Peter hugged me so hard he lifted me a foot off the ground. I hadn't been swept off my feet since childhood.

Life never seemed so full of promise. Air never tasted so good. *Nothing like a near-death experience to make you appreciate being alive,* I reflected.

We found a freshwater spigot and cleaned up as best we could. As we were wringing out our socks, one of the ship's officers came up and offered us each a Coke. It tasted better than any commercial ever said it would. The officer was feeling charitable after the night's ordeal. He told hand-waving stories of the crew's heroics. His eyes widened many times as he told us all about the storm. Unfortunately, his wild animated tale was all in Greek. He didn't seem to notice that we didn't understand a word he said. Once he finished his story and walked away, Peter and I looked at each other and rolled our eyes.

We spread out our gear on the top deck to dry as our fellow passengers staggered out of the hold to bask in the sun. Everybody was friendly and happy to have survived. They talked to us like they thought we understood what they were saying. We nodded and smiled. We understood the emotions if not the words.

It wasn't long before Peter grabbed my shoulder and pointed to the distance. "Look! Look! There it is. Turkey!"

Sure enough, a green and brown layer of earth was slipping into the horizontal line that separated the blue of water from the blue of sky. It was land, all right. It could have been Africa or even China. There was nothing unique about it except that it wasn't water and it wasn't sky. It was Turkey. It sent shivers of eager anticipation down my spine. Visions of the Ottoman Empire and star crescents danced in my head. Of course, the experience would be nothing like the expectation. I had already learned that no place is ever anything like you thought it would be.

It took a long time to reach the harbor. Once the boat finally docked, we exited and were funneled onto a crowded bus that rolled along for a short time before dumping us in the middle of the city. Thousands of people with brown skin and flowing clothing were rushing about, doing business as usual. We were in the middle of Izmir, a city more ancient than the Bronze Age. From the look of things, nothing much had changed for quite a while. People stopped everything to gawk at the white foreign giants.

Peter and I stood out like aliens. We were much taller than the sea of pedestrians that stretched out before us. Our brightly colored packs, patched-leather blue jeans, and long hair quickly attracted an uncomfortably large crowd. Apparently, they'd never seen anything like us. Or maybe they were just looking for a handout.

We pushed our way through to a nearby park, hoping to find a place to rest. There was not a chance the growing crowd was going to leave us alone. People were pushing each other to get near us.

The locals were dirty. Their clothes were tattered. Their shoes were sandals if they had any footwear at all. Their eyes were dark holes of excitement. Their teeth were bad. Obviously, the Cultural Revolution from the West had not reached this international port city. This place had an innocence of primitive culture that had yet to evolve into the cosmopolitan bazaars of Istanbul. Of course, these were the beggars of Izmir, not the business class. People were yelling questions at us in Turkish. They weren't being hostile, just curious; although hostile and curious feel like the same thing when you're surrounded.

Peter blazed a trail through the yammering mass, and we walked quickly to a concrete circle in the park with a twenty-foot statue of a statesman in the middle. "Watch my back," Peter said as multiple sets of hands began touching us. "These people will steal us blind." It was

Peter's turn to feel uneasy. I tried to calm him by saying, "I've got you covered but who's going to watch my back?" I kept spinning around when I felt hands beginning to unzip compartments in my pack.

The crowd was beginning to get quite loud and dense as we arrived at the statue. As we stood back to back, Peter called to me over his shoulder. "Okay, we've got each other's back. What do we do now?"

"Don't worry, I've got a plan," I said. "Stay like we are but step up on this ledge." We stepped up a two-foot foundation step. Once we were looking down on the crowd, I held up my hands and yelled like a carnival barker. "Hear ye, hear ye! Step right up to the greatest little show on earth."

Much to my surprise, the growing crowd fell into an immediate and expectant silence. This suited me fine. All I ever really wanted in life was attention. Now, I was center stage, where I always thought I belonged. All I needed was a spotlight and a microphone. The danger of being swarmed and robbed by these eager street people didn't faze me in the slightest.

Peter smirked at my unlikely and temporary success as if to say, "What are you going to say now?"

"Hear ye, hear ye!" I shouted at the top of my booming voice. "We have come bearing great gifts. Welcome to the big top, the main event, the really big show! We have come from far away to demonstrate for you . . ." The crowd gawked in amazement as I paused for dramatic effect.

"The Swiss Army knife!" I screamed as I held mine over my head and, with great flourish, opened up several blades. The front row was so amazed they actually tried to step back from the shiny knife. Of course, this was impossible as the people in the ever-growing crowd were now straining forward to get a better look at the show.

"Behold!" I shouted. "This amazing device has a tool for everything and anything you could ever possibly want or need to do. It is a miracle of modern science." I snapped out the scissor blade. "You can cut paper or cloth in a straight line with this marvelous invention. You can even cut your own hair!" The crowd cheered wildly as I cut a lock of my own hair and threw it to the second and third rows. They knew I was putting them on, but they appreciated the entertainment.

"But wait! There's more!" I shouted my best imitation of the slice-and-dice hawkers at the kitchen shows back home in the Midwest. "This little baby can open bottles!" I pulled out the bottle opener and demonstrated it in thin air. There were more *oohs* and *ahs* from the gathering. "It can be a screwdriver!" I demonstrated on the side of Peter's head. He played along by flapping his arms in mock pain like one of the Three Stooges. The crowd erupted in laughter. They loved us. We were good together.

"It can be a little knife." I pulled out the small blade and cut the air in tiny circles. "Or a big knife." I pulled out the larger blade and made larger air circles. "*En garde!*" I thrust playfully toward Peter, who fell to his knees, pretending to beg for mercy. He looked like he was beginning to wonder how we were going to escape what had now become a bona fide mob.

"It has a handy toothpick!" I showed the plastic pick and began picking my teeth with all the showmanship of a man swallowing flaming swords. The crowd surged forward in excitement. Up close they smelled like a meat truck in rural Mexico.

"It can be a pair of tweezers!" I held it low for the eager onlookers to examine and try to grab. I plucked an imaginary splinter out of my right hand. The crowd was moving in on us. Peter had to gently and then not so gently push people away from us and off our ledge. He looked at me anxiously. I was beginning to share his concern. Besides, I was running out of attachments to display.

"But wait! There's more!" I hollered, fumbling with the knife. "In fact, the best is yet to come." I paused. They were in the palm of my hand. Actually, they nearly had us in the palms of their hands. "I've been saving the best for last! That's right. You are about to see the very best thing modern science has to offer. Right here. Right now. For free! I now present you with man's best friend, the miracle of the wine bottle, the corkscrew!"

The crowd gasped and fell back slightly as I waved the gleaming device in their faces. In that instant, Peter saw an opening in the tight circle of people around us and began pushing his way through it. I danced along behind, turning round and round, as though I was the corkscrew opening the crowd. People gave us just enough room to get through. At the edge of the mob, I didn't need to tell Peter what to do. We broke into a dead run past a police officer who was trying to disperse the crowd. We didn't stop for blocks until we ducked around a corner and into a restaurant. All those in pursuit were left wondering where we had gone.

"My God, man!" Peter was breathing heavily as we found a table near the rear of the wooden-floor restaurant. "That was a crazy thing to do. I admit it was a wonder. And, yes, you are quite the showman. But it was crazy, man. I have never seen so many people come together so fast for no good reason. I felt like a magnet. These people act like they've never seen anything like us before. Is that possible? Is it going to be like this everywhere we go in Turkey?"

"It can't be," I said. "We must have hit some bizarre beggars' zone. Those people were looking for a handout."

Peter leaned across the table to look at me with raised eyebrows. "Did you see them? Did you see their eyes? They were desperate. I was getting really afraid and you kept exciting them more and more."

We caught our breath and laughed at each other. "You were quite the showman yourself." I poked Peter's arm. "We could take our act on the road here in Turkey."

"Nobody could pay," Peter observed.

"Maybe the storm at sea has transformed us into charismatic characters," I wondered.

"Don't get carried away," Peter said. "We were just something new for them to play with."

That was one of the great things about Peter. The man was down-to-earth, an excellent foil for my wild-eyed dreamer. We'd only been together a few days and it already felt like we had grown up together.

It was in Ankara that I got my first bedazzled look at Afghanistan on a map. We were in the Iranian Embassy, getting visas. We had more or less decided that Iran was the next logical destination after Turkey. Fortunately for us, one of our fellow vagabonds told us you couldn't get visas to enter Iran at the border between Turkey and Iran.

I shook my head. "Imagine getting all the way to the border, then having to turn around and come all the way back to Ankara to get your visa and then head back to the border again."

"It happens every day," the clerk said without a smile.

Peter looked at me sternly. "It is a lucky thing to know."

While we were waiting in line, a fellow traveler told us it would be a good idea to get a visa for Afghanistan as well since there would be similar difficulties at the Iran-Afghanistan border. Peter opened up a map and there it was. Afghanistan! It looked exotic even on the map. I'd never read much about the country, much less thought of trying to hitchhike all the way across Turkey and Iran to get there. It had cities with names I'd never heard of like Herat and Kabul. In an instant, I knew that's where I wanted to go, where I needed to go. I could see my future in that map.

"Besides," Peter pointed out. "You've got to go through Afghanistan to get to India."

Up until that very moment, I had never dreamed I would be headed to India. Perhaps, subconsciously, I'd always been heading there since I was such a rabid Beatles fan, and the Beatles had changed everybody's consciousness by going there to find enlightenment. But I really didn't know that I was going to India until I saw that map of Afghanistan.

"Oh, God," I whispered incredulously as if I'd just seen my future. "We're going to India. This is so cool I can't stand it. Yes! Let's go all the way. Let's do it. Let's go to India."

My travel plans had stretched to Afghanistan and on to India in the space of about one minute. It was a magical moment of truth. Now that the itinerary was laid out before me, it was amazing I hadn't seen it coming earlier. I could hear the Indian musical instruments behind John Lennon singing "Tomorrow Never Knows" from the *Revolver* album.

Ever since the Beatles had gone to India in 1968 to study transcendental meditation with the Maharishi Yogi, Western hippies had been following suit. Suddenly, I knew what I should have known all along. I was headed for India. It never occurred to me that $155 might not get me all the way there.

We hiked over to the Afghanistan Embassy, which was not as crowded as the Iranian Embassy had been. We met an attractive, young Turkish woman there, who turned out to be the secretary of the Consular. Her name was Guzen and she was eager to help and to speak with anybody from the West. We hit it off so well she invited us to her house for dinner after she got off work. Once we arrived, she told us her parents were away for a few days and we could spend the night if we needed a place to stay. Her father was a geologist and her mother accompanied him wherever he went.

The house was very roomy and tastefully decorated with ornamental wood furniture and Persian rugs. These people had money. *Her father probably works for a US oil company*, I thought.

Guzen invited several of her friends over for a wine party in our honor. They were nearly fluent in English and shared our enthusiasm for getting high. We drank wine and smoked hash and listened to the Rolling Stones 1971 record album *Sticky Fingers* as loud as the speakers could crank.

Peter and I learned a lot about Turkey that night. Ankara and Istanbul were "modern" Turkey. The rest of the country was still primitive. This was something we had witnessed on our own. It was nomads scratching a bare existence out of the prairies, tired horses pulling carts of vegetables, no running water even in the hotels and people staring at you like they've never been more than a couple miles from the hut they call home. Guzen and her friends felt a responsibility to close the gap between the two Turkeys but the student uprisings of the late 1960s had resulted in martial law throughout the land. The illiteracy rate was well over fifty percent and unemployment was high.

"Most of the peasants don't believe the US put a man on the moon," Guzen laughed. "As you know, the Moslem religion was never much for modernization."

"You might be surprised how many Americans don't believe in the moon landing," I said. "In fact, you might be surprised how much of the United States is still living in poverty. It's not all big cars and skyscrapers. And, by the way, I'm not sure how much difference there is between the Koran and the Bible. Both religions claim their book is the word of God."

That comment turned the party into quite the metaphysical discussion for a short time, much of it centered on the "God is Dead" headlines of the magazines in the US. Then, we returned to talking about the more entertaining topics of the day: sex, drugs, and radical politics. It was amazing to discover that students and young people in Ankara were pretty much the same as their counterparts in Amsterdam and Indiana. Of course, everyone agreed the war in Vietnam was insane. The Turkish people couldn't understand how it could still be going on since the whole world seemed to have condemned it.

Guzen and her friends were intrigued that Peter and I were going to hitchhike to India. "I hope it works out better for you than it did for The Beatles," one young man said.

"I don't know about that," I said. "I think India did them a lot of good. They might not have found the meaning of life but at least they got a new perspective on the world."

"At least they got out of England," Peter joked. Everybody laughed at that comment even though we all knew the world's most influential rock band had done plenty of world traveling before going to India. Guzen put on some Beatles records. We danced and communicated on many levels. When "I Want to Hold Your Hand" played, we all held hands in a dancing circle. It was an electrifying moment that defied national boundaries. We sang the simple chorus together at top volume.

Music is the international language. It helps people understand each other. I was surprised the Turkish kids knew all the words to the songs. The Beatles was the first rock band to take the world by storm. They were as popular in Ankara as they were in New York City.

The party rolled on until 3 a.m. and then gradually fizzled out. After the last drunken guest had left, Guzen directed Peter and me to the most comfortable carpet in the house. It was hard to tell whether we went to sleep or simply passed out. She kissed both of us goodnight on the forehead.

Late the next morning, we bid Guzen a fond and hungover farewell and started walking out of Ankara. We stopped at a dilapidated restaurant and had just finished the difficult process of ordering food from a foreign menu when Peter noticed two Western girls huddled at a table in the back. They had been watching us. As soon as they saw us notice them, they rose quickly from their table and walked directly to us.

Nervously, the one in pigtails and a blue windbreaker began speaking quickly. "May we please join you? I know this is rather forward, but you are the first Americans we've seen here. Sherry and I . . . excuse me, my name is Danielle. Anyway, I'm from Canada. Actually, I was born in the States but I live in Canada. Sherry's from Sweden, but we met in Canada. We've been in Turkey almost a week now and I'm amazed we haven't been raped."

Peter and I listened carefully as she tried to get everything out at once. Danielle was attractive but slightly on the tomboy side. Sherry was a blond beauty although she was wearing almost enough clothing to hide her curves.

The four of us shook hands all around as the women sat down and Danielle continued in a conspiratorial whisper. "Last night we barricaded the door to our room after two drunk men followed us back to the hotel. Then one of them tried to get in our window. We were on the second floor. The men here are crazy. Walking down the street is out of the question. Women wear veils here. The men seem to think wearing jeans means you're a prostitute. It wasn't this bad in Istanbul, but even there it was a lot worse than Italy."

Sherry leaned back in her chair and began to relax. "And we thought nothing could be worse than the men in Italy."

"Next to the Turkish men, the Italian men look like gentlemen!" Danielle continued. "We've been followed and harassed since we got off the train."

"Slow down now." I tried to sound reassuring. "You're with us now. We'll protect you. Won't we, Peter?"

Peter looked amazed at the cavalier chivalry I could spew forth and get away with. "Sure, we will," he played along. "Why not? We protect ourselves. Why not two more?"

The women looked at him curiously. To answer their unspoken question, he told the tale of the vaudeville act we played in Izmir to escape our own mob scene. Everybody laughed as he told the story. The women were prepared to laugh at anything we said. They needed protection and they needed it now.

We settled into a good conversation as we ate and talked about our origins and travels. We began to feel comfortable with each other and hatched a plan to travel south together to the Mediterranean beaches before heading east to Iran. They offered to pay for lunch. We didn't let them. We went "Dutch," a term Peter found interesting as he explained he was from Holland, not the USA.

"Going Dutch means everybody's too cheap to buy anyone else's dinner," I said. "It's true, isn't it? Everybody's cheap in Holland?"

Peter stiffened his neck and shoulders. "It is absolutely not true. And we do not wear wooden shoes."

We all had doubts about hitchhiking through the more primitive areas of Turkey but decided we'd give it a try. Our original plan was to split into two teams and meet at prearranged towns along the way. This proved unnecessary since many truck drivers were only too pleased to pile four foreigners in the back of their trucks. In fact, they often stopped to buy us tea and cakes along the way. Several times each day we found ourselves the feature attraction in a primitive Turkish truck stop.

One of our best rides was atop a fully loaded grain truck, lumbering down the one-and-a-half lane, patchy blacktop road at a top speed of 40 mph. The driver told us we could sit on top of the truck cab if we took off our shoes. He didn't want us kicking in his windshield. So, there we were, looking like four misplaced hood ornaments and feeling like part of a liberating army of peaceniks. The truck wound through rugged rock formations and over stone bridges as we descended from painted plateaus and followed a river through deep oasis valleys. We passed tent villages where heavily wrapped nomads returned our greetings with surprised waves.

Then came the first real sign of the East. Just as we opened and started munching on a bag of apples sold to us by a goat herder, the truck had to hit the brakes to avoid hitting five camels that were blocking the road. What a milestone! These were our first camels. It was a game changing sign that proved we were leaving the West behind.

We jumped off the truck to get closer to them. The driver warned us to keep our distance, but we got close enough to smell them and even touch them cautiously. Their coat was coarse to the touch and they smelled like dead skunk. As we talked about riding them, one of the camels leaned into Danielle and knocked her to the ground. Our driver rushed in to pick her up and yell at the camels. Turning back to his hitchhikers, he clapped his hands and directed us to board the truck. We took our places back on top and watched as the driver eased his wide vehicle through the stubborn animals. We cheered as the camels parted and we were on our way again.

We laughed a lot that day, bouncing down the rural Turkish road and pointing out the ancient sights to each other. We were free and the whole world was along for the ride as far as we were concerned.

We spent the night in a field outside Konya, Turkey. We were close enough to a large mosque to hear the monks wailing in the minaret. It was a mournful and spooky sound, but it also felt like someone out there in the night was at least attempting to communicate with God. Danielle and Sherry insisted on sleeping between Peter and me. They were afraid of the night and not having a door to lock. Neither one of them had ever done any camping. We didn't make a fire since we didn't want to draw attention to ourselves.

"I can't believe you're dragging us through all this," Danielle said as she wrapped herself in a flimsy blanket on the tarp we'd spread.

I told her, "This, my dear, is hitchhiking. It's the only way to fully experience the culture. You can't really feel the people if you're insulated by hotels and restaurants and fellow foreigners."

"I'd like to be insulated by a hotel right now," Sherry complained. "That wailing freaks me out. It sounds like he's going to kill somebody any minute."

"He's just praying," Peter explained. "That's not a bad thing. If you listen to it with an open mind, it sounds quite peaceful."

The next morning, two Turkish men in a 1967 Buick picked us up. We crammed our gear and ourselves into the car and sped down the road at frightening speed. Thankfully, the two men weren't going our way for long and dropped us off in the middle of a small village. We were immediately surrounded by a horde of well-meaning, curious people. As we pushed our way to the main road, a seedy-looking driver of a horse-drawn cart motioned for us to jump on. We piled our packs and ourselves onto the cart and clopped on down the road with a large gang of children following behind.

It was great fun until I noticed the driver had both the reins and the whip in one hand. By the time I realized where his other hand was, he'd unzipped and nearly emptied the middle compartment of my pack. I made him stop the cart and tried to shame him into giving back what he had attempted to steal. He didn't seem at all embarrassed at getting caught. In fact, he tried to charge us three Turkish lira for the short ride. We indignantly refused to pay. Later, I discovered he'd gotten away with my salt and pepper shakers.

We spent the night in Mut, Turkey. It got pretty cold and the women were shivering in their flimsy blankets. Their complaining was beginning to get on our nerves. They obviously were not prepared for the rigors of our road.

The next day we hitchhiked all the way to Silifke where we met a kind man named Kadir. He rescued us from a crowd at the bus station and invited us to his tailor shop for tea. We spent most of that evening talking about Turkish customs and history. We never met his wife. He didn't talk about her much, although he enjoyed answering our questions about his country. He explained that the Turkish people are lazy by nature although we never did understand his reasons for saying so. He lamented the fact that he didn't have a daughter. In Turkey, a little girl doesn't go to school. She stays at home to help her mother with the house or her father with his shop.

Kadir found us a cheap hotel. The women were fed up with sleeping outdoors. They paid for the room and shared the one bed while Peter and I slept quite well on the floor. There was no romance in the air despite the fact we had naturally paired into two couples, Danielle and me and Peter and Sherry. The more we traveled together, the less likely it seemed anything sexual was going to happen. Hitchhiking is dirty work and the women were never going to get used to it. Fortunately, there was an old toilet in a tiny room down the hall with a cold-water sink. One by one, we did a chilly, personal clean up. The next morning, we headed for the sea.

By late afternoon, the four of us had found our way to the beach. It was deserted for miles and thirty-yards wide as it sloped gently down to the water from grassy hills. We took a refreshing, naked swim in the saltwater. Nobody was shy. We were all commune ready and too grimy to care. The water washed away the dust and took a load off our road-weary bones. The women did look temptingly beautiful with the sunset coloring their wet skin and athletic young bodies.

We smoked one of Peter's nine-paper spliffs while the sun slowly set in a brilliant array of oranges and pinks and reds and sizzled into the Mediterranean Sea. We drank wine and recounted our epic journey. The stars came out like diamonds. The sound of the waves lapping the shore put us into a hypnotic state. The moon came up as a narrow crescent.

"Look," Sherry said. "It's the flag of Turkey."

"Far out." Peter moaned his approval. "All you have to do is move your head to get a star in the right place and you've got the flag. It is a perfect and good omen."

"I'm so glad we met you two," Danielle said. "Thank you for rescuing us. This beach is so much different than the city. It washes away all the turmoil and trouble." She was trying hard to make up for all her previous complaining on the road.

"Think about the folks back home, missing all this," I said. "It's funny how great it feels tonight knowing that nobody knows where we are but us. In this moment we are completely independent and free. It feels exactly the opposite of how it felt in the hold of that ship when it looked like we might be going down. At that point, it felt sad that no one knew where I was. Now, it feels great that no one knows where I am."

"It was sad in the ship. It is happy tonight," Peter said simply and logically. "Nobody ever knows where you are but you."

We thought about that comment for a good long while, silently agreeing with its simple truth. We were all a little homesick. I considered where I was and who I was and how the "where" was beginning to determine the "who." The further away I got from my upbringing the more likely I was to make independent decisions about my future. Something had grown in me since the decision to go all the way to India. I was much more intrepid than the young man who started out from Indiana. Confidence and courage were slowly replacing self-doubt and fear. Each leg of the journey made the next seem less daunting.

The stars were wildly celebrating my decision to keep moving east after Europe.

"Think of this," I said. "Each of us has our own private set of dreams and fears, goals and illusions. But something has brought us all together tonight." The others waited for more. "Everything each of us has ever done and every place we've ever been has led us to the exact same spot in time and space."

"That's reason enough to celebrate!" Peter exclaimed. He grabbed the last bottle of wine and borrowed my Swiss Army knife to open it. "Here it is, folks." He mimicked my performance in Izmir. "The miracle of the wine bottle, the Swiss Army knife corkscrew." We laughed and passed the bottle around for another half-hour until it was empty. The fire was nothing but glowing coals by the time we fell asleep.

Four days later, it was time for Danielle and Sherry to call it quits and take a train back to Ankara. It had been a rough road to Malatya and then to Van, Turkey. Harsh words were finally spoken in a field on the outskirts of Van. The night had grown quite cold and both Danielle and Sherry were complaining bitterly about being hungry and cold and dirty.

"I can't believe you two call yourselves travelers," Peter snapped. "Listen to yourselves complaining. You've done nothing but complain since we left the beach. Of course you're cold. You are unprepared. You have no warm sleeping bags. We can protect you from any danger the road has to offer. But we can't protect you from your own stupidity." I agreed with him by maintaining silence. One thing about Peter: when he was right, he was right on.

Sherry and Danielle never said a word to us after that firm rebuke. The next morning, we awoke to watch them walking away and into the city of Van. We didn't try to stop them or even say goodbye. It was for the best.

We didn't talk about Sherry and Danielle much after that. Being on the move keeps you busy. It felt like we had a job to do. Getting into Iran was the next task.

We took a short train ride across the border to Tabriz, Iran. Word had gotten to us that you could wait for days at the border to get into Iran by road. Evidently, the Shah's government was concerned about the growing number of hippies from all over the world pouring into the country on their way to India and points beyond.

We took the shortest and cheapest train ride we could to cross the border into Iran. Peter smuggled in several grams of hashish despite my serious misgivings about the caper. The guards on the train at the border examined our passports and visas carefully and searched our backpacks thoroughly. They never came close to checking Peter's underwear.

We were fools to smuggle drugs across the border. A life sentence in a Turkish prison could have come out of that search. We never thought twice about it. After all we'd been through, we were beginning to feel invincible.

We were glad to get our stash into Iran. Actually, it was hard to believe we had made it to Iran. It had always seemed so far away. Now, it felt as if we had floated in on a magic carpet.

Playing guitar at Debrecen dormitory.

Working on the collective farm in Hungary, Mark second from left.

Lake Bolaton Hotel with Hanna.

Hiking boots, machete and officer's hat.

Hiking shoes, jeans and machete.

Afghan shirt.

Letters home.

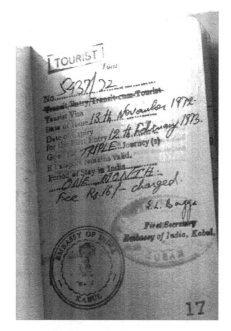

India passport stamps.

Pakistan passport stamp.

Mark and Adriana in Herat.

Mark in Kabul with his trusty passport satchel.

Lake Bolaton in Hungary.

From right" Claines, Borneo, Liza, the HLD and Mark;
sightseeing in Austria.

Getting high at Peace Corp Bob's.

Playing chess at Cigis in Kabul.

Peter on a Hookah..

Rebekah.

CHAPTER TEN

Adriana

AN ARMED GUARD AWAKENED Peter and me shortly after dawn in a park on the outskirts of Tabriz. The guard seemed sleepy himself. He pointed to the six-foot chain-link fence we had climbed the night before as if to say, "You know you're not supposed to camp here." He didn't try to speak to us. He could tell by looking at us that we wouldn't understand a word of his native language, Farsi. He seemed friendly enough, probably wishing he could be off on an adventure instead of patrolling the park. We packed up with great haste as the guard pretended not to watch. He escorted us out of the area. We were surprised when he picked two red roses from a flowering  bush near the gate and handed one to each of us. He wished us well and returned abruptly to his duties as if embarrassed by his random act of kindness.

We were finding it quite common for people, who felt trapped in their daily grind, to applaud and cheer on the travelers who seemed to be escaping the comforting pit of bill-paying routine and social security. For our part, we felt like lunatics escaping the asylum. Peter and I both knew it was crazy and dangerous to hitchhike through Iran. We didn't care. We were ready for anything.

The early wake-up put us on the streets as the shopkeepers and street vendors were setting up for the day. We walked past the peanut salesmen, shoeshine boys, and men who sit by their scales to check your weight for a rial, which was a little more than a penny. We brushed our teeth at a fountain, which doubled as a public watering hole. We didn't swallow the water since several smiling citizens were bathing there.

It was October 15th. Ramadan, the Muslim month of fasting, had begun on October 8th, so many shops were not opening. A few were setting up for the tourist trade. As soon as we started shopping for food, we realized we had arrived in a land where we could no longer read the words or the numbers. Everything was in Aramaic script.

"Wait a minute," I said to Peter. "These numbers aren't numbers anymore. What's with that? We call our numbers Arabic numerals. These guys are Arabs, right? So why are their numbers little squiggly lines?"

"Oh, man, this is going to be trouble," Peter said, letting me know he had no answer to my question. What we both should have known is the numbers weren't different. The only difference was the way they were symbolized.

Peter held up an apple and asked the vendor how much. The night before we had exchanged some dollars at the train station into Iranian rials. The smiling vendor knew his way around the language barrier. He held up his index finger and middle finger as if to say, "Two rials for one apple." Peter put down the apple, shook his head, and said, "Too much."

The finger bartering began. By the time we were done, we had enough food for many meals at what we thought was a bargain price. Our fingers had done the talking. We should have shopped around. Other vendors were calling for us to come over. They knew suckers when they saw them. But we liked our seller. He was fluent in sign language and our first friendly merchant in Iran. We left his place of business feeling pretty good about our trade. It took a couple days to realize we had paid triple price for everything.

We started walking to the main highway that would take us to Tehran. "It's good that no people are following us here," Peter observed.

"Tell that to the taxi drivers," I said as the fourth cab in less than a block pulled up to offer us a ride. The more we waved them away, the more they wanted to give us a lift. It took us at least an hour to realize that waving somebody off means "come here" to Iranians. A couple drivers got out to yell at us angrily as we shook our heads no once they had responded to what they thought was a request for a ride.

"What is with these guys?" I asked. "The more we try to get rid of them, the more they act like we invited them over."

"Ignore them and they'll go away," Peter suggested. Once again, he was right on the money. The taxi drivers left us alone once we stopped inadvertently inviting them to stop.

The world was definitely changing as we left the West and entered the East. It was exciting to get out of Europe and into the Iranian culture. There wasn't a border or an Iron Curtain between east and west. For Peter and me, the West ended and the East began when we could no longer read the numbers or the words. Our camel encounters had been harbingers of Eastern things to come, previews of coming attractions.

We walked out of town and settled down to smoke a joint by the side of the road and wait for a ride. We had no idea if anybody but the police would pick us up. We split our stash two ways so that we could eat it quickly if the police became a problem.

The road was flat and dusty. It was hot enough to make footprints in the asphalt. There were almost no cars on the two-lane highway. The occasional passing truck kicked up great dust clouds that coated our sweaty skin with fine grime. We got good and stoned on one of Peter's massive spliffs. Hours floated by. We saw a vehicle once every ten minutes. Drivers looked at us like we were crazy. Nobody stopped.

"Maybe Iran is not the place to hitchhike," I said.

"No way, man," Peter responded quickly. "I've talked to people who say it can be done. We only need to be patient."

"That was good," I said. "It sounded like something I would say."

We were sitting in the dust by the side of the asphalt, using our packs as back rests, when a four-door Ford came to a sudden halt as it was about to pass us by. We hadn't even gotten up to stick out our thumbs. We had been reduced to simply waving at people as they drove by.

The car backed up to greet us as we clambered to our feet. The driver jumped out and helped us put our packs in the trunk. We made sure he didn't get back into the vehicle before we did so he couldn't drive away with all our possessions. The passenger was friendly as he got out of the car and gestured that we get into the back seat. Both men looked to be Iranian and professional in their backgrounds. They were in their forties and wore Western suits, no turbans. They had obviously been drinking, which is probably why they picked us up, but they were not drunk. They cackled in delight at their foreign cargo as the car roared off and down the road.

The Iranians spoke very little English, but with a few key words, we realized the driver was a doctor and they were headed all the way to Tehran, nearly 400 miles away. Peter and I wondered if we had hit the hitchhikers' jackpot. This could be the ride of a lifetime . . . or it could take us places we did not want to go.

The doctor's name was Hassan. His suit was wrinkled. He had a double chin, a thin mustache, and big watery eyes. The passenger's name was Haseem. His suit was well-tailored and he looked quite fit. He had a gray ducktail flowing out from under his Dick Tracy hat. The two of them smelled vaguely of English Leather aftershave and Dunhill cigarettes, which they were quick to share. These guys were obviously Western influenced and they were doing their best to be hospitable. Their eyes were kind and full of fun. Peter and I had learned the importance of reading eyes.

Our hosts were passing a hip flask back and forth and soon passed it back to us. I took a long pull on the bottle and nearly choked it back up. It was grain alcohol. Hassan laughed so hard he almost went off the road. Peter took a more cautious swig. Haseem urged him to take another. Peter did, and this time choked a little himself. We all laughed together. These crazy Iranians seemed like good people. In a couple more swigs we were drinking buddies, partying like we'd known one another for years. Mercifully, the doctor rationed our consumption, warning us that drinking too much of this stuff would make you crazy. He rotated his index finger next to his temple to communicate in sign language.

"Ah, the international sign for crazy," I said, making the gesture myself. The other three joined in and we laughed together again. It was the wild humor of any good road trip. The language barrier proved to be not much of a problem. It's amazing how much detailed information can be communicated through sign language alone. The conversation eventually turned to women. The doctor was married. He showed photos of his three children. Haseem was single, and from the way he shimmied in his seat, he was an active participant in the nightlife of Tehran.

Peter and I didn't need to say a word to explain our situation. The long hair and backpacks said it all. Our hosts easily understood that I was from the United States. It took a while to explain that Peter was from Holland. They finally understood when he said the word "Amsterdam." They knew that city.

After about a hundred miles together we began singing songs. The front seat would sing the first few bars, then the backseat would mimic them. Then the four of us would sing together. It was such good fun that Peter rolled up one of his hash and tobacco spliffs and passed it around. The Iranians smoked with us like it was an everyday event for them. Before long, the four of us were floating down the highway, chatting away in our respective languages like we could understand each other perfectly.

The doctor stopped for lunch at one of the more modern buildings along the road. He let us know this was a good place to eat by the wide look in his eyes as he rubbed his slightly bulging belly in anticipation of the meal we were about to have. Haseem saw us understanding the doctor's gesture and we all shared a gleeful moment of belly rubbing.

Conversation among the fifty male patrons in the eating establishment stopped abruptly as we entered the large dining room with a vaulted ceiling. Persian rugs decorated the brown tile floor. Two large silver sabers crossed over a fireplace that sat idle in the center of the room, smoke stains stretching up the hard clay bricks to the apex of the ceiling. What had been a rumbling of conversation ceased with a suddenness that made us feel we were walking into a vacuum. Every man in the place, waiters included, seemed to be holding his breath. There were no women in the establishment. The room was staring at Peter and me like we were animals in a zoo. I tried to smile to hide the wave of nausea welling up inside.

The doctor slashed through the silence with a boisterous and friendly introduction and assured the patrons we were his most welcome guests. The hush collapsed in relief as several diners voiced greetings in Farsi. Two men even shook our hands as the doctor led us to an empty table in front of a window with steel bars and no glass.

Not all were happy to see us. Several men in long beards and turbans returned to their food, grumbling displeasure at their guests from the West. Some were abstaining from food in observance of Ramadan. Others were taking advantage of the travelers' exception to fasting. The doctor managed to explain that travelers are allowed to eat so long as they make up the days once they reach their destination. He made no attempt to explain how drinking alcohol and smoking hashish fit into his particular brand of the Muslim religion.

I heard unpleasant mutterings and muffled insults from a few tables. It was my first encounter with an anti-Americanism that had nothing to do with Vietnam. Many Iranians, particularly Muslim fundamentalists, hated the United States and Great Britain. In 1953, the two countries had secretly sponsored a coup d'état that overthrew the democratically elected Iranian government of Mohammad Mosaddegh. They installed Shah Mohammad Reza Pahlavi in order to exploit Iran's rich oil reserves. By 1972, opposition to foreign influence in Iran was well-organized and on the move. The Shah's regime became increasingly unpopular as it resorted to brutality in order to maintain power. Peter and I knew little of these dynamics, but we could feel the cultural collision as we found ourselves the center of attention in the restaurant.

Haseem and the doctor urged us to ignore the hostile elements of the crowd and remained upbeat as we waited for the food to arrive. We were thirsty after hours of dust and smoke and booze. We drank the water after the doctor nodded his approval. The establishment did not serve alcohol.

The food was excellent, steaming plates of rice with wonderfully spiced meat and vegetables. Haseem and the doctor explained Iranian politics in a long discourse over dinner. Peter and I understood almost none of it, although we nodded appreciatively as we continued stuffing ourselves. Diners at nearby tables seemed appeased when they heard the doctor loudly denouncing the Shah and making fun of his regime. The waiters were friendly and brought more food and extra bottles of water. The tension in the room relaxed. By the time we finished eating, we had pretty much blended into the scene. Everyone could see we were just hungry travelers, not agents of evil foreign enterprise. The doctor had won them over. No doubt he adjusted his political commentary depending on who was listening.

When we finished eating and drinking tea, the doctor insisted on paying the entire bill and left what looked like an elaborate tip. Our waiter walked us to the door like celebrities. As any server can tell you, the true measure of a man's character is the size of his tip.

Back on the road again, the doctor drove on relentlessly while the rest of us napped. I woke up when the car pulled off the highway and onto a narrow dirt road that wound back into rolling hills for at least a mile. Everybody was awake by the time we came to a stop in front of a mud shack with a tin roof in an oasis grove of trees and greenery. Peter and I didn't say a word. We wondered what was going on. All Haseem said was "Ahhh," like he was glad to have finally arrived at this private and prearranged destination.

A young boy came running out of the shack to greet us. He greeted the doctor and Haseem warmly, but he was obviously concerned about the Westerners in the back seat. *What have we gotten ourselves into?* Peter and I exchanged wary glances. There was obviously something illegal or at least secret going down.

The doctor convinced the boy we were okay. The youngster ran back into the house and returned with three men carrying what looked to be all the equipment necessary for a backyard barbecue. They wore turbans and sandals and loose-fitting clothing. We got out of the car and followed our guides back into a wooded area behind the house. Nobody said a word. I was beginning to wonder if we were being taken to some kind of sacrifice. I checked the men closely. Nobody appeared to have a weapon of any kind. I noticed Peter was watching their every move and scanning the trees for any sign of other people. The doctor didn't try to reassure us. He had begun what sounded like some kind of negotiation with the guides. The only person following us was the boy, who seemed quite comfortable with our little walk into the woods.

Our group arrived at a grassy clearing in the trees. Blankets were spread on the ground as the doctor and Haseem took off their trousers, revealing bright blue, full-length pantaloons underwear. I looked at Peter as if to ask, "Have we gotten ourselves into some kind of sex thing?"

Hassan and Haseem sat down, cross-legged, on the blankets and invited us to join them. We did not take off our pants to get more comfortable, but we did take off our shoes to sit down. The guides prepared a fire in the small black stove they had been carrying. The doctor began cleaning a smoking pipe. It was a glazed bowl with one small hole in it at the end of a hand-carved wooden stem. One of the guides brought him two small chunks of something that looked like miniature Tootsie Rolls. He preheated the substance with a glowing stick and molded the ensuing goo into the pipe hole. Once the doctor applied a small flame to the goo, I saw Peter's eyes light up as he finally realized what was happening.

"Opium," he whispered as the doctor took a long hit and closed his eyes in ecstasy.

All present murmured our appreciation of the doctor's style as he held the smoke in for at least thirty seconds. When he finally exhaled, his eyes opened slightly and seemed not to focus. He closed them again and breathed fresh air in deeply. His head rocked back, but he did not go down. His body relaxed, and when he finally opened his eyes, it looked like he had gone someplace far away.

Haseem chuckled madly as he sat up straight to take his turn. He had the same ecstatic reaction as the doctor, but he lowered his back slowly to the ground and laid down without opening his eyes.

Peter and I couldn't wait to take a hit. The guides began breaking out snacks and tea as the doctor recovered enough to begin moving in slow motion. Soon, it was my turn. The doctor smiled lovingly as he held the egg-stick pipe to my mouth and lit the goo.

I'd smoked what had been sold as opium in the States, but it hadn't looked or smelled anything like this. This smell was a combination of hash and curry and jasmine. It made me feel like I was in a Chinese opium den where nobody ever gets out of his narrow bunk bed.

I was careful not to choke as I steadily filled my lungs with smoke and held it in as long as I could. Peter laughed approvingly and sounded far away as I finally exhaled what seemed to be a very small amount of smoke.

Everything turned golden. The grass, the trees, the sky, Peter, the doctor, Haseem, the guides. Everything. Even my own hands looked golden. "Whoa, that's some great shit!" I moaned as I fell onto my side. The guides giggled but tried to be polite. I felt a wave of freedom and relief passing through my mind and body.

It occurred to me I had been in pain my entire life, and now for the first time, I was pain free.

My eyes were closed, but my thoughts were vivid. My mind raced until it settled on a glowing vision of my entrance visa issued by the Royal Embassy of Afghanistan in Ankara, Turkey. Beneath the English words was the most indecipherable language I'd ever seen. There was not the slightest hint of an alphabet. The characters ran together. They looked like Muslim architecture, rounded and ornamental. *What kind of people write this ancient script? Have I traveled back in time?*

I felt lost and confused but not afraid. An overwhelming feeling of wellness replaced my disorientation. I was far from home, but somehow, right where I needed to be.

I opened my eyes. The sky was broiling and beneficent. The grass and trees were rolling like an ocean. I was floating on a graceful schooner, following the sun on a well-guided course.

Gradually, the golden hues turned back to green. Peter was on his side, moaning pleasantly. He had taken his turn. The doctor and Haseem were laughing and checking to make sure we were well. It took some time for us to converse again. Neither one of us had been rolled around like that before, even during the intense body rushes of an LSD trip. This stuff was a smooth and uplifting ride without the paranoia of the chemical hallucinogens.

The doctor liked to have a good time, but he was judicious in administering the opium. Medical doctors could legally obtain and prescribe opium at that time in Iran, even though this seemed to be an illegal transaction. The doctor knew how dangerous pure opium could be, especially to people who weren't used to it. He made us wait more than a half-hour for our second hit, which was not as overpowering as the first one had been. Even so, the second hit sent a rush of tingling wellbeing from head to toe.

"Man, I see how this stuff could get to be a habit in a hurry," Peter said after he recovered from the second hit. He shook his long blond hair and red beard to the delight of all present.

"You are the real Wooly Bully," I said, referring to the 1965 song by Sam the Sham and the Pharaohs. Peter made the connection since the song had been a big hit in Europe. We sang the chorus once and the doctor and Haseem joined in the second time around. It's the easiest chorus in the world: "Wooly Bully, Wooly Bully, Wooly Bully." The third time around even the guides joined in. It was a zany good time in the outdoor opium den.

We had tea and smoked cigarettes as the sun began to set and the shadows grew longer. The world seemed totally at peace for once. Even the US Air Force felt like something I could deal with at a much later date. The grassy clearing became a magic carpet floating gently over the troubles of the world. The four of us connected deeply as we lazily chatted together for the next hour. We understood each other perfectly although our conversation had no literal translation. By the time the doctor let us take our third and final hit we were rolling around on the blankets like playful children.

It was getting dark as we made it back to the car and hit the road again. The doctor drove into the night. Peter and Haseem fell asleep, so it was up to me to help Hassan stay awake. After long periods of silence, the doctor would suddenly cry out, "Marsh!" He never could pronounce the "k" in Mark. I responded with a loud "Hassan!" and we laughed and shook hands over the seat. This went on all the way to Tehran.

It was late by the time the highway became four lanes about ten miles outside the capital city. Tehran was well-lit and modern, but there were large gaps of yesteryear in almost every block—tents with people huddled around fires and animals grazing on the park strips nestled between high-rise buildings.

The doctor blasted through moderate traffic and finally pulled into a garage with an automatic door. Haseem grabbed his suitcase and bid us a fond farewell as he walked off down the street. We'd told the doctor we were going to be staying at the Amir Kabir Hotel, but he insisted on having us spend the night at his house.

He had an intercom system and an elevator. His wife buzzed us up. Before we met her, he held a finger to his lips, indicating we should not mention the day's adventure. We knew from the wall-sized cabinet of cut glass in the entrance hall that the doctor was even wealthier than we had imagined. He was also quite progressive since he allowed us to meet his wife. Most Iranians kept their women hidden in back rooms and under veil.

His wife was attractive and well dressed in an evening robe. Even though she was obviously surprised and a little unhappy with her husband's late arrival and unannounced overnight guests, she produced a tray of melons, grapes, apples, and tea. She even served us each an ice-cold Coke, which tasted like home.

"Remember the Coke we had after that wretched night in the ship to Turkey?" Peter asked. "This one tastes as good as that one."

"Ah, yes, Coca Cola," I said with a satisfied *aah*. "It's the real proof that America has taken over the world."

The doctor thought that remark funny, although his wife did not join us in laughing. She made no effort to be one of the boys. She was trying hard to be an accommodating late-night hostess. We were all tired. After a short language-restricted conversation, she showed us to an elegant guest bedroom with two beds and glittering gold cover blankets.

"Man, this is the life," Peter said after the doctor and his wife said goodnight. "This guy's got it made. Look at this. Sheets. How long has it been since you slept in sheets?"

"It's been a long time." I sighed comfortably as I crawled into bed and let my head fall into the thick, soft pillow. "It's been too long." I fell asleep almost immediately. Peter and I slept that night like two hibernating bears.

We took hot showers in the morning, our first in weeks. Hassan introduced the children who were on their way to school. The lady of the house was friendly. No doubt, the doctor had convinced her during the night that his efforts toward international goodwill were worth her time. She served goat brains for breakfast. At first, we thought she was trying to get even for her husband's late arrival, but the doctor seemed pleased with her efforts, so we did our best to enjoy the food. Swallowing goat brains was a new and horrible experience. It felt like oysters and lumpy tapioca pudding going down. It was hard not to gag. The doctor raised his eyebrows in surprise when he realized the vagabonds from the West couldn't eat brains. He passed the bread and cheese.

We left the doctor's opulent home after breakfast and set out to find the Amir Kabir Hotel. It was a well-known, cheap, party crash pad on the hippie trail from Istanbul to Bombay. Thousands of young Westerners were on the road to India in a ramshackle, disconnected caravan of old cars and vans and Volkswagen buses. The Beatles trip to India had opened a cosmic portal and we were all walking through it.

The city was chaotic. Street vendors were everywhere, hawking their dry goods and novelty items. They were so aggressive in their sales pitches they had to be pushed away. One sandal salesman in baggy pants went down hard when Peter straight-armed him on the forehead. I tried to help him up, but the man scrambled away in terror.

"Peter," I said, "you don't have to hurt people!"

"I'm sorry." He hung his head. "The guy ran into my arm."

"Come on, man," I said, laughing at his partially truthful excuse. "Your arm doesn't have a mind of its own."

"Neither did he," Peter joked. "I'm telling you the guy invaded my space."

We walked for miles, mostly in circles, until a young couple from Scotland pointed out the hotel to us. We had already passed under the sign without realizing it. The sign said Amir Kabir Hotel in English as well as Farsi, but you couldn't read it until you knew what it said.

We walked up the steps to the Amir Kabir and into what looked like the lobby of a halfway house in San Francisco. Most of the guests were Westerners with long hair, beads, and fringed leather shoulder bags. There wasn't a pair of jeans in the place without patches and embroidered peace signs. There was guitar, flute, and bongo music coming from somewhere and the place smelled vaguely like hashish. Rope weavings and weird paintings hung on the walls, apparently donated by previous guests. People were sitting around with their gear on the floor, either arriving or departing.

It was like old home week for Peter and me. Many people we'd met on our journey were there. Charlie, Adam, Jack, and Albert were there. We'd met them on the train from Van, Turkey, to Tabriz, Iran. Cindy and John from the Iranian Embassy in Ankara were there. Suzanne and John from Silifke, Turkey, were there. Everybody looked familiar and we all had road stories to tell. Nobody could believe Peter and I had gotten one glorious ride from Tabriz to Tehran. No one else in the room had hitchhiked. Everybody loved the tale of the doctor and his outdoor opium den.

I was standing at the check-in counter when I felt a gentle but firm tug on my right shirtsleeve. I turned to see a beautiful, brown-eyed woman looking up at me. "Hey, where I see you before?"

Her brown, shoulder-length hair was parted in the middle and her round, doe eyes were hauntingly deep and sensual. Her nose was perky and a tiny bit broad, but her mouth and lips were full and sumptuous. She wore a scarf and a vest and baggy pants but even through all that clothing it was obvious she had a dancer's body. Her blouse was slipping off one shoulder. Her breasts were full and needed no support. I had seen her before and desperately wanted to recall where. Her South American accent almost reminded me.

"Hello," I said, immediately deciding to bluff my way through this wonderful encounter. "Yes, I know you. Don't you remember where we met?"

She smiled, letting me know she recognized my tricks. "No, I no joking," she shoved me playfully. "I know I see you before." Her brow furrowed. For an instant, I remembered her, and then the image faded. Something to do with sand in her hair.

I held her shoulders with both hands, studying her face. "It must have been Italy. You remind me of Venus." I shook her a little to let her know I was playing. "Yes, it must have been Italy. In fact, let me guess. It was Florence, about three months ago."

She giggled and shook her head.

"Let's see," I continued. "Was it Turkey, on the beach?"

"What beach?" She leaned into me.

"South of Ankara."

"No, I wasn't there," she pondered, then gushed, "but it was on a beach I meet you."

As we tried to remember our first meeting, a younger and equally beautiful woman joined her. This woman I remembered well. She was the naked girl I'd shared an apple with on Super Paradise Beach on Mykonos Island.

"Rebekah!" Peter beat me to the punch and hugged her off the floor. "You remember me. I'm Peter and this is my friend, Mark."

Rebekah hugged Peter and then gave me a big hug as well. "You guys saved my life!" Seeing her took me back to the island. Now I knew where I had met this woman.

"It was Mykonos!" I exclaimed. "I met you on the beach in Mykonos. We woke up together. You were with some guy with long black curly hair." I turned to Rebekah and said, "That's where I met you too. You were starving and we gave you an apple and asked you to stay with us for the night, but you couldn't because you had to meet a friend."

Rebekah beamed and said, "How could I forget? Actually, I wanted to stay. But I did have to meet a friend. And here she is, in living color. This is Adriana. She is the friend I was going to meet."

Suddenly, everything made so much sense the four of us were hugging each other and jumping up and down in excitement. "Yes, it was Mykonos." Adriana remembered. We laughed together like long lost friends. It was a spiritual reunion even though the four of us had never been together before. The cosmos had aligned to throw us into each other's company, and we all knew it. We had stories to tell about how we'd traveled from Mykonos to Tehran. Before long, we decided to split the cost of a single room four ways.

Adriana and Rebekah did a little dance together. They were glad to have found two big men to protect them and delighted the fates had finally brought us together. "Yes! Perfect!" Adriana exuded. "We have a party, no?"

"Yes!" I responded eagerly, not believing our good fortune in finding two beautiful and excited female companions. "We have a party! What do you say, Peter?"

The ever-pragmatic Peter couldn't help but get caught up in the enthusiasm. "Why not?" he said. "It will be good. I like to save money on the room."

The fact that we'd had a difficult time recently with two women in

Turkey was fresh in both of our minds. But this was different. These women were road-worthy; otherwise they wouldn't have made it this far. Besides, they were sexy beyond belief. The road had evidently been trying to get the four of us together for quite some time.

The desk clerk gave us an old skeleton key on a wooden stick. We lugged our packs into a tiny room on a balcony overlooking a courtyard below. There was only one broken-down double bed and no windows, but there was more than enough room for four people used to sleeping outdoors. The only restroom was the communal toilet between our room and the lobby.

The four of us spent the day exploring Tehran. It was a bizarre clash of Eastern and Western cultures. Men in suits carrying briefcases had to make their way around beggars in rags and veiled women carrying heavy bundles of fabric. Taxis had to navigate around horse-drawn carts. Everywhere someone was trying to sell something, except for the bearded Muslims in turbans who looked like they wanted to kill all foreigners, especially the brazen women.

We ate fresh fruits and vegetables from street grocers. Adriana was careful to wash our meals in bottled water. "It is awful to get sick in these parts of the world."

By the time we returned to our room around 8 p.m., the Amir Kabir was one big party. Adriana quickly organized a happening in our room. She had all the charisma of the perfect hostess. Nobody ever felt left out when Adriana was in charge of the refreshments. She kept the wine flowing and the pipes smoking. She was vivacious and friendly. To her, everybody was part of the show and she was the star attraction.

Our guests came from all over the world, many from Europe, some from South America and even South Africa. Everybody had hashish and was quite willing to share it. A couple guitars, flutes, and percussion instruments materialized and soon we had a musical event on our hands. Our room and the balcony outside were as crowded as a hot-spot nightclub. Belgians were rubbing elbows with Puerto Ricans.

Swedish babes with long blond hair and leather ankle bracelets were turning on to German cats with black vests and long sideburns. The place was jamming, and Adriana and Rebekah were the life of the party. They were each about five feet six inches tall and they could have passed for sisters. They danced through the gathering like nymphs of Grecian mythology.

It didn't take long for me to realize that Adriana was the woman for me, not Rebekah. We were sitting together on the floor in the corner of the room, sharing the last of one of Peter's spliffs. She gave me a "shotgun" by putting the lit end of the joint in her mouth and blowing smoke out the back and into my mouth. She got so close her hands were on my legs and our lips touched briefly. Her touch felt like someone plugged me into a current of sensuality I had never experienced. I felt floaty and furry and fuzzy and funny. I opened my eyes in surprise and she was staring into me like a hypnotist. I backed away slightly and she took the joint out of her mouth. She leaned forward and kissed me softly on the forehead. I was inside her blouse. I smelled her pheromones cleanly taking over my senses. She had branded me. I was hers and she was mine. I reached to grab her, but she was up and off to mingle.

Peter and I had a moment on the balcony. "Those girls sure know how to throw a party," he observed.

"Where else could you find a scene like this?" I asked happily.

Peter nodded and looked down at the courtyard. "It looks like you and Adriana are hitting it off pretty well."

"Oh, so you noticed." I laughed. "Are you jealous?"

Peter shook his head and smirked. He wasn't about to admit he didn't like seeing his traveling companion falling for a woman.

"That leaves Rebekah for you," I pointed out.

"No, she's too young. Besides, I'm not like you."

"What do you mean?"

"I don't know," he started. "I don't look at women like you do. I'm not saying you're wrong. It's just not the way I am."

I knew he wasn't gay, so I asked, "What is the way you are?"

Peter raised his gaze to the opaque skylights over the courtyard. "I don't know. Old-fashioned, I suppose. I'm not looking for lots of women to have sex with. I'm not even looking for a woman. I don't know what I'm looking for."

I didn't respond right away. For Peter, this was deeply confessional. He didn't talk much about himself. He was obviously pretty loaded and maybe a little tired of having his room filled with revelers. Finally, I gave him a hug and said, "Just between you and me, I don't know what I'm looking for either, but I can tell you this. We're going to find it together."

Peter looked down at me appreciatively and smiled. Adriana floated in between us to ask, "Are you two ready to wind down the party?" She was keenly observant and paying attention.

"No, no," I said. "That's already happening on its own. Everything is cool."

The crowd did thin out around 2 a.m. What little management there was at the Amir Kabir never complained about late night noise or anything else for that matter.

By the end of the party, our only remaining guests were a lanky long hair from Czechoslovakia and his graceful, quiet girlfriend. He picked up his guitar and tuned it quickly and perfectly. He began strumming and picking masterfully. He sounded like Eric Clapton. He played mournfully and slowly, eerily melodic and dramatic. It was blues like I'd never heard it. It had no twelve-bar structure. In fact, it had no structure at all. It took us all to a place deep within ourselves that confronted the bittersweet nature of human existence. We were spellbound. I played a little harmonica with him and he switched keys to accommodate my harp. We sounded great together. All I had to do was be careful not to play too much. Anybody would have sounded good with this guy. When he switched keys, he gave me a look that let me know it was time for me to stop playing.

He played for nearly ten minutes before he stopped in the middle of a song, apparently compelled by the music and the atmosphere in the room to tell his story. He had been a leader in the Czech uprising of 1968. He related the euphoria of marching for freedom and the disillusionment of watching those dreams die in the street.

"Ever try throwing a homemade Molotov cocktail at tanks?" he asked with a sly smile. "Let me tell you it doesn't work worth a damn." The smile disappeared and his face turned grim. "The Russians came in and crushed us in the streets. They killed my friends. People I had known since childhood died in front of my eyes with their blood making puddles in the street.

"I was fortunate to escape with only a bullet through my left upper arm. I couldn't go to hospital because they were arresting people who came in wounded. The bullet went through, so I didn't need much of an operation. A friend bandaged me up and gave me a shot of heroin. From that moment on and for the next three years, I was a junkie on the run, underground. I finally escaped my country a year ago. We got out through the southern border under the false bottom of a vegetable truck. And now, here I am. I'm on the road to nowhere, but at least I've kicked the heroin for now." He said he was twenty-eight years old, but he looked forty-five.

"Wow!" Rebekah managed to speak. "That is so heavy. It makes my story seem tame. I never got shot. I did try heroin once, but I liked it so much it scared me."

"Ooh," Adriana added, "I got too much heroin in England and ended up in prison. The good thing, they send me to detox center, and I get clean there."

"I come from Argentina," she began when it felt like it was her turn to continue. "My father was killed when I was young. I am twenty-eight now. I have a small pension from his military. I left home and went to Spain and danced for a time."

"What kind of dance?" I asked.

She dipped her left shoulder and waved her right hand in the air. "It was, how you say it, *exotique*."

"You mean you were a stripper?" I couldn't help but ask.

Rebekah sprang to her defense. She'd heard Adriana's story so she explained, "She was much more than a stripper. Exotic dancers in Spain are like female matadors."

"And we're the bulls," Peter joked.

"Exactly." Adriana laughed. We all did. She told a few stories about dancing in Spain, mostly about what boors and suckers men can be. Her life on the road had left her slightly the worse for wear. One of her teeth in the right upper quadrant was missing. She showed us how she hid that fact with a piece of molded chewing gum. I hadn't even noticed until she pointed it out. Then she looked at me, and it felt like it was time to tell my story.

"Well, I met up with Peter on a bus in Mykonos. Neither one of us knew where it was going so we figured we would travel well together. We had no idea where we were going but, eventually, we realized we were headed for India."

"I'll never forget that first night on Paradise Beach," Peter joined in. "Your harmonica playing was so bad I thought I couldn't last with you. But I must say, it has gotten better. You actually sounded good tonight." The Czech musician nodded in agreement.

"Why, thank you, my friend," I said, genuinely pleased to get a compliment for my playing. "The truth is, I am right now, at this moment, a second lieutenant in the United States Air Force."

Rebekah and Adriana and the Czech couple gasped in disbelief. Adriana asked, "What are you, a deserter?"

I rearranged myself on the floor to sit up a little taller. "No. They gave me eight months leave before going to jet school and I started hitchhiking. Once I get as far as I can go, I'm going back to declare myself a conscientious objector and quit the Air Force."

"Good for you," the Czech musician said. "From what I've seen of Vietnam, the Americans are no better than the Russians. Good for you, man, I hope you make it without going to jail."

"Wouldn't you rather just move to Canada?" Rebekah asked.

"We'll see what happens if I lose my case and they tell me to go to prison," I said.

Adriana gabbed my arm. "What do you mean, 'lose my case'?"

I wrapped my hand around hers. "Well, they won't just let me out. I've been in too long. They even paid my way through college. I'll have to get a lawyer and file a case against the United States to get out. It's been done before. Some have even been successful. The courts seem to be getting more antiwar as the peace movement grows."

Adriana let go of my arm and leaned back to reappraise me. "So, you are an outlaw?"

"I'm not really an outlaw," I explained. "In fact, I used to think I could change the system from within. Now I realize what bullshit that is."

"That's right, man," the Czech agreed. "If you're part of it you only make it stronger. The only way to fight it is from the outside."

He and his girlfriend got up to go. She hadn't said much all evening, but as they were leaving, she said goodbye in perfect English with a heavy French accent. "Thank you so much for having us over. It has been a perfect evening."

They left and Rebekah said, "Wow, that chick had some breeding. She walked out of here like she was leaving a royal wedding."

"She said nothing all night," Peter said. "But she never missed a hit."

"That's what I call breeding," I joked. We all laughed as Adriana punched me playfully on the arm.

It was time for bed. Peter slept on the floor. I got into the old bed with the two women, Adriana in the middle. There were no sheets, so we threw a sleeping bag over ourselves and began drifting into dreamland. Adriana made no secret of her intentions. Just as I was falling asleep, I felt her leg rubbing up and down my leg. I pretended not to notice, but she was turning me on. I was attracted to her in the most wild and primitive manner I had ever experienced. Her skin was hot and exciting to the touch.

I couldn't do it. Not with Peter in the room and another woman in the bed. I rolled onto my stomach and turned to kiss her. She understood my reluctance and giggled as our lips met in a lingering kiss goodnight. She was delicious.

We floated off to sleep in a most wonderful state of expectation. I was falling in love.

I awakened to find her draped all over me in a full-body cuddle, clinging to me as naturally as if we'd been spooning for years. She moaned deeply as she awakened. I rolled over and lifted her shirt to kiss her breasts.

We awakened Rebekah.

"Hey, you two," Rebekah said sleepily. "Keep it down in here. Some of us are hung over." Adriana and I disentangled and got up to get dressed.

The four of us were much the worse for wear as we hit the streets of Tehran in search of food and water and coffee. We found an open-air cafe to lounge in and discuss our travel plans. It didn't take long to hatch a plan to hitchhike together to Afghanistan. "Herat is a beautiful city," Adriana said. "We can live there for a while and then buy horses and ride them over the mountains to Kabul."

Peter looked at me with a deeply furrowed brow. "How much does a horse cost?"

"Too much for me," I said.

"We can rent them," Rebekah offered.

"Don't worry about that now," Adriana said. "All we have to do now is worry about getting out of this city. It's really too much like any city anywhere. Let's head east. We've all got visas, right?"

We all agreed and spent most of the day preparing for departure, buying supplies, and washing clothes. We made sure the party wasn't in our room that night and got a good night's sleep. Adriana and I were getting closer all the time, but there was never a moment for us to be alone.

The next day, we were on the eastern outskirts of Tehran, ready to try our luck at hitchhiking as a foursome. We bought a watermelon and split it into quarters with my machete. Adriana said she loved the way I cut the watermelon with two, smooth strokes.

"In my country," she said, "a man who knows how to use a machete is thought to be a man of fine breeding."

"You should see him cutting his way through the jungle," Peter deadpanned. Adriana and Rebekah looked at me to see if he was joking. One look from me told them Peter was having fun with them.

The melon tasted wonderful and quenched our thirst. Our spirits were high as we waited along the two-lane, blacktop road to Mashhad. Much to my surprise, nearly the first car that came along stopped and gave us a ride. We crammed the four of us and all our gear into the driver's four-door sedan and buzzed off into the mountains of northern Iran, laughing and even singing along the way. Eventually, we settled down as the heat of the cramped car made us groggy.

I was asleep when a loud "bang" from underneath the car awakened me. Our driver was frantically trying to control the vehicle, turning the wheel to the left, then to the right. Nothing worked. We were on a steep mountain road with a rock wall to our left and a severe cliff to our right. The car was completely out of control. A rock in the road had snapped the connection between the steering column and the axle. No one had time to scream as the driver hit the brakes and we went into a screeching skid, heading for the cliff with no steering.

All we could see was the panoramic mountainscape that would be our last image before plummeting to our doom.

We closed our eyes as we came to the cliff and waited for the fall to begin. There was no guardrail or shoulder to the road. The front right tire went over the rock edge and we felt the undercarriage of the car thud to the road. The car pitched forward but did not continue falling. We opened our eyes. The brakes and the car's body contact with the road had stopped the car and left us precariously perched on the edge of the cliff.

I jumped out the rear door and threw myself on the trunk of the car to keep it from tottering over the edge. Adriana and Peter got out and did the same. Rebekah and the driver crawled out the driver's side door.

Our legs were rubbery as we slowly realized we hadn't fallen over the edge into the deep ravine. We looked down into what would have been certain death. The car was tottering on the edge. One push and it could have easily gone over. We retrieved our gear and collapsed in nervous laughter. The driver was thanking us profusely although we had really done nothing to avert the disaster. We had all just gotten incredibly lucky.

People stopped to help our driver pull his car back from the cliff. Two big guys with a rope helped us pull the car back from the edge of the cliff. The driver must have thanked Allah a thousand times for our good fortune. Peter took me aside and said, "I don't know why he isn't blaming Allah for causing the problem in the first place."

Eventually, the four of us decided to push on to the next town. Night was beginning to fall, and we were getting hungry. We said goodbye to our driver and started hitchhiking. In no time at all, a truck stopped to pick us up. It only had room for two. Rebekah and Peter climbed in and, before we knew what was happening, they were waving goodbye as they rolled away.

We shouted out that we would find them in the next town. They disappeared around the bend. Adriana and I looked at each other. We were alone at last. It felt like destiny had removed all obstacles to our being together. We kissed each other deeply and gratefully. It felt like a dream to finally have her to myself. We held hands and looked eastward to the mountains and valleys that awaited.

We walked for a while and then caught a ride into Babol, Iran, where we checked ourselves into a ramshackle hotel. We walked into our room and dropped our packs onto the cracked linoleum floor. The space was small and the walls barren. There was no water source except for a faucet outside in a patio area. The only toilet was an outhouse, twenty yards behind the building. The room had one outside wall with a small, glass window that did open a little. There was only one bed, made of wood and rope with no bedclothes. We didn't mind the accommodations, or lack thereof. We were in love and alone at last.

Adriana turned and kissed me as she took off her shirt and helped me off with mine. Our bare chests pressed together with sexual warmth that felt like the heavens sighing in relief.

Our passions exploded into each other until we were getting much too loud for the close quarters and thin walls of the building. We were making so much noise I barely heard the pounding on the door.

I stopped and said, "Listen. Do you hear that?"

Adriana paused and listened, "Oh, my God, it's somebody at the door!"

Whoever it was certainly wasn't going away. The pounding on the door got louder and louder until I got up and put on my jeans to answer the door.

It was a little old man in a turban who either owned or operated the establishment. He tried to look around me to see what was going on in the room, but I blocked his view. He was not at all happy about the noises coming out of our space. His sign language communicated quite clearly that the other guests were complaining and that we would be kicked out if we didn't quiet down. I assured him we would comply and shut the door in his face.

I waited at the door for him to walk away. He didn't. He was standing outside the door to listen. I waited for a minute and then swung open the door and scared the crap out of him with a loud "Boo!"

He fell to the floor in surprise. I waited for him to pick himself up. He did not appreciate the humor of my tactic. I heard him muttering angrily as he walked away without looking back. *How long was he listening before he started banging on the door, the little pervert?*

I turned back to Adriana. She was posing in the moonlight with my shirt up to her eyes like a veil. She was leaning on the bed with one arm, her legs draped over the edge but not touching the floor. The shirt fell, exposing her naked body, shimmering ghostlike in the pale light. She lowered her eyes and pursed her lips. I had never seen anything more mischievously sexy in my life.

CHAPTER ELEVEN

Iran

TRAVELING WITH ADRIANA changed everything. She was smart and spiritually minded. Her sense of humor and one-world view were instantly contagious. She convinced me in no time that we weren't the ones moving down the road. It was the road rushing toward us to reveal the secrets of the universe.

"There is no need to go to India to find enlightenment," she said with a wrinkle of her nose. "Enlightenment is all around us. All we have to do is let it in. India will present herself to us soon enough."

I lowered my pack to the ground. "I can dig what you're saying, but we still need a ride to Mashhad."

"Our ride is on its way," she reassured with a beaming smile.

I loved the way she told me what I usually had to tell others. The woman was a seasoned traveler. She knew how to have fun with the little things along the way. She could create a social event out of making the acquaintance of a passing bicyclist. She had fun with life and life had fun with her. We made a good couple. I felt exhilarated being with her.

Being with the right woman can make a dirt road feel like a superhighway.

We were standing along the road only miles from the Caspian

Sea, but it never crossed our minds to head to the beach. We had Afghanistan on the brain. We wanted to catch up to Peter and Rebekah. I knew we wouldn't have much trouble getting a lift. There were only two of us, and it never hurts to have a beautiful woman by your side.

Sure enough, a young professional man in a Volvo picked us up and gave us a guided tour of his country for much of the day. The fact that he didn't speak any English did not deter him from waxing poetic about everything we passed. We drove by bazaars with shops made of mud that had baskets of brown and yellow grain and red and black spices out front. We passed through towns that had small brick mosques with tall funeral towers. Livestock freely roamed the roads. Everything smelled vaguely like animal manure. Between the cattle and the cars, it was never certain who had the right of way.

We passed fields of crops and asked our driver what kinds of plants were growing. He stopped, got out of the car, and picked two puffy plants for us. Much to our surprise, it was cotton. He presented them to Adriana like a student with an apple for his fifth-grade teacher. She received them graciously as a queen accepts tribute from her subjects. He was clearly enchanted with her. So was I.

As we stopped along the way for snacks, the sight of Adriana in her flowing and revealing clothing caused a noticeable stir among the local men. A free woman was, indeed, a sight to see. Unfortunately, there was a dark side to all this attention.

We stopped at a primitive restaurant to get a drink and use the restroom. The driver and I went into the large room for men and Adriana was directed to a small room in the back for women. Restrooms had been getting more primitive the farther east we traveled. By this point in the journey, the privy was nothing more than a slit trench with no toilets or paper, just a rusty can of filthy water to somehow facilitate hand wiping.

Fortunately, I didn't have to take a crap. I wasn't emotionally prepared to wipe my ass with my bare hand, and I wasn't about to squat in public. The place smelled like an outhouse in southern Indiana in the middle of a hot summer day. I chuckled to myself about the universal smell of shit in a pit.

I was at the end of taking a long piss when a terrible commotion erupted from the area Adriana had visited. I could hear men barking and Adriana screaming as I hurried out to help her. Running into the hall, I had to step back to avoid two wide-eyed men fleeing my wild Argentinian lover, who was chasing them with a four-inch dagger held over her head. I tried to grab her as she ran by, but she was too quick. The twenty people in the place watched as she chased the two offenders out of the restaurant and into the street. I ran out after her and stood by her side as she stopped and shouted Latin obscenities at the bad guys, who continued to flee.

She was in a full rage and nearly foaming at the mouth. It took some time for her to catch her breath. I watched in amazement as she wiped blood off the dagger and made it disappear in the folds of clothing around her waist. I had no idea she was armed and dangerous. It was obvious from the way she handled herself that this wasn't her first rodeo.

"Far out," I finally managed to say. "Those guys were lucky you didn't kill them. Was that blood I saw you wiping off the knife?"

"I did cut the first one who touched me," she said, regaining her composure with a sly smile. "His filthy arm will remember me for a long time. Maybe he will think twice before attacking another woman."

I looked at our driver, who understood her sentiment. All he did was nod his head. Adriana hugged me. She was trembling from the adrenaline rush she had just worked up.

"I saw you coming to help me," she said.

I grabbed her underarms and backed her up a half step to look her in the eyes. "It didn't look like you needed my help."

She grabbed my arms. "But you would have hurt them for me?"

"Absolutely. They would have been sorry to see me coming."

"Thank you so much." She looked up at me. "You have no idea how much it means to have you in my heart."

Her eyes were deep and sincere. We kissed and held each other tight. My body melted into hers. We untangled when we felt the crowd staring at us in amazement. Public display of affection was unheard of in these parts. "It's okay," Adriana explained to no one in particular. "We love each other. That means we kiss in public, no?"

No one responded to her, but if they had, it was clear their answer would have been a resounding "No, you can't kiss in public under any circumstances." They sat very still and stared at us like we were creatures from another planet. This part of the world was not even close to accepting the notion that women could be free and have equal rights.

Adriana turned away from the crowd of onlookers and tilted her head back like a queen at a Mardi Gras parade. "I no care what they think. Now, I go back to toilet. How you say, to finish what I start?"

Once she returned, we got back in the car and traveled in silence for miles. The violence had unsettled us all. "You know," I said. "I was ready to fight back there. In fact, I'm almost sorry I didn't get a chance to clobber those assholes." Adriana waited for me to continue.

"That worries me since I'm thinking of myself as a conscientious objector. I know I've got a deep violent streak in me. I just felt it rear its ugly head like a ravenous monster. The enraged adrenaline kicks in and I'm ready to fight. Deep down I know I am a violent man. Once the violence gets out, it's hard to stop it. So how can I say it's wrong to be violent?"

Adriana thought about her response for ten seconds before turning to me. "You're not saying it's wrong to defend your woman from a rapist. From what you've told me, you're saying it's wrong for one country to take over the world with its military and kill innocent people for money and oil and power."

The simple truth of her response stunned me. "If that's what I've said, I couldn't have said it better myself."

We laughed together. Our driver joined in the fun even though he didn't understand what we were saying. Adriana's amazingly succinct synopsis of nonviolence had cleared the doubt from my mind. We were all relieved to have transcended the ugly scene at the roadside stand. Meanwhile, the mountains of northern Iran and their wide desert valleys offered breathtaking, ancient scenery. Giant sandstone formations looked like Persian palaces half-buried in the sand. Waves of yellow flowers surrounded crumbling walls and arches of forgotten civilizations. There were vast fields of saffron and other colorful crops in between miles of rocky vacant ground.

Adriana and I felt like lovers on a giant carnival ride. The world was laying itself at our feet. We had hit the jackpot in the game of life. Each had found somebody to love.

After 200 kilometers, our driver let us know he had to turn and head north. He let us out with happy wishes at a place where the bend in the road overlooked miles of valley. There was an outcrop of rocks alongside the road. Adriana and I climbed out as far as we could go and stared off into the distance. We looked to the east. The sun had already set behind the mountains to the west. It was beginning to get dark. We each had one arm around the other.

Something in that moment made me realize how far from home I had come. I took a deep breath and squeezed her hard. She hugged me back. We were staring into our future, heading into that darkening distance. There was no pathway except the rocks at our feet. I half expected to hear a voice calling my name.

As a boy, I read a book about Daniel Boone. In that book, voices kept calling to him from the woods, "Go west, Daniel, go west." I had always hoped, one day, to receive such a clear calling. Now, as I stood marveling with Adriana, I listened. There was no voice, only the silence of the ages. We were on our own. All we had at that moment was each other. That was enough.

We shared the silent epiphany. Right here and right now was all we needed or wanted. It didn't matter where we were going or from where we had come. We were lost and found in each other. All fear and uncertainty faded into the darkness.

There would be no blinding light of inspiration. This was no "Paul on the road to Damascus" revelation. There would be no voice of God guiding us into action.

What we both realized was that we were exactly where we were supposed to be; alone, together, in the middle of the Iranian mountains as darkness fell. I got down on my knees. Adriana joined me. It felt like we were coming together in slow motion as I took her hands in mine. We looked into each other's eyes and acknowledged the gravity of our situation. We were in love.

Our kisses on that rock were more tender than passionate. We were not afraid of the night or the wilderness surrounding us. She was crying softly and gratefully. All the day's adventure and excitement blended into our embrace. I tasted her tears. She tasted mine. The world seemed to be spinning around us irrelevantly.

Only the darkness intruded upon our reverie. We climbed back to the road while there was just enough light to navigate the rocks. There was very little traffic. We walked half a mile to a spot in the road with a good shoulder in case anyone wanted to pull over. No one did for more than an hour. It was dark, but the moon and the stars cast a reassuring glow on the road. We looked around for a place to make camp. There was none. The road was a narrow notch on the side of a mountain.

We were just about to walk on down the road in search of a campsite when huge headlights nearly blinded us as they came closer and closer. The ground shook. We waved happily, hoping for a ride. The lights seemed to be slowing down. Sure enough, we heard the sound of air brakes as a huge oil tanker ground its way to a shuddering stop in front of us.

Adriana squealed in delight, "This is the biggest truck I ever see! The gods are shining on us, no?"

"The gods wish they were us." I laughed as the driver got out and helped me strap our packs to a rack on top. Adriana and I were a tight fit in the cab next to the driver, who smelled of kerosene. I sat in the middle to shield her from his obvious interest.

"The bags are safe up there?" she asked.

"Very safe," I explained. "We used rubber cords with metal hooks and rope as well." Adriana seemed appeased, and we settled back to enjoy the ride as the driver shifted through his gears to get the big rig up to speed. His thick black hair was greased back. He wore a dark green uniform with an indecipherable nametag on his short-sleeve shirt. He was quite chatty, but he kept taking his eyes off the road to look around me at Adriana. I finally started moving forward whenever he did to encourage him to watch the road. The mountain passage left little room for error, especially in the dark. He got the message and laughed in a non-threatening cackle.

After about fifty kilometers, he stopped at a little shack along the road and got out of the truck to go inside. After a couple minutes, he returned excitedly with two bottles of vodka and two bottles of Coke. His smile was broad enough to reveal two missing front teeth.

He told us his plans for drinking the vodka, but of course, we didn't understand him. No matter, in a few kilometers he turned into a wooded area, and we began bouncing down a dirt road. We rumbled down the winding road for about a mile until he stopped the truck, got out and motioned for us to come down and join him. We were in some kind of park. There were tall trees all around and a gravel parking lot. He ran an extension cord from his truck and hung a light from a tree to reveal a campsite with a sitting area of logs and stones beside a bubbling stream.

We made a roaring fire from fallen branches and began to drink the vodka. He took a dangerously long swig directly from the bottle and then chased it with a big gulp from the Coke bottle. I followed suit. Since Adriana didn't drink alcohol, she rolled up a hash and tobacco joint, which the driver tried somewhat reluctantly. He was a cigarette smoker, but you could tell the notion of hashish was a stretch for him. He said no at first, but Adriana convinced him to give it a try.

We kept drinking and smoking, getting higher and higher, until we were drifting into the stars like smoke from the fire. Adriana played her flute and danced smoothly and seductively. She couldn't help herself. Sexy was the only way she knew how to dance. The truck driver was spellbound and totally infatuated. He was drinking much too fast and there was no way to slow him down. It was clear he could not believe his good fortune. His eyes were rolling back in his head. He had stumbled onto a card-carrying goddess.

I pulled out my harmonica and played a bit. Before long, the driver sang us a few Iranian songs. He couldn't carry a tune, but he didn't seem to know it. We laughed together as he told stories we almost understood. The party was magical as we connected on deep levels of humanity and humor. The scene played out like a silent movie with gestures and body language speaking much more than words. We finished off the two bottles of vodka and the Coke in about an hour and a half.

"Who drinks vodka and Coke?" I asked.

"He does," Adriana said as the driver, who couldn't have been more than five feet three inches tall, stumbled to his feet and almost fell into the stream. We jumped up to help him. He couldn't walk. In fact, he just barely staggered to the back of his truck and threw up all over the long row of rear dual tires.

The scene was more than comical, but we tried hard not to laugh.

The poor guy was on his hands and knees, moaning in misery. It became clear to each of us at the same time that he would not be able to drive us any further into the night.

"No problem," I said with all the bluster of vodka courage. "I'll drive."

I showed the driver my international driver's license. I knew the thing would come in handy one day. He nodded in drunken agreement and crawled into the truck to pass out with his head hanging out the passenger window.

Adriana and I gathered up our belongings and rolled up his light and extension cord. This time, she climbed the ladder to check the packs. "Are you sure you can drive this thing?" she asked. "It's a giant bomb filled with explosive fuel!"

I straightened up to attention and tried to speak with conviction. "Nothing's going to explode because I'm not going to get into an accident."

I had driven many a truck in my day, mostly flatbeds on construction job sites and one box truck on the way home from the peace march in Washington, DC. But I'd never come close to driving an oil tanker. This was going to be fun. *How hard can it be?* It wasn't even a tractor-trailer. I was too drunk and stoned to realize the enormity of my calamitous choice.

Adriana climbed into the middle seat and I got behind the wheel. "Wow!" I pounded the wheel with both hands. "My own rig through the mountains of Iran at night, high as I can be."

She grabbed the steering wheel. "Are you sure you're okay?"

"Better than I've ever been," I said as I checked the emergency brake, pushed in the clutch, and turned the key. The engine rumbled to life. I hit the gas and the rig responded with earthshaking thunder. Adriana clapped and squealed in delight. The driver remained passed out.

I released the brake, got the truck into what I hoped was first gear, and hit the gas as I let out the clutch slowly. The back tires spun a little gravel and we were off to a jerky start.

"Lights!" Adriana yelled. "Lights!"

I fumbled around and found the lights just in time to illuminate the turn we needed to make to get out of the roadside park. We picked up speed on the narrow dirt road, so we got back to the highway more quickly than I expected. I didn't have time to downshift as I cranked the wheel for all I was worth to make the left-hand turn. We were going too fast. The top-heavy truck leaned heavily to the side as we hit the turn. I could feel the wheels on the left side beginning to lift off the road.

"Slow down!" Adriana shouted as I struggled to pull the massive beast of a vehicle through the turn. I cranked the wheel to the right and the tires came down to earth. But the liquid load rolled the truck like a ship at sea. I over-corrected one way, then fought her back and eventually wobbled us onto a straight course. Adriana was watching me closely to check for signs of insecurity or panic. All I did was laugh and yell, "Whoa, Nelly!"

Getting into second gear proved problematic. The gearbox sounded like a meat grinder. Finally, I got the hang of it and found the right groove. Third gear was no problem. Fourth gear was smooth as silk. We were off like a prom dress.

"Cannonball Smith of the Persian Express," I shouted. "We'll get you there on time!" Adriana laughed loudly and grabbed my shoulder in gleeful support as the driver leaned out the window and heaved a little more.

I drove that tanker through the night for hours, mostly uphill, or so it seemed. The truck probably had sixteen gears, but I never ventured beyond the comfort of fourth gear. There was a red button on the gearshift I didn't really want to try. We were fine with a top speed of sixty-five kilometers an hour. We felt like king and queen of the road as our driver slept soundly beside us. The night air was brisk from the open windows and it kept us wide-awake. It was fun looking so far down at the rare automobile that passed us by in the night. Each time Adriana honked the mighty air horn she got a bigger kick than before. After one particularly loud and long honk, our driver awakened with a start and promptly insisted on driving. I stopped the massive truck and we got out to change places. He took the wheel and seemed quite surprised when a road sign showed him how far we had gotten without him.

Unfortunately, he had a hard time keeping his eyes open. He kept falling asleep at the wheel. I had to hit his arm to wake him up. Even so, we almost ran off the road on a few occasions. Finally, I convinced him to stop and let us out. *Better to sleep in the desert than die in a fiery crash.* We retrieved our packs, waved goodbye, and wished him well as he disappeared down the highway.

"I hope we don't see a giant fireball in the distance," I said.

"I am so glad you got us out of that truck," Adriana said. "He was really scaring me. He was still drunk."

I stared down the road as his taillights got smaller in the distance. "Hopefully, he'll have the good sense to pull over and take a nap."

"Where do you think we are?" Adriana asked, looking around cautiously into the darkness.

I turned around slowly to assess the entire 360 degrees of our situation. "We are in the middle of nowhere. This is it. We have arrived. At long last, we have found it. The absolute middle of absolutely nowhere."

"Very funny," Adriana deadpanned. "Too bad I can't see a thing."

I helped her adjust her pack. "Don't worry, we'll be able to see as soon as our eyes adjust. Come on, let's find a place to crash."

"Do you think we should leave the road?" she asked as I took her hand and started walking into the darkness.

I turned around to encourage her. "It's dangerous to sleep along the road. It's always best to sleep where people can't see you."

The moon and stars were not as bright as before, but they did barely light our way as we walked into the desert. "This is crazy," Adriana said as she kept her hand on my pack from behind. "We have no idea what we're walking into. This could be a swamp for all we know."

I stopped and grabbed a handful of sandy dirt to reassure her. "There hasn't been a swamp around here for centuries," I said. She laughed halfheartedly and seemed to get her courage up as we walked about fifty more yards and picked a spot to settle down for the night. It was a wide clearing in the brush and rock that seemed to glow a little. I spread out my tarp and we each got in our sleeping bags, hoping to shield ourselves from any snakes that might decide to snuggle up to us. The place had to be crawling with them. I had my machete by my side while visions of barbarian tribes danced in my head. *Snakes might be the least of our worries*, I thought.

Adriana kissed me bravely before pulling her bag over her head. We were too tired to talk. The night was cold. We had no trouble falling asleep. It was 4 a.m., October 19, 1972.

We awoke at about 10 a.m. with the sun beating down on us. Now we could see we were surrounded with yellow and green sagebrush, clumps of ornamental grasses and small flowering bushes. In the night everything had looked like rocks. Adriana got up and disappeared behind a small hill. When she came back, she stripped naked and stretched out on top of her sleeping bag, saying, "Oh, yes! I need a sun bath!" She looked fresh and frisky as a centerfold. Her back had a natural arch to it that thrust her round breasts to the sky.

I got up with a dry mouth and a pounding headache. I went behind my own little hill and took a crap.

When I returned, Adriana beckoned me to her side. I stripped naked and let my body barely touch hers. Our lips were parched, and we smelled dirty and slightly of kerosene, but the magic soon took us over. She kissed me with a seriousness that made me think we had entered a secret chamber of her heart. Her light-brown skin was shining in the sun. I felt like I had captured an angel with my bare hands.

It was afternoon by the time we got back on the road.

We didn't have to wait long for a ride. Nearly the first car that came along stopped to give us a lift. It was the director of television for the city of Mashhad. At last, here was somebody who spoke English. Better yet, he had big bottles of water and he was going right where we needed to go.

He told us all about Iran's vast oil reserves and recent investments in oil refinery equipment. He also explained the wage development programs going on in his country. We asked him about the poverty we had witnessed in the countryside. He acknowledged it but said the government would eventually take care of the people. The man was clearly in favor of Western investment. No doubt his job depended on it. He was friendly. He loved our tale of the drunken oil tanker driver. We talked about traveling and television and were in Mashhad in no time. He was kind enough to drop us off at the Afghanistan Embassy where we hoped Peter and Rebekah had left word of their whereabouts.

They had left us a note. It said, "Adriana and Mark, Hope you two are having fun. Mashhad is boring. See you in Herat." The handwriting was Rebekah's, but she signed it "Peter and Rebekah." At least we knew they were still together. And we realized we had a few more "honeymoon" days to ourselves. We started walking hand in hand.

Mashhad turned out to be anything but boring for Adriana and me. As we set out to discover the second largest city in Iran, she informed me, "We will be looking for a place to stay that has hot water and a bed."

I started in with my usual "We can sleep in the park" routine but she hushed me quickly. "Don't worry. I've got money for a room. You want me to be comfortable, don't you?" She looked at me with eyes that said she would need a bedroom for what she had in mind.

We walked through the modern city that had started off centuries earlier as a major oasis along the ancient Silk Road. Turquoise and golden-domed mosques and museums stood as startlingly beautiful reminders of the city's glorious past. We met another couple with backpacks, and they clued us in to the city's heritage.

"This is one of the holiest cities in Shia Muslim," the longhaired male said. He continued with a fairly learned discourse on the Muslim religion until his girlfriend interrupted and said, "Each year, millions of Muslim tourists make pilgrimages here to pay homage to the Imam Reza Shrine. You ought to check it out. It's only a few blocks away."

They were headed for the train station so we soon parted company with the familiar goodbye: "See you next time."

We ended up touring the shrine by way of its crowded and tiled plazas. We beheld spectacular Iranian architecture with giant golden doors and intricate mosaic walls, tear-shaped domes, and tall towers. From there, we shopped for food and wine and water at a sprawling bazaar. The city was crowded and bustling.

"Let's find a place to stay," Adriana said. "I can only take the tourist scene for so long."

I understood exactly what she meant. We both understood the difference between travelers and tourists. Tourists go places to see the sites; travelers see the sights while headed for destinations unknown.

We wandered the streets of Mashhad until we found a cheap room at the Hotel Karoun. It wasn't much, but it had the requisite bathroom with a toilet and a rickety double bed that took up most of the room. We opened a bottle of wine and got naked and jumped into the water stall together. You couldn't call it a shower since it was only a pipe coming out of the wall into a tile corner of the bathroom. It did have almost hot water. Adriana produced soap and shampoo that smelled deliciously herbal. We washed each other into a lather and rinsed off just as the hot water ran out. I pulled out a relatively clean shirt and used it to dry us. We were laughing, naked as the eyes of a clown.

We ate a little food, drank wine, smoked some hash, made perfect love, and took a nap. We awoke in each other's arms and started making love like we had never stopped. This cycle went on all night and into the next day. We tried every position known to man or beast. She couldn't get enough of me and I couldn't get enough of her. After a while, it wasn't even about the sex. It was about two people trying to climb inside each other. It was about feeling so much a part of each other we couldn't bear to be two separate people. I couldn't tell where her skin ended and mine began. We breathed each other's air and drank wine out of each other's mouths. Our limbs intertwined like two trees that grow around each other. It was an amazing delirium.

We thought it would never end.

I went out on the town to buy cigarettes for us. I was minding my own business when a crazy motor scooter driver offered me a ride. I jumped on the back of his little bike and told him I was looking for smokes. He nodded that he understood and commenced to scare me half to death as he sped in and out of early afternoon traffic. From what little English he spoke, I gathered that Mashhad is the world center for turquoise and he would be only too happy to take me to meet some of his friends who sold the precious stones. I told him I'd go along for the ride as long as it didn't take too long.

He took me to a warehouse on a side street. We walked in the outside door and up a flight of stairs where he had to knock on an inside door with a peephole in it. A man in a turban answered, took one look at me, and closed the door. I thought maybe foreigners were unwelcome, but he soon returned and opened the door with a welcoming flourish. Inside were several stations for cleaning and polishing and setting turquoise, each attended by a bearded man in robes and a turban. There were four other men sitting behind a wide, wooden desk along the back wall. They were pleased to meet me. I could tell they thought I had money because I was obviously from the West.

One man wore a coat and tie with his turban. He spoke English and immediately launched into what was an elaborate sales pitch. From what he said, turquoise could be bought in Mashhad, smuggled through Afghanistan and Pakistan, and sold for four times the price in India.

I listened politely. It was thrilling to be in the back rooms of Arab commerce, making secret deals about smuggling. The man in the tie would make a comment like "They go crazy for Iranian turquoise in India." He would then look back at his cronies and translate. They would then agree with him loudly in Farsi. It was comical but strangely convincing.

I told the entire crew I had to get back to my hotel because I had a woman who would be worrying about me. They didn't quite understand this concept, but the motor scooter driver agreed to return me to the hotel.

When I returned, Adriana wondered where I'd been for so long. I'd only been gone about an hour and a half, but that's a long time to leave your lover for cigarettes.

I explained the interesting scene at the turquoise factory and how the young man on the motor scooter had taken me there.

"You weren't even hitchhiking when he picked you up, I'll bet," she said shrewdly.

"No, I wasn't."

"That's because those guys at the factory send out kids on motor scooters to drag in suckers with money from the West."

"I did figure that much out, but I'm telling you, the stones are beautiful, and we can make a lot of money smuggling them into India."

Adriana looked at me skeptically but said, "We'll go see them tomorrow. Even if it's a scam, I'd like to see these guys in action. Wait until they see you show up with a woman. That will blow their little chauvinistic minds."

The next morning, I returned to the factory with Adriana and without the help of the kid on the scooter. Every man in the place stiffened to attention when they saw Adriana walk in the door. All activity came to a sudden halt. Not only was she a woman, she was a sexy woman wearing tight pants and a loose-fitting shirt that showed plenty of skin. No one spoke for the longest time until the man in the coat and tie finally cleared his throat and said, "Good to see you back, Mark. Please introduce us to your friend."

I introduced Adriana and she played it as cool as if she were wearing a burqa. It took some extended throat clearing for the room to relax in her presence and get down to bargaining. We began learning about the turquoise trade and how to buy it polished in Mashhad, get it set in silver in Kabul, and sell it for a hefty profit in India.

Eventually, we agreed to buy what had originally been priced at $600 for the bargain price of $95. Adriana was implacable in the process.

"You are taking food from the mouths of my children," the Iranian cried in exasperation. He then turned to his partners and translated what he had just said. They responded with a low murmur of disapproval.

Adriana was unfazed. She drove a hard bargain. I would have paid much more than we eventually settled on. We walked out of that upstairs den of turquoise dealing with what seemed like a large amount of precious stones.

I paid cash for the stones since they agreed to a further discount if we paid in US dollars. Adriana and I agreed to split the net profits in India. She also agreed to help me financially until we could sell our contraband. I now had $55 to my name. Amazingly, I didn't feel broke at all. I felt like we'd just bartered our way into a financial investment that would make a lot of money.

We went out on the town that night to celebrate our good fortune. We felt like gangsters after a successful bank heist. We drank enough wine that we were having trouble walking on our way back to the room.

Once we got back to the Hotel Karoun, Adriana lit a candle and turned out the one light in the room. I laid her out naked and put the stones all over her body, one by one. In the flickering candlelight, she looked like something out of Cleopatra's tomb. I kissed her as I slowly removed the stones from her body. We fell back into each other's arms, casting lovemaking candle shadows on the wall.

"It feels like we were destined to come together," I said as we lay on our backs in dreamy afterglow.

"You mean sexually?" She sighed.

I propped myself up on one elbow to look her in the eyes. "No, I mean spiritually."

She smiled. The gum she used as her replacement tooth was missing. She saw me noticing it. "You made me swallow it." She laughed. I kissed her.

"Hey, where I see you before?" She repeated her opening line at the Amir Kabir Hotel.

"I'm sure it was many lifetimes ago," I said. "It feels like we've been together forever." We looked into each other's eyes like nothing else mattered.

She grabbed me around the neck and squeezed tight. "I love you too. And I'm so glad you will not be a soldier. I hold a man who only does what he believes."

In that moment, I knew she was right. Nobody would ever again tell me what to do with my life. I would remain a traveling bard for peace. There is no greater courage than that born from the love of a strong woman. Unfortunately, courage comes and goes.

"You know," she continued, "men have been soldiers since the beginning of time. The history is written in the blood of fool boys who try change with violence."

I rested my head on her stomach. "Maybe the women should take over."

"Hah! You and your women's liberation talk. Men still run the world. They only talk about women's liberation so they can see us without clothing and have the free love."

I raised my head briefly to look at her and then went back to using her stomach as a pillow. "Some people would say women have been in charge of things since Adam and Eve."

"The Christians blame women for all the sin," Adriana said. "Look at me. I am the most liberated woman, and I still have to cut men who would rape me in the toilet!" She got up and poured us more wine, pacing the room like a caged animal, ready to pounce on anything I said. I didn't mind. She looked fabulous. I was ready for naked debate.

"Women are making real progress in the States. They got into the workforce during World War II and they never looked back. They're becoming doctors and lawyers and senators and civil rights leaders. One day a woman will be president," I predicted.

She stopped pacing and bent over to point her finger in my face. "The problem with that is by the time she becomes president she'll be as bad as the man she replaced. It will probably be a woman who starts the Third World War!"

I had to laugh at how right on she was. "So how do we get a woman in charge who can stop the war? That's what I want to know."

Adriana sat down and looked at me. I could see her mind working, struggling to come up with an answer. Finally, she said in a defeated tone, "It's not going to happen. It no matter if man or a woman. The human race is destined to blow itself off the face of the planet."

"How can you say that?"

Adriana got up and began pacing again. "Look at our track record.

All we do is kill each other. It's all we ever do. You say you're not proud of being in the military and you say you're not always proud to be an American. How about being ashamed to be a human being?" She paused to let her question sink in, smiling as she saw me contemplating it.

"I am," she said. "I am ashamed to be a human being. We think we're the most noble beast, but we're not. We're the worst thing that ever happened to this planet. We're like a cancer on the Earth."

"How can you say that?" I asked incredulously, taking her hands in mine. "Everywhere we go we meet beautiful people. People who love their families and who want to help us even though we're total strangers. How can you say that when two people like us can find each other on a foreign beach and fall in love like this? Is our love the cancer you're talking about?"

Adriana's angry despair slowly softened and turned into a smile of surrender. She couldn't help herself. "Our love is the exception to the rule," she conceded, glad to be with a man who wouldn't give in to her incantations.

"No, no," I urged. "Love is the rule, not the exception. Every single human being is the product of a loving relationship."

Her eyes narrowed. "That is obviously not true."

"You know what I mean. Your mother and father didn't conceive you while he was off at war. And I'll bet your family spoiled you rotten." I started cuddling her. "I'll bet they loved this little baby Adriana almost as much as I do. I'll bet they dressed you in pink and took photos of your cute little baby face."

She melted into my arms, proving my point in many ways. "Love conquers all," I said. "Love triumphs in the end. Love has gotten us this far and she'll take us all the way someday."

Adriana and I awoke the next morning awash in buyer's remorse about all the turquoise we'd purchased. "One thing for sure," I said. "We won't be able to return it and get our money back."

"They wouldn't even open the door," she agreed with a deep sigh. "Oh well, we did it and it's done, so we will make the best of it. Let's hope we don't get arrested at the border. Where will you carry it?"

I did a double take. "Where will I carry it? I thought you would be the one to do the actual smuggling."

She looked at me carefully to see if I was joking.

"Don't worry," I said, giving in to being the mule. "I'll pack it in the stake bag in my tent. I've been searched before. They usually don't even unroll the tent but, if they do, they don't look in the bag that holds the stakes. It'll be safe there."

We left Mashhad after two blissful days and headed out on foot for the Afghanistan border and Herat. In no time at all, a colorfully decorated Iranian truck stopped to give us a lift. It looked like a circus truck, brightly painted with little mirrors and trinkets all over it. There were two men in the cab, so we made an exceptionally tight fit. They were obviously intrigued with Adriana and eager to please. The man who wasn't driving produced a watermelon and proceeded to slice it up on the dashboard. Seeds and juice squirted everywhere. We laughed and gave up trying to keep from getting sticky. The melon was as tasty as it was messy. The international camaraderie was refreshing.

About 160 kilometers later, our mobile hosts dropped us off in the town of Torbat-e Jam, close to the Afghanistan border. We walked down the street, listening, and selected the restaurant with the best Persian folk music blaring from within. We sat down to see what we could get to eat and watched the sunset through a wide, open window. We were contemplating our situation when a high-energy blond

American guy with round John Lennon eyeglasses wearing jeans and a bright-yellow Hawaiian shirt came up to our table and introduced himself.

"Hey, hey, hey." He extended his hand in greeting. "Great to see you here. We don't get many hippies passing through. I'm Peace Corps Bob. That's what they call me. I do actually work for the Peace Corps. Been here for almost two years now. Where you from?"

We explained ourselves, and Bob seemed delighted when we invited him to join us at the table. He told us right away that the border between Iran and Afghanistan was only open on Tuesdays and Thursdays. It was Sunday. He helped us order some surprisingly cold and delicious beer and explained the menu to us. "You got lucky coming here. You can't go wrong at this place. The kitchen's clean and the food is as fresh as you can get in these forsaken parts."

We had quite a few drinks with Bob as darkness fell. "What I basically do," he explained, "is teach English to classes of eighty screaming kids. Actually, they're good kids. My first day on the job the principal came into my class, picked out four kids at random, beat the heck out of them in front of the others, and warned everybody to behave for their new teacher. This came as quite a shock to me since my only teaching experience had been at a free school in Southern California. It took me a while, but the kids eventually got back to their old screaming selves. I love them and they love me. I don't know how much English they're really learning. It's hard to tell. It's tough being a kid around here. Lots of them don't have much of a home."

"Where do you live?" Adriana asked.

"Funny you should ask," Bob answered. "I'd say you're about to find out. You don't have any place to stay, do you?"

We shook our heads.

"Then you are invited to stay with me. I've got a huge place and lots of people who wait on me hand and foot. You'll love it."

In fact, we did love Peace Corps Bob's villa. It was a modern, one-story home with big eaves and lots of windows. It had a large courtyard with gardens and trees and a long fishpond in the middle, all surrounded by a high brick and mortar fence. The house itself had three large rooms, complete with Persian rugs of all sizes and a kitchen with a refrigerator.

"I've got a generator, so the power never goes out unless I run out of gas, which I don't."

"This is so far out, man," I stammered gratefully as Bob showed us around and introduced us to our own room with a beautiful double bed.

"The best part about this place is the shower. I've only got one but it's nice. It's down the hall on your right. The water gets hot and stays that way for a long time. It's the modern Peace Corps, man." Bob laughed. "It's not all jungles and malaria. Everything around here is so cheap you can live like a king. I've got servants, man!"

Adriana decided to take a shower while Bob and I split one last bottle of beer at the kitchen table. He was eager for news from the States, particularly about how the anti-war movement was doing.

"It's stronger than ever," I said. "It's not just the college kids any-more. Even Dick Nixon campaigns on ending the war."

"Yeah, he'll end it all right. After he bombs Hanoi back to the Stone Age." Bob sounded bitter. He was spitting out his words. "I got into the Peace Corps to change things. I'm sorry to report that the only thing that's changed is me. I'm learning more from these kids than they're learning from me. What I'm really learning is that kids all over the world are pretty much the same. They need love and attention like a flower needs water and soil. Way too many of them aren't getting what they need. I've been doing my best, but it hasn't been easy. My old lady left me last summer. That's a long story. Basically, she got tired of this lonely outpost where women are treated like dirt. I guess she also got tired of me."

I put my elbows on the table and rested my head on my hands. "Bummer, man."

Bob stood up and went to the refrigerator to hide the fact that he was about to break down and cry over his lost love. Then he turned to look back at me and pretended to lighten up. "Yeah, well, I'll be out of here myself in six months. I'm just serving out my time now. How about you?"

I told him my story and how I intended to go back and declare myself a conscientious objector. We talked for a while about how crazy it was that the war could still be going on after all these years. Nobody even debated the war anymore. It was a given that the United States was the imperial aggressor. Most discussions about Vietnam were simply rehashes of the war's atrocities and criminal cover-ups.

Bob straightened up and regained his enthusiasm. "Good for you, man. I hope you do it. We need more guys like you. Running off to Canada's not going to change anything. We've got to beat the system at its own legal game. When are you going back?"

I hung my head. "I don't know. My orders say I've got to be back by February, so before then. We're headed for India."

Bob waited for me to look back up. "Be careful, man. There's a civil war going on in Afghanistan. They're killing hippies on the road. It gets worse in Pakistan and India. You're headed into the wild country, my brother. I saw your machete. That's not going to do you much good against automatic weapons. These guys hate Westerners, particularly Westerners who flaunt their women."

"What's this about flaunting women?" Adriana said, walking in, looking and smelling better than Bathsheba.

Bob froze in place, paralyzed by her charisma and see-through peasant shirt. "Wow!" was all he could say.

I tried to bring her into the conversation. "Bob was saying it gets dangerous for women from here to India."

Adriana slumped over and pretended to be carrying a heavy load. "Perhaps I could borrow a burqa and walk ten paces behind you."

"I'm not saying that," Bob said as her sense of humor made her seem less like a Greek goddess. "You know what I'm saying. You've made it this far. I'm sure you'll be fine if you stick together and keep doing what you do."

Adriana hugged me and said, "In England, they told me to watch out for the French. In France, they told me to watch out for the Spanish. In Spain, they said watch out for the Italians. It Italy they said watch out for the Greeks. In Greece, they said watch out for the Turks. I'm telling you it's never as bad as they say it's going to be. Besides, we keep running into people like you who surprise us with kindness and hospitality."

Bob looked at the two of us with obvious envy and said, "You know, I think you two will do fine wherever you go."

We ended up spending three glorious days at Peace Corps Bob's "Shangri La." He walked us around the town and introduced us to his wide circle of friends. The local doctor and his wife had us over for dinner. Teachers and merchants came over for tea. Adriana dazzled them all. Bob couldn't take his eyes off her. He lit her cigarettes like she was a movie star. She flirted with him but never beyond being nice. We smoked a lot of hash inside his walls. Bob had a killer stash. He also had an old record collection of mainly classical and Persian folk music, but he was short in the rock and roll department.

His housekeeper scrubbed our dirty clothes and camping gear cleaner than it had been in months. We slept in late and made love every morning. It felt refreshing to be clean. Sunlight poured through the windows. Adriana purred like a cat. She taught me yoga stretches and Spanish. I taught her English and everything I knew about the Kama Sutra. After our morning worship of each other, we stumbled into the kitchen for coffee and breads and fruit. Bob was off teaching, but his house staff made sure we had everything we could possibly want. It was as though we had been declared a royal couple. Bob was happy for our company. He wouldn't accept money for anything. He tried to get us to stay for another week.

It was a time of sweet bliss for Adriana and me. We were happy to take a break from the rigors of the road. Our conversations became quite philosophical. I confided in her.

"I hate to admit this," I said one morning at breakfast, "but I've got a bad feeling that once I get back to the States I'll chicken out and serve out my military time."

"No, you won't," she said like it was a foregone conclusion. "You've come too far for that. And our trip is just beginning."

I looked up quickly from staring at the table. "What do you mean by that?"

Adriana walked around the table and threw her arms around me from behind. "You've already told me. You learned you were ashamed to be in the military and not proud of what your country is doing around the world. Now, we're in the process of dropping out of society altogether. It's not just the military you're quitting. It's the whole material world of getting what you want and wanting what you get."

She was making such good sense I remained attentive so she would continue.

"Look at us. We have nothing and we want for nothing. The spirit world is providing for us in ways the material world never could. Take our love, for example. No one can buy or sell it. It is not material. Material is about our senses: taste, touch, smell, sight, and sound. Spiritual is about everything else. We travel to escape the material world and live in the spiritual world."

Adriana was on a roll. She danced over to a window as she continued. "Yes, but it's about more than being free. It's about becoming connected with the universe. It's about getting out of self. Most people think spiritualism is about finding yourself. That's not it at all. It's about losing the illusion of self, which binds us to the material world. It's about becoming one with everything."

She was saying things I hadn't yet been able to put into words. Her

English was perfect as it sometimes was when she repeated what she had heard others say.

"So, you see, you are leaving much more than the military. It's already much too late to even think about going back to the military. You've already resigned from the world as you used to know it. Now, we're off to find the wizard," she said, "the wonderful wizard of Oz!"

I hugged her and kissed her and smelled her and felt her warmth flowing into me. "Some things about the material world are still pretty perfect. And what does a nice girl from Argentina know about the wizard of Oz?"

"It's my favorite movie. It's Judy Garland. It's the lion that gets his courage when he had it inside all the time. And the tin man who finds his heart and the scarecrow that discovers his brain."

"And it all happened on the yellow brick road," I concluded. "Now, it all makes sense. We're on the yellow brick road!"

Adriana wrapped her arms around me and whispered in my ear. "Watch out for the Wicked Witch of the West."

All in all, Peace Corps Bob's was a major stop on my road to conscientious objection. Adriana and Bob helped me turn some kind of final corner in my mind. They changed my journey from running away from my past to searching for my future. I started feeling less and less like a fugitive and more and more like a seeker. Unfortunately, there would come times in the not-too-distant future when I wished I could click my heels twice and be back in Indiana.

When Adriana and I finally walked out of town with our packs on our backs, an entourage of small boys escorted us. They waved goodbye as we walked with confidence to the deserted Iranian highway.

Forty kilometers from the Afghan border a Volkswagen bus appeared on the horizon and got larger as it approached, holding us spellbound until it glided to a stop beside us. A young German ethnologist jumped out with a huge grin and helped us throw our packs in the back. There seemed to be no shortage of fascinating souls willing to help us on our way. As we rode to the border, he chatted amiably about the ninety percent illiteracy rate and inferior position of women in Afghanistan. He went on to explain that the feudal system still existed for these people and that they had to pay cruel taxes even in the past three years of famine and tribal warfare.

We arrived at the border to find at least fifty vehicles parked and waiting for the guards to begin processing admission. About a third of the people were travelers like us, so the wait turned into a party. Adriana knew the owner of one of the vans from somewhere in Turkey. He had the most prized possession of all, a tape of the new Rolling Stones album, *Exile on Main Street*. He opened the doors to his van and played it at top volume.

When we heard the song "All Down the Line" blaring from his eight-track stereo, Adriana and I started dancing. The second greatest band in rock and roll was definitely on the rise again.

I'd never heard the song before, but it made me feel wild and free and invincible. The double shot of rock and roll removed all doubt from my mind. It was just what I needed. Adriana smiled. We were on the right road.

CHAPTER TWELVE

Afghanistan

HERAT APPEARED IN THE DISTANCE as a green gem in the mountain-studded, yellow-brown prairies of western Afghanistan. It looked as magical in real life as it had on the map in the embassy back in Ankara. Adriana and I were soon walking down the mostly paved road through the center of town like a couple of gunslingers. Our packs were on our backs and we were ready for anything.

"I love this town," she gushed as we walked through the crowded bazaar with a hundred little shops selling everything from embroidered shirts to leather goods and antique rifles.

I held up a black vest with gold trim. "I can't believe we're actually here. It always seemed so far away. And I have to get one of these someday."

We were surrounded by ragged children crying, "Baksheesh, baksheesh!"

"Don't give them anything," Adriana said as she tried, unsuccessfully, to shoo them away. "We get you vest but not now."

We kept walking—past the horse-drawn taxis with their jangling bells; past ghostlike women in burqas with one vent of veil at eye level to see out but not in; past regally-turbaned, leather-faced men with dirty feet in sandals; past one-eyed, no-legged, shriveled-up beggars.

The buildings on either side of the street were no more than two stories tall. The city was quiet, not much motorized traffic at all. Occasionally, an armed tribesman on horseback rode past and glared at the two of us. There were no traffic lights, only a policeman in a slightly frayed dusty-blue uniform at one intersection.

Neither Afghanistan nor Herat had found its way into the twentieth century. This was the land time had forgotten. I was so stunned by the calamity of medieval culture that I kept forgetting to breathe. I was shocked and surrounded by the barter system. Every time I filled my lungs it smelled like something I would never understand.

Nobody but the beggars and merchants paid us much attention. The townspeople had seen plenty of hippie backpackers passing through on their way to India.

Adriana stopped and turned to look up at me. "How will we find Rebekah and Peter?"

I took both her hands in mine. "We'll check the cheap hotels. They're here, all right. I can feel it. This is Peter's kind of place."

About halfway through town, we stopped to look into a likely hotel. It was rundown and dusty and there were some longhairs from the West hanging around the small lobby.

"Hey, man," I asked one of the guys. "Have you seen a real tall Dutchman with blond hair and a red beard?"

"Oh, you mean Peter?" the man said with a stoned smile. "Yeah, he's kind of hard to miss. He and some babe from California are staying right across the street. You two must be the ones they've been waiting for."

Adriana and I didn't hang around to chat. We made a beeline across the street to find our friends. Peter and Rebekah were walking out of Hotel Pardess when they saw us coming. All four of us started screaming in delight and dancing in the street as we hugged each other in glee.

"Where have you been?" Peter laughed. "We've been waiting for days. This town is so cool. You're going to love it. We met this Afghani named Canaga who turned us on to some of the best hash you've ever smoked."

"We thought we'd lost you forever," Rebekah shrieked. "We didn't know that truck only had room for two. I couldn't believe it when we drove away without you. Where have you been?"

I hugged her then backed up to look at her. "We've been looking for you two. We thought we'd find you in Babol. Then we thought we'd find you in Mashhad."

"Did you get our message in Mashhad?" Rebekah asked.

"Yes, we did," Adriana answered. "Thank you so much. We were worried about you. We ended up having a great time in Mashhad. Then we spent some time at Peace Corps Bob's waiting for the border to be open."

Peter and Rebekah looked like they wanted to hear all about Peace Corps Bob, but I had a suggestion. "Hey, guys, let's get out of the street and go get some of that hash you're talking about. We ditched all our smoke to get through the border. Turns out they didn't search us that well."

We went up to the room Peter and Rebekah were sharing. It had no heat, no hot water, and mats on the floor for bedding, all for the bargain price of thirty cents a night. It was perfect, enough of a hotel for Adriana, enough camping for me. We quickly checked into the open room across the narrow, wood-floored hall. Things got a little awkward at first, as Rebekah thought she and Adriana would be sharing a room.

Adriana held her gently by both shoulders and looked her in the eyes. "No, no, Mark and I will sleep in this room. Look, it has a window that opens." With that, she creaked open the old wood-and-glass, sliding window.

"What happened in Iran?" Peter joked. "Did you two get married?"

I shrugged my shoulders as Adriana deflected the question. "No worry, Peter, I no steal your friend. The four have two rooms and we all live in both of them."

What a perfect thing to say. Everybody was instantly ready to start getting comfortable with the new communal arrangement. Peter sat down to roll one of his patented nine-paper spliffs. Rebekah peppered us with questions about Iran. I ended up showing off the turquoise to the delight of our freshly stoned group.

When I said we'd paid $95 for the stones, Peter deadpanned, "I'll bet you can get $50 for it in India after you spend $40 to have it set in Kabul. And that's only if you don't get busted at one of the borders for smuggling."

"Don't be such a killjoy," Rebekah chided him. Peter laughed to show he meant no insult. It was obvious the two of them hadn't become romantically intertwined. They didn't touch each other like a couple. Nonetheless, they had become a traveling pair and it was easy to see they had worked out a delicate balance for themselves.

"It's probably a good thing we split up," Peter said. "We had no trouble getting a ride with just two of us."

"Especially when one of you is a beautiful woman," I teased Rebekah.

Adriana punched me playfully on the arm and said, "Hey, I did pretty good for you, too."

"No doubt about it." I laughed. "Every driver in Iran wanted to pick us up."

So, there we were, in a dive hotel in the middle of a frontier town on the edge of Afghanistan, and we all felt like homecoming just to be together again. There was something very right about the four of us. We balanced each other well. Peter kept me down to earth and Adriana was a big sister to Rebekah. Rebekah brought out Peter's sense of humor and I helped Adriana be in charge of everything. It felt like we had known each other for years, even though it had only been days.

We sat down together on the floor of our room and told each other tales of how we got to Herat.

The storytelling hit its peak when Adriana told about the Iranian oil tanker we took over. Like most stories, it was better in the telling than when it actually happened. The oily little truck driver with no front teeth became quite the comic genius at the hands of Adriana. She played his role to perfection, from his bad singing to his watching her dance with his tongue hanging out to almost falling in the stream to puking over his rear duals. She sang my praises as a truck driver and her own as a horn blower. We were all laughing by the time she recounted being dropped off in the middle of the Iranian desert at "O-dark, thirty."

Peter and Rebekah had as many road stories as we did, mostly about crazy drivers and getting dropped off in the middle of nowhere. The common theme seemed to be how many people we were meeting who were happy to help strangers along their way.

They had scouted out Herat pretty well while waiting for us to arrive. "The best place is the Turkish bath," Rebekah said. "You can get really clean there for twenty-five cents. They've got steam rooms and hot baths and cold showers, anything you want. You two could have some serious fun there."

"That sounds great," I said, standing up. "But I'm a little too stoned for comfort." In fact, I was dizzy and had to sit back down. Peter roared with laughter and showed me the hash bar he had purchased. "Look at this, man. This is the real deal. See the gold seal? That's from the government of Afghanistan! That's the national seal of approval. I never thought I'd see a government stamp on hashish. You will love this country."

We freshened up as best we could at the common toilet and sink at the end of the hall. Peter assured us our packs and passports would be safe in the rooms, so we floated on out to the streets of Herat.

The ten-year-old hustlers were out in full force. "Hey, meester! Come look in my shop. We make deal!" Peter and Rebekah knew how to make them go away with a wide, sweeping wave. Soon, we were off the main drag and exploring the local shops, bargaining for shirts, rugs, weapons, and Afghan vests. I fell in love with those vests the first time I saw one.

"How much for this vest?" I asked a street merchant with a table of vests, each one hand-sewn, padded, and multi-colored.

"Five hundred Afghanis," he replied with a straight face. That was about seven US dollars.

"What do you take me for, another stupid tourist? I didn't fly in on a jet plane," I said with a smile. "I hitchhiked from Portugal. Ever hear about Portugal? No? Well, let me tell you, it's a long way from here and there's guys like you all along the way, looking for suckers." The poor guy didn't understand any of my little monologue, so I said, "I'll give you fifty Afghanis and no more."

The others were laughing at my aggressive bargaining attempts as they dragged me off to get something to eat. "The food's not that great here," Rebekah said. "But we did find a place that's pretty good and the kitchen is sort of clean."

We got a table at a little hole in the wall joint that was crowded with locals, all men in beards and turbans. They didn't pay us much heed, but the way they stared at Rebekah and Adriana made it obvious they did not approve of our female companions being treated like equals. They didn't smile when they looked at us; they just stared and turned away abruptly.

Adriana and Rebekah were not shy about staking their claim to equality even in these remote regions. They waved happily at the men and pretended not to notice their disapproval. Peter and I looked at each other warily, knowing we might have to defend them at any moment.

"Don't worry, boys," Rebekah said, sensing our discomfort. "If push comes to shove, there will be four of us fighting, not just two." She rolled down her cloth belt to show her concealed dagger. That made four of us with knives. Peter had his six-inch knife in a sheath on his belt, and my machete was always on my side. I had told Peter and Rebekah the story of Adriana getting attacked in the Iranian toilet.

"These blades won't be much use against a gun," Peter said.

"At least they can see we won't go down without a fight," Adriana said boldly. "That will keep the cowards away. The men with guns are off killing each other in the mountains."

Over a mediocre meal of greasy rice with meat bits and cold, grassy spinach and bottled water, we discussed our previous plans of taking horses through the mountains to Kabul.

"Can't be done," Peter concluded. "She's right about the mountains. There's a civil war going on. Occasionally, they kill tourists on the road for their vehicles and their money. Nobody will guide us through the mountains. It's much too dangerous. Besides, it's almost winter and we couldn't get through the snow."

"Horses are much too expensive," Rebekah continued. "We checked it out. We couldn't afford to buy them, much less feed them."

So much for riding into Kabul on a big white horse.

Delusions of grandeur had always been a problem for me. It occurred to me it was my vision of flying jet planes that had gotten me into the Air Force. It had all seemed so exciting in high school, screaming through the clouds in my silver spaceship. Now, halfway around the world, the reality of killing innocent people had pretty well grounded me. Meeting the people I would be killing to get my aerial kicks had been a serious game changer.

"So, let's hang out in Herat for a while," Adriana said. "I'm ready to soak this place up."

"Let's go back to the rooms so we can drink to that," Peter said. "I've got about five bottles of pretty good wine. They make it around here. We can have some people over to christen the commune."

We ended up partying the night away with at least twenty fellow travelers from all over the world. Everybody had stories to tell and we all ended up learning from each other about the history of Herat. For one thing, I learned the city was much larger than I had originally experienced. As it was the third largest city in Afghanistan, the population was well over 100,000. I was told of towering fortresses, wide tree-lined avenues, and beautiful mosques, all just waiting to be explored.

"Herat was an important stop on the ancient trade route of the Middle East and Central and South Asia," one lanky lad from Florida who called himself a writer told me. "Man, we're all taking the silk route to India. Can you dig it?"

"Yes, I can."

A musician from England told me Herat looked like an oasis because it was located in the valley of the Hari River, a fertile region traditionally known for its wine. He had a pretty good guitar and he knew how to play it, but he was currently short an A string, which cramped his style. He tuned up to my harmonica and we sounded pretty good together for a few songs. Then he pulled out a briefcase full of chillums—straight, conical pipes carved out of marble that you smoked by cupping your hands around the bottom and lighting the hash on top.

"Oh, yeah," Peter said. "I've seen these in Amsterdam. What a great way to get high. It's much less trouble than rolling the big spliffs. Let me try a hit."

He took a giant inhale and held it in until he fell on his back and let out the smoke like a volcano erupting. We all cheered and took turns imitating his style. No doubt about it, Afghani hash was the good stuff. It wasn't as good as Iranian opium, but after a few hits you could hardly tell the difference.

Getting stoned in a flop hotel in Herat made it easy to forget who you were or where you were. The communal disorientation made us all feel like cosmic explorers. Transcendental meditation was a favorite topic. Many of our fellow travelers had already acquired complex mantras. Adriana and I relied on the simple "Om" to help us orchestrate our breathing. Rebekah sometimes spent hours meditating. Peter even gave it two twenty-minute sessions per day.

"The thing about it for me," Rebekah explained, "is that breathing is an unconscious thing. When you turn it into a conscious thing, you connect your conscience with your subconscious and that's your ticket to the universe."

On our third day in Herat, Peter took me to meet Canaga, one of the smoothest operators in all of Afghanistan. He had a windowless room filled with traditional artifacts. Pipes, sabers, rugs, and musical instruments hung everywhere. Quite incongruously, one wall was covered with rock posters from San Francisco, no doubt gifted, or traded, by previous customers.

He tried to come off as a spiritual guru, but he was more of a drug dealer than anything. He sold everything from LSD to hash to heroin. The best thing about him was he was not in a hurry. His English was excellent. He talked slowly and listened carefully to what we had to say about ourselves and how we got to his neck of the woods. He boiled water ceremoniously on his kerosene stove to make chai. He offered sweet treats as he began to talk about the mysticism of Afghanistan. "This country is full of mystics and shamans. They heal illness and foretell the future with the help of spirits. They use sacred drums and animal blood and human skulls to create magic." He could see we were fascinated. "If you would like, I could take you to one."

We told him we were more interested in the music than the shamans. "For a slight fee," he said without missing a beat, "I will take you into the mountains to hear the most fabulous concert you will ever hear." Canaga had all the angles covered.

"How much?" Peter asked.

"For you," Canaga smiled, stroking his half-gray beard, "for you, I will only take three US dollars."

"For both of us?" Peter bargained.

Canaga cackled. "No, you know it is three US for each one."

"That is too much," I threw in. "I have no money. I'm a musician and a writer. Actually, I'm more of a wandering minstrel. Or really, if you want to get technical, I'm just wandering."

He looked at me with deeply searching eyes. We stared into each other for a full ten seconds. I could feel his depth of soul. He could see I was telling the truth.

"I tell you what." He clapped his hands. "For you two, and especially for the musician, I will do it for three dollars for two."

"What if we bring two women?" I asked.

Canaga looked at me as if I had suggested murder. "No women," he said, holding his hand over his heart. "Women cannot go where I will take you. It is sacred music. Women are not allowed. And you must pay me now so I can make arrangements. Not many Westerners can go. I can only take so many. This is a great honor. I do it because of what I see in your eyes."

I felt the spirit of John Lennon smiling over my shoulder.

"Let's do it!" I said excitedly. "Pay the man, Peter."

Peter dutifully paid up, and two nights later we found ourselves following Canaga up the mountain for our mystery concert. It had not been easy convincing Adriana and Rebekah they could not join us, but, in the end, they decided it would be good for us to have an adventure on our own.

Up and up we walked. The path became quite steep. Canaga had to be at least fifty years old, but he didn't seem to tire as much as we did. He kept saying we were almost there. Stars pierced the black night like all-white Christmas lights as they lit the narrow rocky trail. The moon was behind the mountain, but we could see its light.

The farther up the mountain we walked, the more I wondered if we could really trust our guide. He could be taking us anywhere. *Maybe he knows a tribe that needs some hostages?*

I stopped and turned to look at Peter as he stumbled into me. "Can we trust this guy?" I whispered.

Peter laughed. "Don't worry. He's just making money on us, that's all." That simple explanation satisfied me. We turned back uphill and hurried to catch up to our older guide.

After about an hour of walking, we came to a long, low-slung hut that was barely visible at first against the side of the mountain. As we got closer, we heard angelic music coming from inside. It sounded like nothing I'd ever heard. We walked around to the rear of the building. Canaga held his finger to his mouth so we would remain quiet as we entered through the woven, back-door curtain of the establishment. He knew the armed guard at the entrance and slipped him some money. The guard looked us over closely but did not search us.

The scene inside was like a low-hung circus tent. The highest part of the ceiling was barely ten feet tall. Even so, it was much larger than it looked from the outside. At least one hundred men in turbans were on carpets facing a dimly lit stage that was only one foot above the floor. On the stage were eleven musicians making the most sublime music I had ever heard. In that instant of sound recognition, I experienced the soul of Afghanistan. I felt the power of the mountains and the people who carved out their rocky living. The melodies soared like the topography itself. I could hear caravans crossing in the night. The folk music conveyed a fierce independence. It was unique to my welcoming ears and mind. No invading army could ever conquer this.

The percussive sound of the tablas and the nylon-stringed domburas was hypnotic. The rhythm was ominous and joyous at the same time. There was a sitar player at center stage, a tambura player to his right and, to his left, two men playing rhubab, a lute-like, stringed instrument quite a bit smaller than the sitar. They played off one another like guitar, banjo, and mandolin from a bluegrass band, yet blended chordal harmonies like the string section of a symphony orchestra. I heard complex jazz and even basic blues progressions coming out of these cats. It sounded like the fierce and foreboding mountains of Afghanistan had blended all the world's music into one earthquake-avalanche of swinging soul.

One microphone hung from the ceiling by its chord and the singer had his own microphone. I was surprised the performance was being amplified at all. *They must have a generator. How else could the light bulbs be working?* A small speaker was on either side of the stage.

The singer's chanting was at once mournful and uplifting. He introduced each song with an eloquent Arabic description and the musicians began playing together without a vocal count.

The dynamics of the Afghani orchestra were beyond stimulating. They could climb to crescendo and fall to near silence in startling speed and unison. The melodies made me want to fly at some points and cry at others. They rose and fell like the mountains themselves. Up to that point, my only involvement with eastern music had been what George Harrison had brought to the Beatles. Now, I was beginning to understand what all the minor scale tonalities and deep, ocean-like rhythms meant to each other. The sounds were dancing with each other like wild spirits coming down to earth to have a little fun. I had goosebumps on my skin. The hair was standing up on the back of my neck. My epiphany was visceral. The music made me feel like I might be reincarnated someday, like I might live forever in a thousand lives. I felt liberated, part of something infinite.

This was the moment I decided to become a musician. It felt like a ray of sunshine breaking through a cloudy sky. I had reached a state of mind where my love of music would compel me to create music, not just listen to it. No more wondering whether I was good enough to do it. The joy of the Afghani music told me I had to make my own music.

It felt the same as the night the grieving North Vietnamese man in Hungary had finally turned me into a conscientious objector. A switch flipped on inside me and I saw the light. Now, the music of Afghanistan was turning me on. These mountain musicians sent an awakening signal that could not be ignored. It tingled my entire spine. I wanted to sing for joy.

The road had taken me to a place I would never have found on my own. It was teaching me how to be what I always hoped I could become.

The band played on. I looked over at Peter and saw tears streaming down his face. He smiled at me and shook his head in disbelief. The music was making our hearts soar to new heights.

Canaga smiled knowingly and nodded as he saw the gratitude on our faces.

We had listened to about twenty songs when Canaga let us know it was time to leave before the show was over. He wanted to keep his Western guests as unobtrusive as possible. We slipped out the same way we came in and began walking back down to Herat. We could see our breath in the cold night. The sudden silence was stunning.

There were no words that needed to be said. The moon was over the mountain and seemed to fully appreciate our heightened musical and spiritual condition. We bid Canaga goodnight and went back to the hotel to try and explain what we had just experienced. We had a delicious taste of what it meant to be Afghani.

We ended up staying in Herat for ten days. By the sixth day, I was down and out with a combination of dysentery and pneumonia. I had a high fever and a ringing in my head. Lack of sleep, too much smoke and booze, and not enough vitamin C had caught up with me. My friends took good care of me as I took to the mat to sleep it off. Peter provided vitamins, Rebekah kept making me herbal tea, and Adriana faithfully nursed me back to health.

I actually stopped smoking hash, which meant I had some crazy dreams. Some were about the military and Vietnam. I saw a lot of napalm wiping out jungles and found myself rescuing screaming children. Most of the dreams, however, were about Afghanistan and its music and colorful tribal heritage. I was climbing up steep mountain trails to get a better look at something. I didn't know what it was I was hoping to see, but I knew I had to keep walking up and up in order to see it. There were often musicians along the way providing directions and musical accompaniment. During one dream, I made it to the top of the mountain and discovered a broad vista of nothing but more mountain peaks. I woke up sweating and told Adriana about the dream.

"You see," she soothed. "You are getting better. You are reaching the top of the mountain. It will all be downhill from here."

"I don't think so," I said sadly. "It didn't feel like I was getting better. It felt like there were only questions and no answers. It felt like once I answered one question, a thousand more would spring up to take its place."

Adriana put a wet rag on my forehead. "Why do you think there should be an answer? You Americans are always looking for the answer or 'enlightenment,' as you call it. Don't you see? There is no answer, so don't spoil everything by asking the same question over and over. We should just live our lives and be happy with what we have and who we are with."

I raised my head off the pillow and sat up. "That sounds like the answer."

"Maybe it is," she said, helping me into a clean shirt. "Maybe it is."

In two days, I was well enough to get up and walk around Herat again, grateful to not have to go to a hospital. We'd all heard nothing but horror stories about health care, or the lack thereof, in Herat.

One morning we introduced Rebekah and Adriana to Canaga. We took the ladies right up into his den of wheeling and dealing. Canaga nearly leaped to his feet when he saw us coming. He was not used to having female guests, but he was obviously eager to make an exception.

"Oh, my, my," Canaga stammered. "I am overwhelmed by the beautiful women you have brought into my life. My, my, my. Let me look at you. Oh, yes, you are flowers of the desert. I can smell your perfect perfume. I am so pleased to have you here in my humble, humble quarters. Please sit. May I make you some chai?"

"That would be lovely," Adriana said as she allowed him to kiss her outstretched hand. "What an amazing home you have. Mark and Peter have told us so much about you. It is wonderful to finally meet you in person. Do you have a wife?" Adriana was nothing if not direct.

Canaga went about making the chai and answered, "No, alas, that is my great sadness. My wife and two daughters were taken by the sickness many years ago."

"I am so sorry," Adriana stammered. "I had no idea. I did not mean to pry or bring up sadness."

"No, do not worry," Canaga soothed. "It was many years ago and I have found happiness here in Herat, meeting people from the West like you and your friends."

He ended up giving the ladies much more of a detailed explanation of the artifacts in his room than he had ever given us. He was clearly delighted by their interest. He served chai and sweets and hosted a marvelous tea party. "You must allow me to show you around the city. I know all the best places to shop."

"That would be lovely," Rebekah cooed.

"He'll want a fee," Peter warned.

"I'm sure he will be worth it," Rebekah said as she flirted with him by holding his arm. Canaga beamed. I caught him looking down her blouse, but I didn't say anything. Who could blame him?

By the time we left, both Rebekah and Adriana were quite impressed by his charm and social skills. "You see," Rebekah remarked. "These Afghanis can get along with women if you just give them a chance."

"Canaga is hardly your typical Afghani male," Peter commented. "Even so, you two made him very happy. I never saw him hustle and bustle like that before."

The five of us explored Herat to our heart's content. Canaga guided us off the beaten path to meet his friends. The people of Heart turned out to be quite welcoming once we had our entrée. We took long walks and tried to go a different way each time we went out. The weather was sunny and unseasonably warm. Our days melted into each other like hot chocolate sauce and ice cream. In fact, Canaga showed us a place that served chocolate sundaes. It became our favorite spot, always the last stop on the tour for the day.

"If there's one thing this trip has taught me," I said one day over ice cream, "it's that people everywhere are pretty much the same. They want love and kindness. Nobody I've met wants to fight or be in a war."

"You always say that," Rebekah chided.

"People are people," Peter observed dryly. "They want good food, good fun, and a nice place to sleep at night."

"I'm amazed that the women around here put up with being treated like slaves by the men," Adriana said.

"All it's going to take," Rebekah said, "is telephones and television and these girls will take to the streets like our grandmothers did."

We laughed in agreement. Our little group didn't argue much. We didn't see ourselves as missionaries or ambassadors or agents of change. We were simply passing through to soak up whatever it was we were supposed to learn. We all had faith in the road. It had brought us together and we knew it wouldn't let us down.

Rebekah crossed the line one afternoon when Adriana was out with Peter and I was alone. She came into the room and sat down to have a chat. As we made small talk, she casually loosened her top to partially expose her fabulous figure. She was offering herself to me. She got close enough that I could smell flower gardens in her freshly washed hair and skin.

"I always hoped I would find a man like you," she purred. "It doesn't seem fair that Adriana should have you all to herself. After all, we're a family, aren't we?"

This was more than temptation come to call. This was fate knocking down the door. I had wanted this young woman since I first saw her naked on the beach on Mykonos Island. She made me weak in the knees. I could feel my entire body slipping into a sexual tremble.

She leaned closer to kiss me. Her eyes were closed. She was positively glowing with sensuality. I was about to let her lips melt into mine. Our foreheads touched gently. She opened her eyes. They were brightly innocent and darkly hypnotic at the same time. I nearly fell into her well of desire and longing. But I knew there would be no way out, no turning back.

A bell went off inside my head like an alarm clock. *This can't be right. What would Adriana say?*

Rebekah put both hands on my thigh. I pulled my head away from hers and grabbed her hands. As much as I wanted her to continue, I knew she had to stop before it was too late. I pulled her hands away gently and got to my feet. "I'm sorry, Rebekah. We can't do this. You know why. I'm not saying I don't want to or that you are not attractive. I'm just saying we can't do this. Come on, let's take a walk."

Rebekah stood up with me and hung her head. "I'm sorry. I feel like such a fool. I don't know what got into me. You're right. I must think of Adriana. Yes, yes, I am being selfish. You are right. We should walk."

We ended up having a reconciling stroll. What Rebekah needed was intimacy, not sex. We had a good talk about traveling and missing home and wondering where the road would lead. She admitted to being jealous about Adriana having so much romantic fun. And I was taking away her traveling companion.

I nudged her playfully. "Your time is coming soon. Mr. Wonderful is already on his way." Rebekah smiled coyly like she knew it was true.

We resolved not to tell Adriana about the incident. Rebekah, however, felt so bad about it that she spilled the beans to Adriana as soon as they got together. It was not a pretty picture. Instead of being proud of me for remaining faithful, Adriana flew into an instant rage.

"How could you let her come on to you? You know how young she is. You know how much she means to me. She is like my little sister. You are a man pig. I throw you in the mud where you belong."

Then it occurred to her that, perhaps, Rebekah was at least partly to blame.

"And you. You little whore! You keep your filthy paws off my man. He is my man. He is no your man. Do you understand?"

Rebekah nodded and hung her head. "Yes, it was my fault. He stopped me."

Adriana slapped her on the shoulder. "Now get out of my sight. I no want to see you for a long time. Go. Leave us."

Rebekah left and Adriana turned back to glare at me. I wasn't about to laugh at her, but her reaction had been completely irrational. I wasn't backing down either. For once, I had done the right thing. But her reaction was not what I expected.

Peter burst into the room. "What's going on?" he demanded. "Rebekah's in tears. What did you do, Mark?"

I held my hands up and proclaimed my innocence. "Why does this have to be my fault? I did absolutely nothing wrong. Rebekah came on to me and I turned her down and then she told Adriana."

Peter looked at Adriana quizzically. Seeing his concern and hearing my defense, she realized she had overreacted. Her shoulders sagged out of rage mode. She brushed past Peter and left the room to go talk to Rebekah.

"Is that true?" Peter asked. "Did she come on to you?"

"Without a doubt," I confirmed. "But she got over it with no trouble and we don't have a problem. Man, that girl is ready for a man. Why have you not taken care of that?"

Peter didn't respond for almost a minute. I waited as he formulated his explanation. He furrowed his brow and put his hands on his hips. "I don't know. She's so young and, I don't know, I've had nothing but bad experiences when I go for the sex without the love. She's not the one for me. She knows it and I know it. That is all I can say. But I will say this. We need to move on. We've been in this town long enough. That's why things like this are happening."

Eventually, we all agreed it was time to hit the road. Adriana and Rebekah kissed and made up. We decided to split up into two teams and hitchhike to Kabul by the southern route through Kandahar. Peter and Rebekah left first. We gave them an hour head start so as not to interfere with their hitchhiking. By the time we got to the edge of Herat, they were nowhere to be seen, which meant they had gotten a ride.

Adriana and I didn't have to wait long. A large flatbed truck filled with bags of flour pulled over and motioned for us to jump in the back on top of the flour. We climbed aboard, laughing aloud at our good fortune. The truck bounced on down the road. The bags of flour jostled up clouds of white powder. We became white as ghosts.

I began coughing. "This is what they mean by flower power."

Adriana laughed so hard she started to cough as well. Then her coughing turned into choking. The road was getting rough. The flour powder was making it hard to breathe. We were still laughing until the truck hit an unpaved stretch in the road, which caused the entire load to bounce up and down and emit a thick, white dust. By now, our hair and clothing were caked in white. We were making flour dough in our mouths. Funny as it was, we were both choking and unable to breathe.

I banged on the roof of the truck cab until he pulled over. We jumped off and collapsed on the side of the road, still choking and coughing. The flour was so thick it had nearly closed our eyes with a thick paste. The driver took one look at us and laughed out loud until he realized we were in real respiratory trouble. He ran back to the truck and returned with a large bottle of water. When he saw us beginning to breathe a little better, he asked if we would like to continue riding with him.

"No. No thank you," I coughed. "You go on. We'll be fine. Don't worry about us. We're not getting back on that truck for anything."

It took quite a while after he drove away to brush off and wash out the flour. Adriana fluffed her hair and danced away from her thick cloud of a flour shower. "I am the ballerina of bread," she joked. "Wherever I dance, people will have bread. I am the hunger fairy."

She was funny in the face of adversity. She didn't take herself too seriously. I loved that about her.

We brushed each other off. No sooner had we gotten ourselves relatively clean than a giant oil truck pulled over to pick us up. It looked a lot like the one we had commandeered in Iran, but the driver wasn't the same.

"I wonder if the warring tribes would hijack a truck like this for the fuel?" I asked as we rolled into Kandahar, waving at onlookers like we were the king and queen of a Mardi Gras parade.

It was November 4th, three days before the presidential election in the United States.

The next day it was easy to locate the hippie center of Kabul. There were hundreds of us, and we tended to form our own little community wherever we went. Adriana and I checked into the Green Hotel, an establishment particularly tolerant of Western travelers and our partying ways. We knew half the guests from our travels and quickly became friendly with the other half. For lunch, we went down the street to a restaurant-bar named Cigis, which proved to be party central.

The sun was shining and longhairs and hippie women from all over the world were lounging on the lawn for picnics and guitar jams. The center of the lawn was a giant chess set, with three-feet tall pieces, surrounded by a white wall about four feet tall. The place felt like something out of *Alice In Wonderland*.

Hipsters and hustlers got high on the fence and watched the chess game like a concert. Rock music was playing loudly from a sound system inside the restaurant, which served Italian spaghetti and French cheese and American hamburgers.

The whole vibe was something straight out of Tom Wolfe's book *The Electric Kool-Aid Acid Test*. We were all trying to be Merry Pranksters in our own right. The favorite Prankster line was, "You're either on the bus or off the bus." In fact, the Prankster Bus had been through Kabul about a year earlier and people were still talking about it.

"I don't know what's so cool about the Pranksters," I said to Adriana. "It sounds like they had it pretty easy. They were tourists on a bus. We don't even have a bus."

Instead of being proud of our hitchhiking, Adriana said slowly, "I wish we had a bus."

"Come on, girl," I chided her. "You're already in the running for greatest female hitchhiker ever."

Adriana smiled wearily. Hitchhiking through Iran and Afghanistan could take the wind out of the sails of even the toughest woman. It was hard and dirty and scary. "Sometime I feel like prostitute standing on side of road."

I tried to be funny and lift her spirits but ended up saying exactly the wrong thing. "You're no prostitute. You don't charge money. You're free."

She opened her mouth and eyes wide, clearly shocked by my lack of sensitivity. Before I could apologize, she walked away and disappeared into the restaurant. Peter watched her walk away and came over to sit down next to me. "What did you say this time?"

The group of travelers at Cigis was the cutting edge of the counterculture. With all the feather and leather and fur and headbands, we looked like a tribe of wild Indians from the American West. We were all fugitives from the American Dream.

There was a little bit of the "hipper than thou" attitude going around the group, but mostly, there was true camaraderie, particularly once acquaintances had been made. Many had tales to tell of being robbed and even beaten along the way. Sickness had been common. Everybody was thin. We were all travel weary and resting up in Kabul before making the move across the Khyber Pass to Pakistan and India.

I was eager for news from the States since the presidential election was coming up. It had been weeks since I'd seen or heard any real news. I found several recent newspapers at Cigis that helped bring me up to speed on current events. Richard Nixon, of course, was promising a negotiated end to the war. None of the longhairs believed a word Nixon said, but it was becoming all too clear that he was going to soundly defeat the anti-war candidate, George McGovern. Nixon was the incumbent and McGovern's campaign was sputtering to an ineffectual stall as the election drew near. Nixon winning the election would mean most people in the States were still afflicted with Cold War mentality.

"It doesn't matter who wins the election," a French girl in a long, colorful, patched skirt said. "America will keep fighting the war because it is in the business of making war."

"The US hasn't stopped colonizing the world since World War II," a dark-skinned man in a ponytail chimed in.

The US bashing continued from every corner of the lawn. Even the chess players had to jump in with their anti-American rhetoric. Adriana looked at me to gauge my response. She knew I was at once ashamed and proud of my country. Unfortunately, when it came to Richard Nixon and Vietnam, it was downright embarrassing to admit you came from the United States. I said nothing and kept reading the papers.

It had been a big year for the anti-war movement. In July, Jane Fonda was filmed in North Vietnam with soldiers on an anti-aircraft gun and broadcasting her anti-war message on Hanoi Radio. Amazingly, I hadn't heard about it until I saw her poster at Cigis.

By August, the last US combat troops had departed Vietnam, a fact much heralded by candidate Nixon. But Operation Linebacker had continued until the end of October. In that "operation," US warplanes flew 40,000 combat missions and dropped over 125,000 tons of bombs to disrupt the North Vietnamese Eastertide Offensive.

"If Nixon wins," I said to Adriana one cloudy afternoon, "the Air Force will stay plenty busy in North Vietnam, dropping bombs on innocent civilians and military alike."

"Aren't you glad you won't be part of it?" she asked, knowing I still had a few reservations about my peaceful course of action.

"Absolutely," I said, more to myself than anybody else. "This election news makes me sick." That brought out a chorus of groans from our little circle of newfound friends.

"Look at this," I pointed out from the newspaper. "That group, Black September, hijacked a Lufthansa Boeing 727 over Turkey to demand the release of three of their comrades being held for the massacre of those Israeli athletes at the Munich Olympics. Man, those guys don't know when to stop."

"What's going to happen to the passengers?" she asked.

"It's hard to say," I replied, continuing to read the paper. "They usually end up letting them go, don't they? Oh, hey, here's a story that'll cheer you up. Some guy named Alex Comfort has published a sex manual called 'The Joy of Sex.' Now that's a book we ought to get."

"Oh yeah." Adriana laughed. "That sounds much more interesting than all this talk about elections and wars."

Try as I might to change the topic, I couldn't get the war out of my head. I wanted to share with my country what I had learned from my travels. I wanted to scream from the rooftops that I had met the communists in eastern Europe, and they were not the enemy, that I had met the North Vietnamese and they were not the enemy. The only enemy the American people had were the power-mad warlords of the military industrial complex, the unholy souls who make up enemies to manipulate the masses through a climate of fear. These are the guys who would get Richard Nixon reelected.

It occurred to me I wasn't even writing about these obvious truths in my articles for the *Fort Wayne Journal-Gazette*. I knew they wouldn't publish a load of anti-war rhetoric, so I had censored myself and reduced my writing to a travelogue. My father had already withheld a pro-communist article I'd sent home from Hungary.

So, what was I doing to help end the war? I was doing a big fat nothing. My travels had become a lot like the peace movement itself. They were more about sex and drugs than peace. I was growing anxious about getting started with my own personal anti-war crusade.

"I've got to do something about it," I concluded out loud.

Adriana was surprised by my comment. The last she had heard we were going to buy a book about sex. "Do something about what?" she asked.

"Something to stop the war. It's obvious we're going to lose the election and that means the war will go on for years. Maybe Nixon will pull out ground troops, but he won't stop the bombing until it's too late for a whole lot of people."

"You can't stop the war all by yourself," she reasoned. "All you can do is not be a part of the insanity. You can't change the world. All you can do is change yourself and your own situation. You will do more than your part when you go back and quit the military."

"Maybe it's time for me to do that," I responded glumly as the truth of her comments sunk in deeply.

Adriana was silent for a long time. "Would you leave me now?" she asked quietly.

I saw the fear and uncertainty in her eyes. "No, don't worry. I'm not going to leave you. We've got a long way to go before I even begin thinking about going home."

She paused again before asking, "Will you take me home with you?"

"Of course I will," I said, hugging her. Yet even with my arms around her I wondered how things would actually turn out.

Peter and Rebekah did not arrive for two days. Their hitchhiking luck had not been nearly as good as ours. Meanwhile, Adriana and I explored the city, taking long walks, holding hands, and chatting happily.

Kabul, the capital of Afghanistan, is surrounded by rugged, snow-capped mountain ranges. There are two lonely mountains in the center of the city, positioned like the center of a bull's eye. One clear, warm afternoon Adriana and I joined some new friends and climbed the mountains in the middle to get an aerial perspective on the city. The two-hour climb was not that steep, but at the top we were sweating and panting and more than 2,000 meters above sea level. Looking below, we saw an amazing view of a city caught in the throes of modernization. What a contrast between the old and the new! There were high-rise apartments with aluminum and glass gleaming in the sun right beside what looked like little lakes of mud huts. Grand avenues trailed off into dirt roads. Horses and trucks struggled in the same traffic.

One of our climbing partners was an anthropologist from Denver.

"Look at all that," he marveled. "You're looking at the result of 3,000 years of history. This place was once the center of Zoroastrianism, then later it was home for Buddhist and Hindu kings. The Muslims invaded in the seventh century and introduced Islam. Then the Hindus took it back. This city was even invaded by Mongols under Genghis Khan. It has survived all of that so well that they now call it the Paris of Central Asia. It's still a clash of culture, though. You can see a girl in a mini-skirt passing by a woman in a chador or burqa."

"It's like the Columbus Nightclub," Adriana said. "It's right downtown in Kabul. It's divided into the west room and the east room. The west room has loud rock and roll, whiskey, and crazy, sweaty dancing. In the east room people sit on carpets, drink tea, and listen to Afghani music."

"Which room do you prefer?" the anthropologist asked as we began our descent. The lights of the city were getting brighter and brighter as darkness fell.

"I like them both." Adriana laughed. "I dance like crazy in the west room until I get tired and then I go to the east room to catch my breath. Sometimes, I even dance in the east room."

That assessment was vintage Adriana. She loved it all. In that regard, we were so much alike it was frightening. We made a great traveling couple, although we sometimes encouraged each other much too far down the trail of intoxication..

I spent the next day writing while the others were out exploring and socializing. It was a rare, emotional downtime for me. I even resorted to making a list of all my friends back home. I missed them more than I ever thought I would. Mostly I missed my parents and sisters on good old Sunset Drive in Fort Wayne. I wrote this letter:

Dear family,

Enclosed are articles 25 and 26. I think they're pretty good. I'm beginning to look forward to coming home, but Thanksgiving is just impossible. I've decided it's worth the $375 for the plane ticket from Bombay to Lisbon to be home for Christmas. I'm coming home for the express purpose of facing up to the Air Force and work however long it takes to pay all my debts. Then South America is next before I even think about a career. Got to learn Spanish.

If for some reason you can't get the money, please at least send $100 so I can hitchhike overland to Lisbon. That would put me home about the 30th of January. You might think it's a little dirty to use this Christmas thing as a lever, but the way I look at it, it's my money and my decision and only a short-term loan. I've been saying this for years—but never again.

The only way I'm assured of getting the $400 is if you cable it through American Express New York to American Express Bombay. I should be in the States around the 13th of December and home by the 22nd. My money situation is desperate, but whatever danger I might have been in is past now. I'm taking a bus to Delhi then to Bombay—then fly to Lisbon and use my return ticket. Got a short letter from Dad in Kabul. Happy to hear you're all okay. This experience has been worth more than money could ever be. See you soon.

Love,
Mark

Article 26 was the one about Kabul and entitled "Me and Mr. Murray":

To get an Indian visa in Kabul you must show $100 in travelers' checks. But since I had only $45 to my name, I had to borrow $55 from Adriana and wait all day in an incredibly inefficient bank in Kabul to change it into good old American Express. Then show the checks for the visa, change them back to dollars and pay Adriana back, and get to Delhi on $45 to sell my turquoise. Oh, the problems of poverty.

But during a moment of panic I figured I'd better talk to the American Embassy to find out the sure-fire way of getting money cabled to me in Bombay. That's where I met Mr. Murray, the assistant American ambassador in Kabul.

He looked patronizingly at me in my Afro hairstyle, ragged beard, black leather jacket, hiking boots, and dirty army pants, and I caught a trace of pity in his eyes. I felt like I was back in third grade getting a lecture from the principal. He handed three photos across the mahogany desk to me.

The first photo showed a Volkswagen van parked alongside a road in southern Afghanistan. A typical traveling mode of the young American couple off to see the world before they maybe settle down and raise a family. The second photo showed the inside of the van. The usual messy array of dirty clothes, Coleman stove, sleeping bags and pots and pans. But this van looked like someone in a big hurry had rummaged through it.

The third photo showed the young couple sprawled in the ditch, as dead as the ground that had soaked up their life's blood. One bullet in the spine for each of them from a thief's rifle. They'd probably lived for about an hour after they'd been shot, lying bleeding in the Afghan night, unable to move or believe the nightmare that had befallen them for no reason at all, hoping desperately that a passing vehicle might stop to save their fading lives. Their bodies were only 45 feet from the road and weren't found until four days after the shooting.

Actually, Mr. Murray turned out to be a nice person and we

had quite a talk about his job and all the down-and-out hippies that come to the embassy looking for help, even though I could tell he was hoping his son didn't grow up to be a "bum" like me. His mouth dropped open when I told him I'd hitchhiked and slept outdoors all the way from Turkey.

"You've been taking quite a risk. These people weren't the only unlucky ones."

I remembered the many times I'd been absolutely defenseless in the middle of nowhere, hut, restaurant, truck stop, with Adriana surrounded by dark-looking men who never stopped looking at her. Frightened, and at the mercy of near-starving people whose language I don't speak, and who've been known to kill for a lot less than a woman.

But then I remember the *Newsweek* magazine I read while waiting to see Mr. Murray that told about the murder cult, the Mau Mau, in the supposedly civilized USA. So I realize that living itself is a risk and that the only decision we can make about our safety is "Is the risk worth the experience?" And when I think about all the beautifully hospitable people I've met hitchhiking that I wouldn't have met traveling by bus, I know that my experience has been well worth the risk I've taken.

Mr. Murray is convinced that my fellow "international bums" are a bunch of very lost dope smokers. But I know that we're all searching, eyes open and hands dirty, for whatever we can find.

And I know that he'll never experience at his formal embassy parties the strong sense of community and mutual understanding that exists among the young people (and old people) who give up their security to go feel the motions of the rest of the world.

I felt quite a bit better after finishing my travel articles and writing the letter to my family, so I headed out to mail them at the post office. I was walking down a crowded street when I heard a vaguely familiar voice call out, "Hey, Smitty. What's happening?"

Turning around, I saw H.L.D., one of my old traveling friends from Austria, Italy, and the Fiat van. "H.L.D.!" I cried. "It's really you. We had to come all the way to Kabul to get back together again." We embraced heartily.

"What took you so long to get here?" H.L.D. joked.

I held him at arm's length to look him in the eyes. "Man, I've been here for almost two weeks."

H.L.D. held his arms out and looked at me with raised eyebrows and sadness in his eyes. "Last time I saw you, you left without saying goodbye in Athens. What happened?"

I let go of his shoulders and shook my head. "I know I should have said goodbye. I'm sorry. But it was time to go and I knew you would talk me into staying."

He nodded his head to accept my apology. "Yeah, we knew you were gone when we saw all your gear gone. We were a little surprised you didn't leave a note, but we all knew you were getting ready to head out on your own. I left the van a little after you did," he said. "Things were getting a little crowded. I figured you'd be back in the States by now. I was hoping you didn't end up in jail. What goes on with the Air Force?"

We walked together as I told him my plans. "I'm headed for Bombay with some folks, then I'll be headed home to quit."

H.L.D. stopped me in my tracks. "Right on, man! I knew you wouldn't cave in. Hey, bummer about the election. Nixon took every state but Massachusetts. Can you believe it?"

I hung my head and looked at my dusty hiking boots. "I hate to say it but, yes, I can believe it. The farther away I get from the US, the crazier it looks."

"I hear you, my brother," H.L.D. said, "but I sure do miss it. I remember we used to talk about never going back, but I can see now that's not going to happen. I'm getting kind of sick of these little brown people." We laughed, knowing the comment was not so much racist as it was a comment on being a stranger in a strange land, as well as an acknowledgment of missing home.

We spent about a half-hour telling each other how we made it to Kabul. H.L.D. had not been hitchhiking. He thought that was a little too crazy in these parts. "I just hang out until I see somebody cool who looks like they've got some room in their ride," he explained. "Then I offer to help pay for gas. As you can see, it works like a charm."

"Hey," I suggested, "why don't you come with me back to the Green Hotel? I've got some far-out people for you to meet."

"Oh, man, I'd love to," H.L.D. said, "but I'm just headed out. In fact, I've got to get moving or I'll miss my ride. Tell you what, I'll check you out in Delhi."

"Cool."

We embraced and off he went. I watched him disappear into the crowded street market. I noticed he was wearing an embroidered Afghani vest, much like the one I was wearing. I knew it was time for me to get moving too. The road was calling.

CHAPTER THIRTEEN

Pakistan

KABUL KEPT US intrigued and entertained for two weeks. We took long walks along the river and reveled in the sights of more than three thousand years of civilization. The diversity of architecture reflected the many empires that fought over the narrow valley between the Hindu Kush mountains for its key location on the Asian trade routes. We walked through miles of primitive neighborhoods where people looked like they scratched out a living from the

dust itself. The women wore burqas and the men wore turbans. They eyed us with a suspicion of foreigners that had been passed down from generation to generation.

We hiked to the old post office, hoping for word from home or news from fellow vagabonds. Two weeks was a long time to stay in one place, considering we were travelers on the move. It was long enough to rest up and get ready for the next round of getting from point A to point B. The farther away from home I got, the longer my travel breaks needed to be. The road was beginning to take its toll. I had lost thirty pounds and my energy level felt low. Everything smelled like horses. There were some horses on the streets, but it didn't seem like there were enough of them to make everything smell the way it did.

One afternoon, for no apparent reason, I had a sudden attack of homesickness and melancholy.

"What's the matter?" Adriana asked, sensing my sadness.

"Nothing," I started to cover up, then decided against it. "I guess I'm homesick."

"Oh, you poor baby," she said sarcastically as she sat down to cuddle up next to me. "Momma's right here to take care of you."

I put my arm around her and kissed her cheek. "Don't you ever miss home?"

Adriana softened and got serious. Her voice sounded soothing as a mother's lullaby. "Yes, of course. We all do. But home is someplace you can never really go back to. You know it. You've been away. Once you come back, you realize everything went on quite nicely without you."

I let out a deep sigh of agreement. "Going home will be very difficult for me."

Adriana leaned out of my hug and pulled her hair back behind her head. "Because of the military?"

"Quitting the Air Force is only the tip of the iceberg," I said. "The hard part will be all my parents' friends calling me a coward and saying how unpatriotic their son is. It won't be easy for them either. Fort Wayne is a small city. They call it the city of churches and all those church people believe in serving their country."

"Maybe you serve best by no fighting," she suggested.

"That is exactly the way I feel about it," I said, taken aback by how squarely she had hit the nail on the head.

"You're going to be fine," she encouraged. "You watch. It will all work out for the best."

"We're going to find out," I said, hoping she was right and getting up with a renewed sense of purpose. "Come on, let's go to Cigis."

Cigis was always a grand time, telling stories and smoking hash and making music and dancing around fires at night. That enchanting place, along with Adriana's companionship, cured my homesickness in no time. People were hanging out and playing chess on the giant chessboard and reading books and painting canvases and meditating and doing dance exercises. The smell of hashish and incense and pa-tchouli oil was in the air.

The cast of characters was constantly changing and there was often a reunion of travelers. New arrivals poured into town, full of curiosity and eager for pointers on how to get around the ancient city. People who had been around for a while were moving on in search of adventure on the road to India.

It didn't take long to obtain seniority at Cigis. Adriana and I were soon holding court and conducting mini seminars on where to go and what to do in Kabul. We weren't spending much time with Peter and Rebekah. They were hanging out at a nearby campground for people with vehicles.

Peter came into our room at the Green Hotel one morning and announced he was headed out. "I've found some guys from Germany who have room for me in their van. They're leaving in about an hour." He looked at me somberly. "I guess this is goodbye. Or maybe I should say I'll see you in Bombay."

I jumped up to hug him. Ever since Adriana and I got together, I knew this moment would arrive, but I hadn't thought it would be so soon. "You can't leave me now," I said in mock desperation. "Can't you see I'm being held captive by a crazy woman!"

"What about Rebekah?" Adriana asked, jumping up to join our hug. Peter laughed at being the center of a group hug. He didn't need to be the center of attention. It made him uncomfortable.

"Rebekah's been living with that Italian guy for three days now," he said. "She's in love. She's finally getting laid. She'll be fine. She doesn't need me."

Peter wasn't petulant about being the odd man out. He was ready to move on. "I'm going to miss you, my brother," he said to me. His deep voice started to crack into a higher pitch like someone giving a eulogy at a funeral.

"I never would have made it without you," I said with tears beginning to well up in my eyes at the awful reality of saying farewell to Peter.

"Me too," he said as we embraced again. "I remember when we first saw the map of Afghanistan in the embassy in Ankara. You looked at me and I looked at you and we decided to go all the way to India."

I hugged him again. "Up until that time we had no idea where we were going."

"Come on you two," Adriana scolded good-naturedly. "We'll be together again in Bombay or probably before that."

We sat down to smoke a chillum and reminisce. I got out my journal to check dates. "Look at this," I said. "We got together on Mykonos on September 27. It's now November 17. That's less than two months."

"Man, it seems like two lifetimes," Peter said.

"Being on the road is intense," Adriana said. "Why is that?"

"It's because you never know what's going to happen, where you're going to sleep or eat or wash your clothes," Peter explained in his matter-of-fact fashion.

"And it's dangerous," I said.

Peter shrugged his shoulders. "Not for us."

"We've been lucky," I agreed. "I thought we were goners on that boat ride to Turkey with all those puking animals."

Peter's big laugh rumbled out of his throat. He smiled. I could tell he felt good to laugh again.

Adriana looked up at the two of us and stood on her tiptoes to insert herself into the conversation. "The two of you are too big and mean to get in trouble."

We smoked another chillum and told tales of running from crowds in Turkey, the women from Canada, smoking opium in Iran, and following Canaga around Herat. We had been through a lot together.

Then it was time for him to go. It was hard to say goodbye. He never asked if I wanted to come with him. He could see I wasn't ready to leave Adriana. Even so, his departure made me realize there might come a time in the not-too-distant future when I would have to say goodbye to her and find my way back home alone. The party was wearing thin. It was time to go back to the States and do what I could to stop the war. Nixon's reelection had dealt a severe blow to the peace movement. We all knew he'd kill a half million people if that's what it took to achieve "peace with dignity."

Things were changing fast between Adriana and me. The heat was beginning to fade from our sex life. I was feeling a little too much like a "husband." I didn't like being told what to do. Neither did she. We had squabbles over money. She was beginning to question our deal of splitting turquoise profits in India. I was down to $17 and didn't like being dependent on her. Worst of all, she became insanely jealous when she spotted me talking to another woman. I was beginning to feel like a kept man.

After Peter left, she looked at me with her big, soulful brown eyes and beckoned me to kiss her. I couldn't resist. She tasted sweeter than ever. The chewed Chiclet gum she always molded into a fake tooth kept her breath fresh. She pulled me close as if she sensed my doubts. "Stay with me," she purred. "The gods are happy we are together."

"It's hard to believe Peter's gone." I sighed. "He's the only guy who could pick me up off my feet when he hugged me. I feel like I should have said something more important to him before he left. Meeting him on that Greek island was like something the fates had ordained. He came along at the perfect moment. We were both on a bus not knowing where it was going. I mean, how many people pay for a ride when they don't know where it's headed?"

"Peter loves you," Adriana soothed. "He loves you so much he didn't try to come between us. He didn't like watching me take you away from him, but he could see we were happy, so he never complained. People like Peter are rare. My father was like Peter. He cared more about others than he did himself, until he was killed in the war."

I shook my head to shift gears from Peter leaving to her father's death. "How old were you when your father died?"

Adriana took my right hand in both of her hands. "I was fifteen, going on twenty-one. I was so in love with my new boyfriend I barely understood why my mother was so devastated. I loved my father dearly, but he was gone so much that it almost felt like a stranger had died when he passed. I miss him more now than I ever did. I miss the way he picked me up off my feet. Isn't that strange? Just like you and Peter."

I put my left hand on top of her hands. "The thing I liked best about Peter was the way he cut to the chase."

She looked at me curiously. "What does this mean, cut to the chase?"

"It means he always got right to the point."

"So why say cut to the chase?"

"It's from the old silent movies. When the plot was getting slow, the director cut the scene and changed it to the chase scene so the audience could get to the thrill before they got too bored."

"You know what I love about you?" Adriana cooed. "I love the way you make me understand everything. You are a good explainer."

Who is this woman? I wondered to myself. She had appeared right on cue, as if my journey had been scripted. I suspected on the beach at Mykonos she would be important to me. That meeting had only been a matter of glances. Later, in the Amir Kabir Hotel in Tehran, my suspicions were confirmed. The woman came into my life like a hurricane and swept my beaches clean. She had taken my consciousness to a new level. Suddenly, it hit me. In a flash, I understood the pivotal importance of women in the world. *Women guide men through life, like Sacajawea guided Lewis and Clark. Women teach men who they are.*

The more I pondered this epiphany, the more sense it made. Adriana was, in fact, the third woman on my journey to help revolutionize my worldview. Danny, in Portugal and Spain, made me realize my shame in being in the Air Force. Hanna, in Hungary, made me question my country's role in the world. Now, Adriana had me wondering whether or not being a human being was something to be proud of.

I was beginning to realize I wasn't in charge of anything. I wasn't the center of the universe, much less the chief executive officer. This was quite a revelation to the eldest child of an affluent baby-boomer family.

"What's the matter?" Adriana interrupted my thoughts.

"Nothing," I said as she put her head on my shoulder. "I was just thinking how much you mean to me."

She fell asleep in my arms as I began to refine my newfound philosophy. *It's not just women who guide men. It's more like everybody you meet is a guide, created by your own imagination. Our guides teach us what we need to know and what we are ready to learn. Actually, we don't create the guides; we create learning opportunities by choosing the people we accompany. In this way, we make up our own reality.*

Things were starting to make some kind of intuitive sense. I realized it was time to start paying more attention to the people around me.

We found Rebekah later that afternoon at Cigis with her new Italian lover, Bernardo. The two of them had blended into each other. They were glowing. Rebekah had obviously found the man she needed.

"Did you say goodbye to Peter?" Adriana asked in a motherly fashion.

"Oh, yes," she answered. "We all had breakfast together. He's fine. He found a couple guys from I'm not sure where who wanted him to help pay gas. He'll be fine. We'll see him again."

"Mark and I are leaving too," Adriana said. "I've met some old friends from Madrid, and they're going to take us all the way to Delhi if we help with expenses. They've got a baby, but there's plenty of room in their big van. I'm not sure when we'll be leaving, but it won't be long. Are you two going to be all right?"

"I'll take care of her," Bernardo said. "My brother and his wife have a van and we all love Rebekah. You should come on over. We've got a campsite. You'll love it."

We took him up on his offer and spent a luxurious time bonding with Rebekah and the Italians, who had the best food and wine and smoke we'd had in some time. They had two guitars, so we got a good jam going right away. In no time at all, at least twenty people joined the party. We all sounded great on "Hey Jude." It was the first time I learned how to play a D7 chord. We sang the outro—"Na, na, na, na na na na"—for fifteen minutes straight. Paul McCartney would have been proud. So would John Lennon, whose spirit still seemed to be following me around, if not guiding me.

The journey had given me confidence and convinced me that I could become a musician if I kept working at it. This was a giant step for me. Once again, I thought of how my musical growth had been severely stunted in the fifth grade when Mr. Broom flunked me in song flute for being the disruptive class clown of the music room. The 4'10" bastard of a bald-headed teacher even stood up in front of the whole school and said, "Congratulations to all the fifth graders who passed song flute and can now choose which instrument to pursue. Only two students failed, John Hume and Mark Smith."

Yes, he actually said our names. The humiliation was crushing and complete. I didn't touch an instrument for ten years after that. It took meeting John Lennon and hitchhiking halfway around the world and the music of Afghanistan to finally find the courage to make my own music.

The shackles of ingrained self-doubt are always the hardest to break.

The jam with the Italians went on most of the night. It was a happening of the finest order. But something had been bothering me most of the night. Once we returned to the Green Hotel, I asked Adriana, "By the way, who are these people from Spain and why do I only hear about our travel arrangements, secondhand, during a casual conversation?"

She dismissed me with an imperious wave of her hand. "Don't worry, you'll love these people."

"Did you say we'll be traveling with a baby?"

"Do you have a problem with that?" she challenged, tired and bitchy.

"Not really. How much is it going to cost?" I asked, actually quite pleased to have a ride to Delhi.

"I've got it taken care of," she said in a way that made me feel like less than an equal partner. I decided not to quarrel and tried to not let it bother me. A ride is a ride.

The couple from Madrid and their baby seemed like friendly people when we met them the next day. Juan, twenty-nine years old, was an ex-engineer who had dropped off the professional treadmill six months earlier. His British wife, Leslie, had been a professor of English literature. Their two-and-a-half-year-old baby named Rowan was cute enough to be on jars of Gerber baby food. He had big dimples on his fat cheeks, blond curly hair, and jack-o'-lantern teeth. His birth had delayed their plans to travel until he was old enough to withstand the rigors of the road. He was able to walk and talk a little and he was amazingly well-behaved.

"Where are we going, Rowan?" Leslie asked playfully.

"India!" he shouted with glee as we all laughed. It was funny the first fifty times they did it.

Adriana and I threw our packs in the back of the large Ford van and settled in for the trip. We were all excited to be on our way. The road was rough. We bounced around quite a bit even though Juan did his best to avoid the larger holes in the asphalt.

Once we got to the Khyber Pass, the road became frightening. The fifty-three-kilometer pass that connects Afghanistan to Pakistan is one of the most scenic yet dangerous stretches of road in the world. It winds through the towering snow-capped mountains of the Hindu Kush, carved into the side of the mountains and only four meters wide in some spots.

Nothing moves fast through the Pass—not the tall tanker trucks or the leaning buses piled high with baggage or the overloaded trucks that don't look or sound like they can make it another mile.

The scenery was breathtakingly majestic. The mountains looked like palatial monuments to crown the Earth itself. They stretched out much farther than the eye could see. Everywhere you turned, never-ending mountain silhouettes controlled the jagged skyline.

We couldn't resist the temptation to ride on top of the van on the steel luggage rack. Juan wasn't wild about the idea, but Adriana talked him into it.

"We promise we'll be good," she said flirtatiously.

"Just promise you'll hang on tight," Leslie said as her husband relented.

The sun was shining, which took the edge off the high-altitude chill of nearly 4,000 feet above sea level. We waved gaily at passing motorists. Almost everybody waved back. The difficulties of the Pass bred true camaraderie. Looking over the edge of the road down to hundreds of feet of nothingness made us realize a wrong turn would mean certain death. We didn't care. We were invincible. We were on top of the world.

"Think of all the people back home who don't know what they're missing," Adriana said as she tilted her head back and let her hair blow in the wind. "This is what we live for. Look at these mountains. They've been waiting for us forever. They are so happy we came to see them they are shining all their glory on us!"

I wrapped my left arm around her as we faced forward and crossed our legs to keep them from blocking Juan's view out the windshield. "This is how I always hoped it would be. Riding over the mountains on top of a van with the most beautiful woman in the world. I'll bet even Alexander the Great didn't have this much fun."

"He have no truck," Adriana said as she squeezed my hand against her stomach. "You know, I think I do this before—in a dream or maybe former life. Something is the same."

I took a deep breath to take it all in but all I got was diesel exhaust. "It does have a real déjà vu feel. This whole scene is so overwhelming it feels unreal."

Adriana bounced a little on the truck top. "Yes, déjà vu. That word I know. And think, we miss it if we stay home. Safe and sound, no?"

At that moment we were on a narrow spot in the road, moving quite slowly around a blind corner. It felt like something was coming around the bend from the opposite direction. We listened and, sure enough, heard the growling of an oncoming truck, still not visible to us. I banged on the roof of the van and Juan slowed to a stop. No sooner had he hit the brakes than the truck came roaring around the corner. He was less than twenty yards away.

"Look out!" we screamed as we waved our hands over our heads in a futile attempt at warning. We could see the oncoming driver's eyes widening as he tried to stop. He was going much too fast for the dangerous road. Juan was completely stopped with nowhere to go. We braced ourselves for an impact that would push us off the road and straight down the mountain.

Miraculously, screaming brakes brought the truck skidding to a stop, only inches from our front bumper. Not a word escaped my mouth. I felt shocked that we weren't plummeting down the mountain to our deaths.

It didn't take Adriana long to let loose a torrent of Latin insults. Juan carefully backed up to a spot where he could let the truck pass. Leslie got out of the van to calm Adriana and avoid a scene as the truck rolled past. The driver shook his fist at us like we were to blame. Adriana was so mad I thought she was going to chase him down on foot. It took a while to settle her down. We were all pretty shaken.

"So much for the glory of leaving our safe little lives." I laughed in relief. Adriana relaxed a little at the reference to our previous conversation. Juan and Leslie saw little humor in my attempt to lighten the moment. Adriana's temper surprised them both. Leslie gave me a stern look that said she did not appreciate a woman who could not control her anger.

When we finally got up the nerve to drive around the blind corner again, I walked ahead as a scout. There was no oncoming traffic this time and we made it through the narrow stretch without further incident. After that, Juan and Leslie insisted Adriana and I ride inside the van. We didn't protest. The views were still astonishing, but they didn't feel nearly as triumphant as they had on top.

It was hard to imagine how all the conquering armies of the past had managed to make it across the Pass. There were crumbling arches, empty stone guardhouses, and abandoned bridges along the way. The road was nothing but semi-level rock at some points. I was glad to not be hitchhiking. No doubt it was prohibited on this treacherous stretch of the road. We didn't see a single pedestrian.

We had no trouble getting into Pakistan other than a long wait at the border. The guards took one look at the baby and waved us through without a search. Juan and Leslie had insisted we ditch our hash before getting in the van, so we felt a little cheated at not being searched.

We made it to Peshawar, Pakistan, and pulled into a park that many travelers were using as a free campsite. Juan and Leslie set up camp for the evening while Adriana and I took Rowan for a walk in his stroller. We were all happy to be out of the van. Rowan insisted on walking so Adriana held his hand while I pushed the empty stroller. People greeted us like we were a happy little family. Adriana was good with the boy. At one point she gave me a look that clearly said, "We should have a child of our own." The look terrified me.

We bought fruits and vegetables for dinner, which Leslie cooked up quite expertly with some rice in a pressure cooker on a Coleman stove. Our spirits were high. We were in Pakistan. Once again, I was reminded of the great thing about being on the road—you feel like you're getting somewhere in life.

After dinner, we relaxed by our fire and the conversation turned metaphysical. Nothing beats arriving in a new country for stimulating discussions on the nature of reality. Juan brought up *The Teachings of Don Juan: A Yaqui Way of Knowledge*, a book by Carlos Castaneda.

I'd heard about the book but hadn't read it, so I asked, "What do you think of Castaneda?"

"I'm trying to base my entire life on his teachings," Juan said so earnestly it was hard not to be intrigued.

"What does he teach?" Adriana asked.

"Don't get him started," Leslie warned. "He's an absolute Castaneda freak."

We convinced Juan we were really interested, and he started explaining how there are levels of reality going on all around us that we aren't aware of and don't utilize. The basic notion is that there is more to the world than the material realm we perceive with our five senses. This concept had long appealed to me. It was the same thing Adriana had been saying all along. She squealed with delight as Juan kept talking.

"It's not about God like we all learned at church," Juan explained.

"It's about the 'nagual,' which is a way of perceiving more of reality than most humans think possible."

Adriana and I listened to his analysis of Castaneda until we were all ready for sleep. Something inside of me clicked as he was talking that night. I was finally getting somewhere spiritually, although still laboring under the delusion that one day I would figure it all out.

I borrowed his book the next day, and Adriana and I both started reading it. I loved the notion that what you see in life is not what you get. It occurred to me that what I had been looking for all along my journey was a way out of reality. I had a sneaking suspicion that the whole notion of "self" was mainly an illusion. Most of my drug experimentation in college, particularly with LSD, had been an attempt to "Break on through to the other side," as Jim Morrison of The Doors sang. The LSD trips had taught me that the mind could take you places you didn't think were even there. The problem had always been that, once you came down, reality was always waiting to bite you in the ass harder than ever. Now, here was a guy writing about increasing consciousness without drugs. Adriana and I were ready for Castaneda, as was a good percentage of our generation. He smacked us right in the middle of our third eye.

We continued our rugged drive through Pakistan. Traveling with a baby added a whole new dimension to the trip. Rowan was no ordinary boy. He could sleep through a riot. He patiently toughed it out with us in the marketplaces, even when surrounded by a wall of curious strangers. Riding in the van, he squealed with delight when we passed by camels or trains or anything unusual. His enthusiasm gave all of us a fresh outlook on the world.

Coming into a crowded city, Rowan would go nuts jumping up and down on the seat, waving to all the people with exuberant energy.

At night, after dinner, he'd fall asleep in somebody's lap while we talk-ed softly around the fire about the day's experiences.

"What would you think about having a baby?" Adriana asked one night as we were falling asleep in our sleeping bags. The question made me wonder if she was still taking the birth control pills she had care-fully displayed and explained at the beginning of our relationship.

"I think it would be a terrible idea right now," I answered carefully.

She waited a short time before continuing. "I don't mean now. I mean someday."

"Someday, in a few years, it might be a good idea," I said, "but I'm nowhere near ready to be a father. I've got some personal battles to fight."

"Do you think I'd be a good mother?"

I sat up at that question, realizing the importance of giving the right answer. I threw my arm around her and said, "You will be the most wonderful mother in the world. You will love your babies like you love me and they will be the happiest babies in the world."

Adriana sighed sadly. She had come to realize she could count on me for reassurance. She was also beginning to suspect I wouldn't be around long enough to have babies with her.

The road through Pakistan was the worst for driving I had ever seen. With close to seventy million people, the developing nation was under continuous construction. The road was always congested with sluggish, cow-drawn carts, bicycles, pedestrians, and road construction crews. It was traffic jams without cars.

The roads were in poor repair, and from the looks of the workers along the road chipping rock into gravel, things were going to get worse before they got better.

After a long day of driving we decided to get cheap rooms at the Swat Hotel in Lahore, Pakistan. Leslie asked me to go out and get food for Rowan, so off I ventured into the sea of pedestrians clogging the street market. After some haggling, I got a pretty good deal on what looked like perfectly fine cakes for the boy. I returned them proudly to Leslie, who took a bite out of one and immediately spit it out.

"This is much too spicy," she snarled. "How could you think this would be good for him? This wouldn't even be good for you. Did you even taste it?"

I hadn't tasted the cakes. Feeling foolish, I took them back from Leslie without comment to avoid what was obviously an emotional explosion getting ready to happen. Evidently, something was getting on her nerves—probably traveling with a baby and two extra passengers. We kept our distance from Juan and Leslie that night.

Adriana thought the cakes were too spicy, but she agreed Leslie had overreacted. She ate some bread and potatoes and carrots we had left over while I ate the spicy cakes myself. They tasted fantastically hot and flavorful, like I always thought fine Pakistani food would taste. I ate them thinking the others were fools for not sampling the local cuisine. As it turned out, I was the fool.

About 4 a.m., a terrible gurgling in my entire digestive system awakened me. I tried to ignore it, but it soon became quite painful. Suddenly, I had to run outside the room to become violently ill in the grass. I was puking and had a terrible case of diarrhea at the same time. Adriana heard the awful noises and came out to check on me. She found me sprawled in the grass next to the jeans I had taken off in the nick of time.

"Oh, my God," she said, holding her nose. "What happened to you? It smells like you just died out here."

"I did," I moaned. "It was the cakes. It was the goddamned cakes. This is my punishment for trying to poison the baby."

"You didn't try to poison the baby," Adriana tried to comfort me.

"Tell that to Leslie," I choked as I rolled over for another round of retching.

I changed my position on the ground to find fresh grass and dirt. Adriana could see I was in no shape to come back inside so she let me sleep outside. In the morning, she brought out the rope bed from the room. I barely had enough strength to lift myself off the ground. At least I had finally stopped emitting noxious elements from both ends. I fell again into a fitful sleep. The next time I opened my eyes, I saw Juan and Leslie and Rowan looking down on me like I was already dead.

"I'm sorry, Leslie" was all I could say.

"It was the cakes wasn't it?" she asked.

"No doubt about it. I'm sorry. I'd hate to think what would have happened to Rowan if he'd eaten them. I should have tasted them before I bought them."

Leslie softened and said, "I'm sorry I snapped at you. It wasn't your fault. You didn't know. I've just been so tired lately. I think Pakistan is doing me in."

"Hang in there, Mark," Juan said. "We'll stay here for a day while you get better. We're going to explore Lahore by foot today, so you just relax and get some rest. You look terrible and much too thin."

I waved them goodbye and slipped into a day of fitful dreams. I kept getting chased by people I didn't know who wanted to do me great harm. Every time I thought I'd lost them, they'd reappear and seem closer than ever to catching me. I woke up periodically when Adriana moistened my lips and put a wet towel on my forehead and tried to get me to drink water.

"You are burning up," she said with a look of alarm on her face. "This fever cannot be good. I've been watering you all day and you still look pale and you still feel hot." She held her hand on my forehead. She was a good nurse. "Yes, you have fever. If this doesn't break by tomorrow, you will have to go to the hospital." She made me sit up and take a big drink of water, which I threw up almost immediately.

I watched from my rope bed as the sun went down, watched the shadows lengthen into darkness and thought seriously about how I might be dying. *What a way to go. I'm so close to India it would be a shame if I never made it. What will they do with my body? What could they do? They'll have to burn me like the common pauper I've become. No, maybe my parents will retrieve the body. But, so what? I'll be too dead to care. Oh, man, this is not how it's supposed to end. This is not how it's supposed to end.*

I must have been talking in my delirium because the next thing I heard was Adriana saying, "You're not going to die. Here, we've boiled some plain rice. Eat this and you'll get better. And drink some water, it's distilled and safe."

I ate the rice and drank the water and waited to throw it up. Thankfully, I kept it down and fell asleep. I had a terrible dream about being hauled away to prison in handcuffs while my friends and family watched helplessly. The dream felt real as I rode in the transport truck and ended up in a military prison. The guards were saying terrible things to me, calling me a coward. I was unable to respond. It felt like they might be right, and I would never get out of that metal cell. I hung my head and sobbed at the notion of losing my freedom.

When I awoke from the nightmare in the middle of the night, every star in the sky was shining down on me as if to say, "You are freer than you've ever been. It's not time for you to die."

I thanked my lucky stars and went back to sleep. The fever was breaking.

The next morning, I was still shaky but able to walk. We decided to hit the road. Everybody was a little sick and Rowan was uncharacteristically cranky. I noticed that every time I got sick, I felt like heading for home immediately. Nothing makes you more homesick than thinking you're going to die in a foreign country. Being sick also temporarily weakened my resolve to quit the Air Force.

I never seriously considered heading to the nearest Air Force base and hopping a free ride home. I could have done it at any time on my journey. I had my orders and my passport. One thing about the planet Earth is you're never far from a United States Air Force base.

There was no way I was going to ask the Air Force for help. I was to the point where I would rather die than admit defeat. The road would take care of me.

We met a major in the Pakistan army at the border, near Amritsar, India. The man must have been bored. He was chatty beyond belief. He bragged that the military was one of the highest paid and respected professions in his country. He also opined that the Pakistani army would have wiped out Bangladesh had his country's leaders not foolishly submitted to pressure from the United States and the Soviet Union.

"Your country is not the only one with a military problem," Juan scoffed as we continued through the border. "And by the way," he said to Leslie, "whatever happened to the United Kingdom? Didn't they once rule both Pakistan and India?"

Leslie didn't take the bait. She was busy keeping Rowan in line as we endured the border delays.

The Pakistani-Indian border was only open one day a week, Thursday. No surprise, since the countries were constantly on the brink of open war. It took us eight hours to get through exit stops, custom stops, entrance stops, and more customs with long lines of bewildering bureaucracy at every stop. The crowd of people seeking passage was quite a sight to see. There were backpacks everywhere, hundreds of them. Hippies and longhairs were cooking food in their vans and cars and buses like some party at a music festival. People knew each other from previous encounters and adventures on the road. A picnic atmosphere prevailed despite the culture of delay we were enduring.

Adriana and I were worried about the turquoise being discovered.

We hadn't told Juan and Leslie about it, but we knew we would all be in some kind of trouble should it be discovered.

It turned out to be safe and sound, secretly stowed in the bottom of the stake bag, rolled into the middle of my tent. There were so many people at the border that the searches had to be quick. No one came close to unrolling the tent.

When we finally finished with the red tape, we realized that all of India was waiting for us with open arms. It was the place we had been heading for so long it often felt like we would never arrive. Now that we were here, it felt almost anticlimactic.

"So, this is it," Juan said as we drove into India. "It doesn't feel any different than Pakistan, or Afghanistan for that matter."

"Were you expecting instant Nirvana?" Leslie laughed.

"I wasn't expecting anything," Juan said a little testily. He was tired of Leslie making fun of his spiritual quest. "I just thought it would be different. That's all."

We spent the night in a campsite in a little town fifty kilometers from New Delhi. We didn't talk much. The thrill of being in India had worn off quickly, like Christmas morning after the gifts have been unwrapped. India was a little bit greener than Afghanistan. But that was the only difference. The roads were still narrow and in poor repair and crowded with too many people in makeshift carts and wagons.

The next day Juan and Leslie dropped us off at the Crown Hotel in Old Delhi, the next stop on the underground hippie railroad. They tried to remain upbeat, but they were obviously glad to be rid of us. It was time for their little family to get back to being a family. Adriana and I were also glad to be on our own again.

The Crown Hotel was five stories high with a fabulous flat roof that afforded an aerial view of the city and a perfect place for young Western travelers to party. It was the usual assortment of wandering musicians, would-be authors, disillusioned scholars, import-export dealers, Hari Krishna freaks, and vagabond prophets. Getting high was everybody's favorite pastime. Hash and wine were the drugs of choice. Life at the Crown was a non-stop party.

The rooms were tiny and cheap and dirty, but a sleeping bag would keep the bed bugs away and a rupee would buy a bucket of hot water for a bath.

The roof felt spacious and even glamorous. We were high above the fray of the hoi polloi. We could see the Red Fort in the distance through the rising dust of the teeming masses below. We thought Pakistan had been crowded. It couldn't compare with Delhi. Delhi was the poster child for overpopulation.

There was a different shop every ten feet. We did not stop to shop. The streets were so jammed it took a real effort to make forward progress walking. Motor scooters and little taxis were zipping everywhere, nudging pedestrians out of the way. There were tall Brahma bulls pulling overloaded carts and sacred cows wandering around like they owned the place. People, people, people were everywhere; people who comprised a strangely civilized mob. People who were not too aggressive and who seemed oblivious to the crush of the crowd. By the time we got back to the Crown, we were speechless and traumatized. The city was a claustrophobic experience.

I was ready to get out of Delhi almost as soon as I arrived. Adriana couldn't leave. She was expecting money from home to arrive *Poste Restante*, or general delivery. I was completely out of money. I hated not being able to eat without asking her for money. On our second day at the Crown, we decided to hit the backstreet markets and try to sell the turquoise.

We asked people on the street where we could sell turquoise. Following their directions eventually led us to a labyrinth warren of cave-like shops with creepy-looking merchants wearing turbans sitting on pillows. We had obviously found the heart of the black market. It felt like you could get your throat slit at any second. It smelled like chai, hash, curry, incense, and dirty feet. Every hair on the back of my neck was standing on end. I looked at Adriana. Even she was unsettled by the vibe of the lair into which we had stumbled.

We selected the shop of a nice young man who spoke good English. He made us chai and set about trying to sell us his wares of gold and silver. It took some time to make him understand we had come to sell, not to buy. I took the small bundle of turquoise out of my shoulder bag and unwrapped it on the low table between us.

The man began laughing as soon as he saw our stones and said, "Mashhad, right? Mashhad, Iran. That is where you buy these stones?"

Adriana looked at me and I looked at her, both realizing in an instant that we'd been conned and swindled back in Iran.

"Yes, we see these stones all the time," the man continued. "The thieves in Mashhad do a big business, convincing tourists to buy these stones. The truth is they are worthless in India. I would not give any money for these stones. I am sorry. I can, however, offer you a true deal on these silver bracelets."

We left his shop without saying much more. We were dejected. Here we were, broke in India, with nothing but a bundle of worthless turquoise to our name. "Maybe we should check with some of these other guys," I suggested halfheartedly.

Adriana stopped and spun to face me. Her face was contorted in anger as she spat out her bitter response. "Why? So they tell us same thing? I should know they play us. I did know. I did it for you. You think everything is good. I was a fool to listen to you."

"Oh, so this is all my fault?"

She turned away and stomped off alone into the squirming marketplace. I let her go and followed behind in case she got into trouble. She never turned around to see if I was shadowing her. She knew I would be. It pissed me off that she could make me follow her without saying a word. It also upset me that she could make me feel guilty for doing something we had mutually decided to do. She had no right to be mad at me.

I followed her back to the Crown Hotel and watched her walk inside. Instead of following her in, I set my sights on the Red Fort and kept walking. Nothing I could have said to her at that point could have done either one of us any good.

The colossal Red Fort stands on high ground. Its tall ornamental walls of red sandstone with their huge gates and pillars and cupolas make it easy to keep in sight as you walk through the crowds. The closer I got to it the more my anger at Adriana subsided. Events of the day often pale in comparison to the monuments of history.

I spent the rest of the afternoon at the massive fortress and palace, marveling at the combination of Persian, European, and Indian art. I had no money for a guided tour, but there were several professor types around who were happy to share their historical knowledge. I was mainly amazed that something built in the seventeenth century could remain such a powerful architectural force in the tumultuous city of Delhi.

It occurred to me on the walk back to the Crown Hotel that it had been some time since I had done anything on my own. It felt good, not having to keep track of someone else. I felt liberated.

I wasn't prepared for Adriana's response when I got back to the Crown Hotel and found her on the roof as the sun was going down.

"Where you been?" she growled. "I worry sick about you. You no care my feeling?"

I tried to deflect her anger. "What you meant to say was, 'Honey, I'm so glad you're home. Come join me for this marvelous sunset.'"

She stomped her right foot down hard on the roof. "Don't tell me what I say. Where you been? Off with some woman you meet in the street?"

"Adriana," I said carefully, noticing that others on the roof were paying attention. "I believe it was you who walked away from me in the market without saying a word."

"You throw away all our money on magic beans in Iran!" she

shrieked. Now, everybody was tuning in to the show. Her temper had slipped out of control. It was my turn to face her Argentinian wrath. "You no care about anybody but yourself. You walk off and leave me like I some rag you can throw away when you want. Look at me when I talk. You treat woman like dog. You take my money and treat me like servant!"

Her face was flushed and twisted with rage. There was nothing I could say to calm her down. I'd seen her like this before. I looked around the roof to see the faces of some very stoned sunset watchers who were wondering what my next move would be. That's when I made the mistake of turning my back on Adriana. Not a smart thing to do. Before I knew it, she jumped on my back and started beating me on the head and shoulders with both fists.

I spun her off me and grabbed her hands. She started kicking. I tripped her to the ground and got on top of her long enough to subdue her. People watched in horror, but no one intervened. They could see I was only acting in self-defense. I wasn't hurting her.

"Adriana! Stop it! This is crazy. I'm here with you now."

"You left me," she shrieked. "You're going to leave me. I know it."

"No, no, I'm not going anywhere," I said as I let her go.

She looked at me and began to shake. Her tantrum dissolved into tears. I helped her up. She let me hug her. The sun had just slipped below the horizon, but it was still lighting up the Red Fort like a neon sign. "Look at the Red Fort," I calmed her. "That's where I went today. It was amazing. I'm sorry if I made you worry. Maybe tomorrow we can go there together."

We stood in silence for a long time, watching darkness descend on Delhi. Millions of lights began glowing from the city to outshine all the stars in the cloudless night. The city was shimmering. Adriana gradually returned to her sane self. She was quick to anger but equally quick to forgive and move on. She had a little money left so we went out to dinner at a cafeteria-style restaurant. We didn't talk much. I told her I'd have money once we got to Bombay. She said she was sorry for getting so upset about our financial situation. She knew what was going on even though she wasn't ready to admit it to herself. That's why she got so mad on the roof. She knew I was getting ready to leave her before I knew it myself.

Her money came in on our third day at the Crown Hotel. We celebrated by buying food and wine and water and cigarettes at the market and sponsored a sunset party on the roof. Our fellow travelers were surprised but pleased to see that our relationship had recovered from the night before. Actually, it hadn't. After the party, Adriana wanted to make love. I told her I couldn't because I was still feeling sick. She knew that was more of an excuse than a real reason. Everybody on the road in India was at least a little sick all the time. Adriana was not used to being turned down sexually.

Some switch had clicked in the back of my mind. I was mad at her for blaming me about the turquoise. I was mad at her for being so controlling. But what I was really mad about was my total dependence on her financially. And she wouldn't let it go.

"Why don't you get money from the Air Force?" she asked on our fourth day at the Crown. "I'm still getting money from my father's military, and he's been dead for a long time."

"Let me try to explain something to you, Adriana," I said slowly. "At this very moment, thousands of tons of bombs are being dropped on innocent people by the United States Air Force. I wouldn't take money from the Air Force if I were dying of hunger, which I damn near am. Thousands of young American men got drafted and sent to Vietnam to kill people. They burned villages and blew up tunnel systems and went out on ambush patrol while I was sitting in a college classroom." I was getting angrier by the second. "I've already taken too much money from the military. It's blood money and I won't take any more. In fact, I'm going to repay what they gave me."

She had no response to my angry summation. We didn't talk to each other much the rest of the next day. Traveling was beginning to feel less and less like an adventure and more and more like running away from what I knew I had to do. It was time for me to get back on my own and do what I could to end the war, or at least my personal involvement with the military.

The next evening, the social scene at the Crown was hopping. The sunset party on the roof was livelier than ever. A couple good guitar players were playing and singing wonderfully together. The wine was flowing, and the hash was smoking. At the height of getting loaded, Adriana said, "Tonight we make love, yes?"

I agreed, but when it came time to go to bed, I turned her down again and tried to go to sleep. I felt no affection for her. I was mad at her. She was turning out to be even more strong-willed than me. I was punishing her for making me feel inadequate. I was being an idiot. She deserved better, but I couldn't give it to her. The last thing I heard her say somberly before I fell asleep was, "You no love me anymore."

At dawn, I awoke to see her holding a dagger in her hands, staring at me with a murderous look in her eyes. It was frightening. Even worse, during the night she had painted a giant set of blue eyes on the wall. They looked like a monster sticking its head into the room. By the early morning light, I read the Spanish word for blue, *azul*, painted in large letters beneath the eyes.

The scene was straight out of a horror movie. She had blue paint all over her face and hands. Tears had streaked her face. How had I slept through all this? She obviously had not slept at all. The wall was the most frightening expression of "Hell hath no fury" I had ever seen. Was I dreaming?

No, I most certainly was not. She started pointing the dagger at me in a thrusting, threatening motion and then raised it over her head to stab me. I did not wait for her to cut out my heart. I grabbed her knife hand with my left hand and choked her neck with my other hand. It was instinctive self-preservation. She was screaming in Spanish. I rolled her onto the floor and banged her hand on the wood hard enough to make her let go of the knife. She didn't put up much of a fight. She looked at me with dull surprise and sad confusion. I had never seen the look she gave me. It was pure madness. I waited for her to start crying. Instead, she began to laugh.

"Look at you, afraid of a woman. What a big strong man. You took knife away from a broken-hearted woman. Why don't you pick it up and stab me with it? Go ahead. Stab me right through the heart like you did last night."

That was it for me. I was done talking to her. She had slipped into full crazy sometime during the night. I threw the knife hard into the corner of the room. It stuck and quivered in the wall just above the floor. I got dressed quickly and threw everything I had into my pack. It didn't take long. By this point in the journey, I was down to two changes of clothes, four pair of colored underwear, a sleeping bag, a tent, a machete, a black leather jacket, a toilet kit, and some writing materials. My passport and orders were in my shoulder bag, as was the turquoise. I didn't look at her directly, but I kept a watch on her out of the corner of my eye.

It occurred to me she could have cut my throat before I woke up. Small consolation to think she must have awakened me so I would have a fighting chance. Maybe she only wanted to shock me so I would see how deeply I had hurt her.

I didn't even say goodbye. She was crying by the time I walked out the door and down the stairs to the already crowded street below. Twenty yards into the pedestrian chaos, I stopped and turned around. I could feel her watching me. I looked up. There she was, standing on a balcony outside the hall on the fourth floor. She was wearing a see-through nightgown. The wind pressed it into every contour of her lovely body. She looked like the carving of a goddess on the bow of a mighty warship. Her hair was a mess but still beautiful in a Medusa kind of way. I could see the blue streaks on her face. She waved to me like an absent-minded beauty queen, wondering where she had lost her crown.

I waved back to her sadly and turned to walk away. I knew she didn't think I would really leave her. What would I do with no money? I could feel her watching as I walked away with my pack on my back. I did not turn around.

I walked away from Adriana with the deepest feeling of sadness I had ever experienced. It felt like I was swallowing my heart. Her spell was still upon me. I had to keep walking. I couldn't turn around. One look in her eyes and I might not escape.

My mind's eye remembered her waking up on the Mykonos beach and smiling more brightly than the morning sun. I could still feel her dancing seductively in the firelight for the drunken truck driver in Iran. I wanted to go back and thank her for nursing me back to health in Pakistan. How could everything we'd been through end so suddenly and in such ugliness?

Even from thirty yards away, her spirit reached out to draw me back. Every fiber in my being wanted to turn around and try to make things right. But the road was calling more loudly and clearly than any siren's song. I kept walking. I did not turn around.

CHAPTER FOURTEEN

India

I NEVER FELT SO ALONE as walking through the crowded streets of Old Delhi, leaving Adriana standing on the balcony of the Crown Hotel. I had no money, a lingering case of dysentery, and an Argentinian lover who tried to stab me in my sleep.

All I could do was keep walking into the jostling bustle of people and carts and animals and scooters. The morning smelled like gasoline and an open sewer. I tried not to breathe through my nose. I didn't know it at the time, but I was finally headed home.

Every fifty feet or so I had to whirl around when I felt little beggar hands trying to unzip a section of my pack. It was about an hour after dawn and the kids were already working the streets for breakfast. I was hungry and thirsty but in too much emotional turmoil to think about it. I kept seeing the blue paint smeared on her tear-soaked face.

I wondered if her dramatics had been staged to make me stay or to make me leave. Probably she didn't "stage" them at all. Adriana was an emotional competitor. She wasn't a good loser. But I felt like a loser walking out on her. The woman had shown me so much about life and love and how to live spiritually with faith instead of fear. I loved her, but there was no doubt it was time to leave. We both knew it. What I had to do could only be done on my own. Even so, my head was spinning over how we could fall apart so quickly. We'd only been together for six weeks. It felt like forever.

Part of me was exhilarated at my newfound freedom. The rest of me was already beginning to wonder how I would survive. Without a dollar or a rupee to my name, I was treading water in a sea of drowning humanity, surrounded by beggars and thieves.

Many Western hippies in my position had resorted to panhandling. Never once did I seriously consider begging. That would have been too much an expression of defeat and too much a loss of faith in the road. I refused to beg or steal. My mind raced to find a *soul*ution. It didn't take long to remember, *Hey, I'm not morally opposed to borrowing.*

Walking south through Delhi, I remembered the Sarawali expedition and where they were camping. Sara and Wali were a young couple, temporarily retired teachers from Canada who had driven their van overland to India. We partied together at the Green Hotel in Kabul and they recently stopped by the Crown Hotel to check out the scene. They supported my decision to quit the Air Force and declare myself a conscientious objector. Wali had even offered to loan me money for the cause. It was clearly time to take him up on the offer.

I walked until I was engulfed in the squalid, semi-living conditions of the starving masses of Delhi. I was surrounded by the kind of poverty that will make a man sick to his stomach. There was no shelter from the storm of starvation. The lucky ones had some kind of sheet metal protection over their tiny fire pits. Eyes were bulging because faces were skin and bone. Even the babies were too thin and wrapped in rags. Mothers were shivering in hunger. Many instinctively held out their hands as they saw me staring in disbelief. I got so deep into the slums it felt like there was no way out. Everywhere I turned were makeshift tents and choking smoke and people staring at me like I might be their next meal. The injustice of it all was overwhelming. Only blocks away, people were dining in fine restaurants and changing money.

The morning sun showed me which way was east. It was blood red from the desperate dust of a million forgotten souls. I kept heading south. *Why am I the only one fleeing this scene?*

I finally got out of the human stench of the slums and found Sara and Wali at a refreshingly clean campground. They were lounging in folding chairs under a tarp, stretched out from the top of their van, having morning coffee. They looked like they might be on safari. Their site was neat and well stocked. They were both barefoot, wearing jeans and tie-dyed shirts. Wali had shoulder-length, brown hair. He wore glasses and was handsome and square-jawed. Sara was a brunette and had a sunny disposition. Her loose shirt barely concealed an athletic, sexy body. These two had great teeth and infectious smiles. They looked like they could make beautiful babies and be fine parents.

"Hey, look who the cat dragged in," Wali said as he stood up to greet me. "It's Mark, isn't it?"

"Yes, it is," I said. "Good memory. How's the Sarawali expedition going?"

"Good memory yourself," Sara said as she rose quickly from her chair like she was genuinely pleased to see me. "Hey, where's that woman you were with?"

"That's a tough topic," I said.

"Oh, oh," Wali guessed. "You just broke up and now you're on your own."

I looked at him like he'd slapped some sense into me. "How could you possibly know that?"

"Well," he began. "You look miserable and you're alone and you've got all your gear on your back. You don't have to be Sherlock Holmes to figure it out."

"Come on in, sit down, have a cup of coffee," Sara invited. "You don't have to talk about it if you don't want to. Here, I'll get some water and food too. You've got to be hungry. My guess is you're completely broke."

"What are you guys? Mind readers?" I laughed, relaxing in their hospitality.

"Don't worry," Wali said. "We'll lend you enough to get by for a while. Or you can ride with us to Nepal."

It was nice of them to take me in and not make me ask for a loan. They were pleased to have a social caller, even if I was a little down and out. They were ready to help.

"I don't really know what happened with Adriana," I said as we began breaking bread and drinking coffee. "Last night she got really weird on me and it was just time to go. I was getting a little tired of being 'married.' Plus, I've got to get back to the States and quit the Air Force before they declare me AWOL."

"How are you not AWOL already?" Wali asked.

I took a long drink from a water bottle before answering. "When I graduated, the Air Force gave me eight months leave before I had to report to jet school for pilot training. I took off hitchhiking and here I am. I'm not due to report until early February."

"That gives you plenty of time to do Nepal with us," Sara said.

"No," I answered slowly. "I always thought I wanted to go there, but now all I really want to do is get home and get on with it."

Sara handed me a chunk of cheese. "What happens if they throw you in jail? You could always go to Canada."

"I'm not going to run to Canada," I said. "I'm going to stand and fight the government through its own legal system. They'll have to beat me in court before they throw me in jail. Lots of conscientious objectors are winning their petitions these days. The government's case for Vietnam gets weaker every day."

"But isn't being a conscientious objector about more than just Vietnam?" Sara asked.

"Vietnam, Korea, World War II, World War I, the Civil War, the

Crusades, it's all the same," I said, trying to hide my bitterness. "Take World War II, for example. We killed millions of Germans and Japanese in the 1940s and within a decade we were buying their automobiles and drinking their beer. I could go on."

"You're preaching to the choir." Wali held up his hands in mock surrender.

"So, what happened with . . . what was her name?" Sara asked, trying to change the topic.

"Adriana," I said, wincing inside at the sound of her name.

"Yes, Adriana. What happened with you two?" Sara couldn't help but ask.

I stopped eating and drinking and looked at them both while formulating my answer. "I don't know. It was just time for me to go. She knew it, but it made her angry. She started getting crazy more often than she was sane. Last night she tried to stab me in my sleep." I paused to let my last comment sink in.

Sara's eyes widened in horror. "What? Stabbed you in your sleep?"

I waved my hands at her to bring the story down a notch. "Well, she woke me up before she used the knife. At least I think she woke me up. Something woke me up, and there she was with the knife and a giant painting of blue eyes on the wall. I had to take the knife away from her by force."

"You've got to be shitting me," Wali said.

I hung my head and shook it slowly. Telling the tale only made it more difficult to endure. "I wish I was."

"It sounds like something out of a horror film," Sara said.

I lifted my head and looked at her with tears in my eyes. "It was. It is."

Sara and Wali fell silent and looked at each other, wondering what to say.

I broke the silence. "Still, it's hard being without her. We were practically joined at the hip."

"We could tell," Sara said.

I dried my eyes and took a long drink from the water bottle. "I guess it's mostly my fault. I got tired of being so dependent on her for money."

"She was holding it over your head," Sara said, springing to my defense. "I heard her bitching about having to pay for everything way back at Cigis in Kabul. I don't know how you made it this far. She's a character, that one. A beautiful, sexy character, but I'll bet she's a lot to deal with. Don't get me wrong. I liked her. She was a lot of fun, but she was just a little too much . . ."

"The star of the show," Wali finished her thought.

"Yeah," Sara agreed. "You two were a little too much alike."

"You had to compete for air-time," Wali joked.

I had to laugh. It was funny to see Adriana and me through someone else's eyes. Evidently, we had been colorful if nothing else, constantly upstaging each other for attention.

I managed a weak smile. "I don't know. I feel kind of strange and empty without her."

"You two were good together," Sara said. "You always seemed to be having more fun than anybody else."

I straightened up, knowing Sara was right. "She's probably back at the Crown Hotel right now. Waiting for me to come back with my tail between my legs. I'll tell you right now, that's not happening. I'll walk all the way to Bombay if I have to."

"What's in Bombay?" Wali asked.

I lowered my chin and raised my eyebrows. "Hopefully a plane ticket home. I've contacted my parents and they're wiring the money there."

Sara got up and handed me a slice of bread with peanut butter on it. "Sounds like you're ready to stop wandering for a while."

I took a big bite. "Oh, man. Peanut butter. Best thing ever. Haven't had this in a few countries. Yeah. You know, I'm tired of always being broke and sick and just doing sex and drugs for a living."

"The sex and drugs for a living sounds pretty good," Wali said.

"No, that's not what I mean," I said. "It's more like I've made up my mind to go back and quit the military and now I don't need to keep traveling to convince myself what I have to do. I'm just ready to do it."

"Wowie zowie!" Sara said in amazement, and then turned to Wali. "Do you think that's what we're doing? Are we just on the move to try and decide what to do with our lives?"

"Pretty much," Wali agreed as he started loading up a hash pipe. "We've talked about heading home too. It's tough being on the road and dealing with the masses. But I've got to see the Himalayas before we head back to Canada. I was never one of those guys who thought he would find enlightenment in India. Hell, the Beatles didn't find it here. Maybe George Harrison did, but he was going to find it anyway. All I'm looking to find is the Himalayas."

I took a big drink of water to unstick the peanut butter in my mouth. "I'm just tired. I'm tired of all these people. They're everywhere, all the time, and it seems like they're all begging or hustling or plain old stealing."

Sara laughed when she saw me trying to talk through the peanut butter. "Yeah, when you're living on the street, that's what you meet. Street people."

"Here, smoke this." Wali offered the pipe. "You'll feel better."

He was right. Getting high was just what the guru ordered. The hash Wali had was good enough to make the morning roll by like a float in a Mardi Gras parade. By noon, we were opening up a bottle of wine. Wali tried to talk me into heading north with them.

"Come on, man," he urged. "You're this close to the greatest mountains in the world. It would be a shame not to finish your trip on top of the world."

"No thanks," I said. "I got enough of the top of the world on the Khyber Pass."

"So, what happened that made you want to leave?" Sara pressed for details. She was stoned and jacked-up on coffee and wine and forgetting her manners. It didn't bother me.

I told her the whole story about falling in love with Adriana and how I really wasn't ready for a wife and how she had a terrible temper. Sara and Wali listened like they were watching a soap opera on television.

"Did she really try to stab you?" Sara asked.

"I'm not really sure. I had to take the knife away from her, but I think if she'd really wanted to kill me, she could have easily slit my throat while I was asleep."

"Far out," Wali said in a whisper. "Hell hath no fury . . ."

"Like a woman scorned," Sara completed the phrase.

I hesitated before continuing but decided to get it all out. "Yeah, it got to the point where I just didn't want to make love to her anymore."

Sara and Wali waited for more, nearly holding their breath in anticipation.

"You guys know how it gets," I deflected their curiosity.

Sara looked at Wali. There was an uncomfortably long pause. He laughed to ease the silence. "We've been through some tough times," he admitted, and then added hastily, "We always work it out, though." Sara nodded.

"No, there was no working this out," I said. "She got too crazy. You should have seen the look she had when I woke up. There was murder in her eyes. To tell you the truth, she scared the crap out of me."

"I'll bet she's calmed down by now," Sara said. "I'm sure she's worried to death about you. Maybe you should go back and try to say goodbye."

I acknowledged Sara's good female instincts with a nod. "I know what you're saying. But I'm not going back. She'll find somebody at the Crown to team up with. She'll be fine. It's time for me to be on my own again."

We all decided to change the topic. Wali brought out some maps and we began studying how best to hitchhike to Bombay.

We stayed at their campsite all day, lounging in cool breezes, talking about how nothing makes much sense until about two years after it happens. "Someday," Wali waxed, "We'll look back on this afternoon and realize how meeting up in Delhi changed our lives forever." We chuckled over that comment. And then we sighed. It was a little sad that we'd rather get stoned than brave the crowds to explore the city.

There was a pretty clean toilet with a water source at the campground. A few people we'd met along the road dropped by to share stories and travel plans. No one was ready to remain in Delhi. We talked about Buddhism, Castaneda, the breakup of the Beatles, tricky Dick and his FBI henchmen, the horror of the Old Delhi slums, and where to go in India.

By the time we rolled up in sleeping bags for the night, I was feeling resolved and determined to stay on my own. Still, Adriana's voice was in my head. She was calling to me. It was terribly sad. I missed her. I offered her best wishes in a long, silent prayer as I drifted off to sleep.

I was off for Bombay on my own with fifteen borrowed Canadian dollars and a few rupees in my pocket. I hoped that one day soon I would be able to pay back the Sarawali expedition for their kindness and insight and understanding.

My first ride out of Delhi was with a peanut-eating frustrated socialist on a motor scooter. He was so busy shelling nuts and shouting political opinions over his shoulder that he didn't have much time for driving. He complained about the lack of education, which led to the increasing population problem, which led to the staggering poverty, which allowed Indira Gandhi to buy all her votes and those with money to buy off the police force. Several times he drove right off the road in his indignation. He was the first of many angry young men I would talk to in India. Unfortunately, there were no foot pedals for a rider on his scooter. I was painfully reminded of my first ride on the scooter in Italy. I hung on as long as I could and then signaled the driver to let me off. I was, once again, glad to be alive when I got my feet back on the ground.

I didn't have to wait long for an English-speaking man in a small car to pick me up. The countryside of India was nothing like the city slums. It was colorful and expansive and nearly tropical. Most of what I'd heard about India involved famine and flood and disease. Much to my surprise, the driver pointed out that rural India is bountiful farmland. The fields were yellow and green and lush.

The driver let me out after a short hop, but I continued to enjoy the countryside on one short ride after another. People were eager to pick up a Western traveler, but they never seemed to be going very far.

After a few short lifts, six English hipsters in an old customized hospital truck took me all the way to Agra, home of the Taj Mahal. My hosts obviously hadn't been traveling long, as the road was still a big party to them. They seemed immature. For me, the road had become a deeply personal and spiritual experience. It had taught me to watch the world come and go as it pleased and to have courage and faith in where the road would lead me. It wasn't about seeing who could drink the most beer.

We arrived in Agra at sunset, just as the evening glow was turning the marble symmetry of the Taj from white to gold. The English guys left to go find a bar. I decided not to join them. The last thing I needed was a wild party. I thanked them for the lift and said goodbye. They couldn't believe a hippie from the States was saying "no thanks" to a party.

I was feeling reflective, so I took a walk and sat down by the edge of one of the long pools in front of the Taj.

My first reaction to the ancient shrine was that it wasn't very big by modern skyscraper standards. The guava-domed marble mausoleum was only about 115 feet tall. The minarets around it were slightly taller. Even so, the dome, with its four smaller domes at the corners and tall, arched doorways, made a royal first impression.

I knew the story about how it had been constructed in 1653 by a ruler mourning the death of his beloved wife. The thought behind the marvel was that even a guilty person who sought asylum here could become pardoned and freed from sin. This notion appealed to me. I felt the need for absolution. I was feeling guilty about letting myself get bribed by the military so they could teach me how to kill from the sky.

There was a calming influence about the ancient shrine. As the sun went down a little further, the Taj changed colors again, this time from gold to pink. Completely entranced by this natural light show, I made no effort to approach the gardens to gain entry. I was content to view it from a distance of fifty yards or so. It had a subtle, healing influence on me. It made me feel like everything was going to turn out all right. After thirty minutes in a quiet meditative state I realized in a sudden shift of consciousness that this wonder of the world was more human than architectural. In fact, it was more godly than human. I felt like the Taj could read my mind.

Darkness began to change the Taj's image from regal splendor to a temple of timeless mourning, shrouded in shadows of tears. The scene became highly confessional for me. I needed to talk about how lost I felt. I poured out my broken heart to the Taj. Not just about Adriana, but about all the suffering and hatred and killing in the world. And about how I felt so alone in the universe. I talked about my guilt for being part of the killing machine and for being too wrapped up in myself to care about the suffering of others. I felt tears rolling down my face as I recalled the horrors of the slums.

I was breaking down emotionally in front of some kind of spiritual mirror. I hadn't realized it until that moment, but I was desperate to get back home. I'd seen enough suffering. I'd felt enough suffering on my own. I was broken beyond wounded pride, a lost child crying for its cosmic mother.

A group of begging children passed by my location. I waved them along without making a contribution or even eye contact. Awash in self-pity, I looked up at the Taj, now nearly invisible in the darkness. I was looking for some kind of consoling message or sign.

That's when it happened. Out of the shadows enveloping the Taj, a disturbing question came to me. *How selfish can you be, wasting energy feeling sorry for yourself?*

I stood up in shock. *Had the Taj spoken to me?* It certainly felt like it. Something, or someone, told me to get up off the pity pot and get back on the road.

There was no question about it. The soul of the ancient shrine had taken me by the shoulders and tried to shake some sense into me. The Taj had become assimilated into the spirit of the road. The universe was calling.

I got down on my knees and bowed my head to the pavement in thanks. I felt cleansed and refreshed. Suddenly, I knew what I had to do. It was time for me to get back on the road.

I shouldered my pack and went looking for a place to spend the night. I felt completely rejuvenated and ready to do whatever it would take to get myself right with the world. The Taj had broken me down and built me back up in one unforgettably therapeutic session. I was back with renewed purpose. I didn't have to worry anymore. My faith had been restored.

Sure enough, as I was passing a gas station, the owner came out of his small hutch and invited me in for dinner and offered me a rope bed out back for the night. He said all this in pretty good English as though he was surprised at making the offer. "I don't know why," he said, "but I know you need to stay here tonight." He was a short, brown, bald man wearing sandals, blue pantaloons, and an open-neck shirt with at least three gold necklaces adorning his hairless chest. He squinted at me like he needed glasses, but he wasn't wearing any.

"Why, thank you so very much," I managed to say, wondering if this unexpected good fortune was some fallout from my session with the Taj Mahal.

I had been walking in the darkness just outside the dull glare of a light on a telephone pole. "Come with me," he said as he grabbed me by the arm and showed me an open-air bed out back. "Your things will be safe here," he said as I put down my pack and left it by the bed. I knew I could trust this man. The spirit of the Taj was with me.

"I have wonderful food for you," he said as he ushered me into the company of several men sitting around a fire in front of his place of business. This was not a gas station like you would find in the States. It was a small shanty along the one-lane, blacktop road to Bombay. The men around the fire wore turbans and beards and loose clothing. They seemed intimidating at first, but they welcomed me warily into their company as a guest of the owner. They were obviously truck drivers, their rigs parked at various angles along the highway.

The owner brought me a delicious cup of chai. "This is good for your soul," he said with a bow and then turned to encourage the men to feed me. One of the drivers handed me a long stick with some meat on it and a bowl of rice and beans. I joined the group in cooking the meat in the fire. It smelled like a Texas barbecue.

The food was indeed wonderful. They watched me gobble it down with some amusement. But they didn't speak much English and seemed uncertain of my company. Once we'd finished eating, there was a long pause of uncomfortable silence, almost like they were waiting for me to introduce myself. I knew I had to break the ice, so I decided to tell them about my experience with the Taj Mahal. I started off by simply saying, "Taj Mahal," and holding my hand over my heart.

To the man, they repeated, "Taj Mahal," and placed their hands over their hearts. I wasn't sure if they were mocking me or empathizing with me. My host encouraged me to continue. "Ah, so you are familiar with our temple."

I decided to tell the story of my inspirational encounter with the Great Spirit. Before I knew what I was doing, I was standing up and pantomiming the story. I held out my arms, entreating the great Taj for advice. The drivers murmured their approval. Our host applauded, obviously pleased that his guest was able to provide meaningful entertainment.

I held my head in my hands to show despair at losing my woman and being alone in a foreign land. The drivers understood the loss of a woman when I held my arms around myself and then opened them up quickly to show an untimely departure. Now I had the crowd in the palm of my hands. Every driver was with me. They shouted words of condolence and encouragement.

I called out to the sky, "Adriana!" as sparks from the fire flew into the night. It felt good to shout out her name. The drivers could feel my catharsis. I paused for dramatic effect and looked each man in the eye, one by one. Their smiles had changed to wide-eyed wonder.

I asked the Taj for help, once again holding out my arms to the fire. I stopped and listened with my hand to my ear to let the drivers know the Taj was communicating with me. Then I put my hands back over my heart to show the message that everything was going to be all right as long as I stopped feeling sorry for myself. By now, the story was telling itself. It surprised even me as the message was so clearly delivered around the fire without much benefit from the spoken word.

Finally, I held my hands over my head in triumph to show how the message from the Taj had miraculously uplifted me and led me to their particular fire ring and the owner's unusual invitation.

The drivers loved it. They loved that a Westerner was actually getting the essence of their culture and that he was including them in his epiphany. They cheered and laughed and began passing bottles of water and plates of dried fruit and olives and bread around. I ate and drank everything handed to me. I knew it wouldn't make me any sicker than I already was. The chai felt good going down and even better settling in my stomach.

It was clear they regarded me as a sign of good fortune and good fun. After my initial success in the conversation, I settled back and listened to their tales. I didn't understand much of what was said, but it was obvious they were happy to be together, and that they had allowed me at least temporary membership into their fellowship. I did understand they were Sikhs. They explained their beliefs very carefully. Sikhism, like Islam, believes in one Supreme Being, not many gods as in Hinduism. Sikhs eat meat and reject the caste system, which is probably why they were so willing to accept me. They don't believe in idols. They identified with my Taj Mahal experience more as a cultural exchange than as worshipers at a shrine. They weren't smoking hash or drinking alcohol. Sikhs oppose hedonism and the five evils: lust, wrath, greed, materialism, and egotism. Even so, this was a fun-loving bunch of guys. We laughed and sang and told stories until it was time to sleep.

I awoke to the sounds of doves and monkeys and pandas and parrots. By the light of day, I could see we were beneath a vast canopy of banyan and eucalyptus trees. The forest came alive at dawn with animal noises. I tried to keep sleeping but they were too loud.

Upon awakening, I looked around for Adriana until I remembered I was alone in the back of a Sikh truck stop. My thoughts were so clear I could hear them breaking through the trees like radio waves of light:

Something wonderful happened to me last night. I was communicating with God. I got outside myself and became part of something much greater than I could ever understand. I escaped the material world and got in tune with the universe. The spirit of the Taj Mahal put me in touch with the most unlikely allies I could ever imagine, Sikh truck drivers.

I gathered up my pack and went around to the front of the business. The owner welcomed me to the fire pit. "Good morning. I see the trees and all their little friends have you up with the sun." He had prepared a marvelous breakfast of hot cereal and chai and bananas. The bananas were small and looked to have come from the surrounding trees.

"I slept like a baby," I said. "Thank you so much. Last night was a joy. I think the Taj brought me to you. I hope you agree."

The man began a celebratory dance. "Yes, yes, yes. Agra is a place of many miracles. You are one of the many."

The faces around the fire had changed, but they were still Sikh drivers. The owner talked a couple of them into giving me a ride toward Bombay. They agreed without hesitation and looked at me like they'd heard all about me. As I piled into their truck, I realized there were four of them and me all packed into their double-sleeper cab.

Truck drivers in India were in the upper-middle financial ranks and, once I gained entry into their Sikh subculture, they took excellent care of me. Evidently word had gotten around that I was an okay guy, if not just a little crazy. I looked like one of them, in my twenties, long hair and beard and an Afghani shirt. The only thing missing for me was the turban and loose-fitting shorts. They were all quite curious about my patched jeans, which by now were nearly covered with leather and cloth patches. Adriana and Rebekah had worked on them together.

The trucks themselves were ready for the circus. They were painted bright blue and green and yellow with mirrors and bells and drawings and flags all over them. The long panel trucks made of wood always seemed to be leaning and on the verge of tipping over.

At first, I thought my new friends would resent me for taking up a sitting place on the floor of the cab. There were no hydraulic or even conventional truck seats. It was cushions on the floor, except for the driver who had a small, metal seat, which was elevated enough so he could shift gears and hit the pedals.

Almost immediately, I began earning my position as guest of honor in the cab. Since the road is only one lane wide in most spots, the truck drivers' favorite game was "chicken." As a truck approached from the opposite direction, we all began shouting and waving our arms, encouraging our driver not to back down. Here was a game I was ready to play. At this point in the journey, I was perfectly ready to go out with a very large bang if that's what the universe had in mind. My hosts appreciated my unbridled enthusiasm and Kamikaze attitude.

"You good man," the driver said with respect and a toothy grin.

"No," I said, "You are the good man." We bumped shoulders in solidarity.

On a couple occasions, at slower speeds, our truck and the oncoming truck had to screech on their brakes to stop just short of collision. Everybody from both trucks jumped out and started yelling and waving their arms. Whoever was loudest or largest got to stay on the road. My presence seemed to unnerve our opponents. They looked at this crazy hippie like they'd seen a ghost. We always returned triumphant to the truck with back-slapping congratulations as the other driver begrudgingly gave his ground.

I ended up bouncing along the highway with them for twenty-four hours, during which time they bought me four meals. The makeshift truck stops with the earthen stoves and fire pits didn't seem to be very sanitary, but I ate everything they put in front of me and drank chai, lots of it, at every stop.

My hosts were extremely friendly and loved pointing out the sights with huge, handsome grins. The black beards and colored turbans framed perfectly the thin, chiseled features of their faces. One minute we'd be rolling through an archway of big-leafed trees with twisted trunks, the next we'd break through into fertile flatlands with yellow and purple crops and people pushing carts and carrying baskets on their heads. I found it hard to believe that a famine was going on at the time. The main driver, who spoke limited English, eventually explained that the drought hadn't hit these parts.

We made terribly slow progress thanks to stopping constantly for customs checkpoints with big stacks of forms to fill out that I was quite content to not understand. My hosts complained bitterly about the paperwork, as do truck drivers everywhere.

I didn't mind the snail's pace. I had reached a new level of acceptance regarding the road. My eyes were wide open, and my mouth was mainly shut for once. I had a lot to think about. It didn't do much good to talk because of the language barrier. We didn't need conversation. We were shoulder to shoulder, watching the world come at us like a freight train. The cab didn't feel too crowded. It smelled like curry and tea and a locker room.

I did almost jump out of the truck in excitement when I saw my first elephant lumbering down the road with a guy in a red turban riding him. The scene looked exactly like a photograph in my sixth-grade geography book. Even as a child, I had marveled that such a small human could control a beast as huge as an elephant.

After the first elephant sighting, there seemed to be elephants everywhere, as though the first one had primed the elephant pump. My hosts were delighted that I got such a huge kick out of the massive beasts.

Once darkness fell, the truckers insisted on giving me the best bunk, a wooden crate over the cab with some padding on the floor. As I drifted off to sleep, it occurred to me that my stomach was feeling much, much better. In fact, the last time I had squatted to take a crap, my stools had been semi-solid. It had been a long time since anything but liquid came out.

Besides a couple bumps in the road that nearly bounced me out of the sleeper, I was riding high that night. I even thought about hooking up with Peter in Bombay and maybe using money from home to catch a boat all the way to Vietnam. After all the news coverage, it might be a good idea to see the place causing all the commotion. That notion faded quickly, before I'd even nodded off to sleep.

My hosts let me off at one of the checkpoints, informing the guard in Hindi that they were leaving the road to Bombay and that I was their friend and needed a ride. We embraced like the road brothers we had become. The guard took me right into his little hut and whipped up an excellent cup of chai. The tea thing blew my mind. Everybody drank tea every chance they got. Tea for breakfast, tea break in the morning, tea for lunch and then big deal tea during the middle of the afternoon, obviously a British thing. By now, I was sure it was the tea and milk and sugar that were slowly curing my tortured intestinal tract.

In the time it took to consume two cups of chai, the guard had secured a ride for me. Little did I know I was getting into a truck being driven by the greatest truck driver in the world.

The first thing I noticed about the driver was that he was alone. Every other truck I'd seen had at least three people in the cab. I could tell right away he was happy to have company and ready to show me what he could do with his truck. He took off quite quickly but smoothly and ran through the gears cleanly and effortlessly as he brought us to full speed in a short span of time. He turned to me and smiled slyly. I applauded with both hands like he had just played a bass solo in a jazz band. He nodded happily, pleased I understood fine driving. It didn't take long to realize that nobody I'd ever ridden with, from San Francisco to Kabul, could handle a big truck like this driver.

"What is your name?" I asked after our first hour together.

"My name?" he asked like he was surprised I cared.

I nodded and explained, "My name is Mark," hoping he would understand I was simply being friendly.

"Oh," he nodded in understanding. "My name is Ravindar. It means god of sun." He checked my reaction and then said with a chuckle, "You can call me Ravi."

I held up my arms. "Like Ravi Shankar!"

"Yes, but no sitar for me. I have this as my instrument." He ran his hands around the steering wheel.

"You play it like a master," I said.

"Thank you, it is good to have you in my sitar," he said as he held out his right hand for a shake.

As we rolled through the Indian countryside at a breathtaking pace, I told Ravi my story. He nodded appreciatively, but it was obvious he understood little of what I had to say. He did comprehend I was on my way to Bombay to get money to fly home to the United States. He didn't talk much about himself. After our initial conversation, we spent long periods riding in silence together. I fell into the trance of his high-speed road ritual.

Ravi had a three-tone horn that he used sparingly and only at exactly the right moments. We came barreling over a hill and saw a herd of bulls in the middle of the road. I started to brace for impact. Ravi didn't flinch. He simply employed a super-smooth, double-clutching downshift and a short blast from the lowest tone of the horn. The bulls cleared a narrow path just in time and barely wide enough for us to pass through as though they were responding to some mysterious command.

"Unbelievably cool!" I exalted as he resumed speed with a knowing grin. He had a hawk nose and a prominent warrior forehead. He was a predator behind the wheel. The road was his hunting ground, even though he wasn't killing anything.

The same parting-of-the-waters magic happened when we came

upon pedestrians in the road, except he used his high tone for them. As soon as we passed through with no room to spare, the hole closed. Other drivers would have had to come to a complete stop and lay on their horn. It seemed everyone understood Ravi's high-toned horn meant he wasn't stopping for anybody.

He only used the middle tone on oncoming trucks. It was menacing, like an air horn on a ship in the fog. I never saw another truck even think about challenging him, even at slow speeds. His truck seemed to lean forward into the road with total confidence.

Ravi drove incredibly fast, hanging just right on the curve lines and gunning it in the straightaways. He was a speed demon. I caught him checking me out from the corner of his eye. "Don't worry about me," I said, pumping both fists in the air. "I'm built for speed!"

He laughed and stepped on the gas.

He must have done something to customize his engine. It growled like a Harley Davidson motorcycle and had plenty of acceleration even at top speeds. He pushed his truck like a Ferrari driver at Monte Carlo. At many points, we were airborne on the bumpy road.

The strangest thing about his driving, though, was the sudden widening of the road whenever he needed to pass a slower truck. His timing was incredible. He never got stuck behind anything and he rarely needed to slow down. Every time he needed to pass another vehicle, the road got wide enough for him to execute his maneuver. The man knew the road to Bombay. And the road knew Ravi.

When the sun set and turned the tar road golden, Ravi was headed due west for optimal viewing. He glanced over at me and laughed loudly as though he'd paid the sun for its performance.

"Nicely done." I applauded again. "This sunset must have cost you a fortune."

"This sunset is God talking to both of us." He chortled. "The world is good."

I began to think of him as my truck-driving guru. He looked

the part with his long black beard and baby-blue turban. Beneath his rugged brow, he had laughing eyes. Although he was mostly ruthless behind the wheel, I did see him slow down on several occasions so as not to alarm parents with children or elderly people with animals.

He often stopped to buy us chai and win a few rupees playing gin rummy with his fellow drivers. Everybody knew Ravi. He must have been in his late forties, but he still seemed youthful. He loved introducing me like his trophy hippie. It felt like I was riding with the king of the road.

He never wasted a gesture, casually pointing out hidden temples and monuments along the road and, sometimes, even stopping so I could get a better look. We didn't need to talk much. He chuckled deeply when I expressed delight in the multi-faceted road show.

I rode with him all day, and at nine o'clock, when I was beginning to nod, he stopped the truck and tucked me in under two blankets in a bed on top of the cab with a thick, canvas cover on top to shield me from the wind. He stopped once more, and another driver joined us. Ravi must have slept in the bunk behind the cab while his relief driver drove through the night. He woke me up in the center of Bombay.

It was as though I had floated into the bustling city on a cloud. I stretched and climbed down to gather my pack. The whole Sikh trucker phenomenon seemed like a dream. I had been snatched from despair in Agra and flown by angels to a bright new day in Bombay.

I felt like bowing as we said goodbye. Instead, we gave each other a big hug. "Good driving," said my driver somberly.

"Good driving," I said.

He got back in his truck and drove off through the crowded street, parting pedestrians with his high-tone horn. *There goes a man who knows who he is and where he's going.*

As I watched Ravi's truck disappear, I realized I was in the middle of one of the most populous cities in the world, the commercial and entertainment center of India, surrounded by high-rise buildings of glass and steel, with no idea of my exact location. Anxiety approaching fear began to well up in my throat. I took a few deep breaths and started softly chanting, "Om, Ah, Hum," as I shouldered my pack and went off in search of directions. I knew the three syllables comprised the mantra of the Buddha and that they stood for the body, speech, and mind. Beyond that, I had little knowledge of the many layers of meaning they actually convey. All I knew was the three syllables had a great calming influence whenever I repeated them while breathing deeply. I was beginning to get it together when I found a shop that offered the "Tourist Map of Bombay," free for the taking.

I sat down on the marble seat of a large pool of water with a fountain and opened up the map. This was an unusual event for me since I had come to consider maps as unnecessary contrivances. But in this big city, I needed the map. It showed me Bombay was a peninsula on the West Side of India, surrounded by the Arabian Sea and something called Back Bay. I knew I was near Mahatma Gandhi Road so all I had to do was take it south to get to the water and the Taj Mahal Hotel. I was anxious to finally get to the sea after so long on desert and mountain roads. Also, I figured the American Express office wouldn't be far from the famous hotel. I was excited to pick up my money from home and get a decent meal and a room.

I walked past a large cricket field and stopped to watch a game in progress. Without an understanding of the rules, the sport had little entertainment value. It did remind me, however, that the British East India Company had been working Bombay since the seventeenth century. I kept walking and passed the Yacht Club and several other civilized watering holes I couldn't afford to enter.

The Taj Mahal Hotel was stunning in its size and majesty and seaside location. It was much bigger than the temple in Agra but had none of the spiritual magic of the original shrine. In fact, it was a depressing symbol of opulence in the face of mass poverty. I sat down at the water's edge next to the Gateway of India arch to smell the saltwater. It smelled like dead fish. The dock was clean but trash and chemical trails floated in the water. The party beaches of Goa were a long way away.

It didn't take long to find the American Express office. I knew I'd be in trouble if my money wasn't there.

Sure enough, it wasn't there.

The clerk had no sympathy for my dilemma. Fortunately, I had enough money to send a telegram home, which basically said, "Hello, I'm dying in Bombay. Please send money fast!"

I had to pull myself together in order to survive. I didn't know a soul in Bombay. It was so much bigger than I had imagined. Finding Peter in this mass of humanity would take a miracle.

I spent the rest of the day looking for a place to spend the night. Unfortunately, the parks were extremely well patrolled since homelessness was obviously a growing concern. I finally found a back street, which several fellow travelers and a few locals were calling home.

My first night sleeping on the street in Bombay was a nightmare. I knew theft would be a problem, so I slept with my shoulder bag under my head and draped one leg and an arm over my pack. Those precautions turned out to be no deterrent whatsoever. Every time I drifted off to sleep, somebody was trying to pull my pack out from under me. They were pretty stealthy about it. They only moved the pack a millimeter at a time and they took their time. Even so, I could always feel my gear slipping away. I got angrier every time I had to fend off another thief. Finally, I landed a punch on the jaw of one creepy crawler. He laughed it off as he scampered into the night.

This was clearly a game I would not be winning. I was outnumbered, twenty to one. I gave up trying to sleep and spent the rest of the night walking around the docks. By morning, I was so tired I spent most of what little money I had on a sleeping room at a flophouse called the Rex Hotel. Actually, it was more like a sleeping closet, large enough for a single mattress on a wooden shelf. At least the door to the closet had a lock so I could store my pack with some small hope of security. My shoulder bag with my passport never left my side.

I slept most of the day. By the time I hit the street around 4 p.m., I was hungry and had three rupees to my name. That would not be enough to survive until my money came in, if it ever did. No, I would have to make other arrangements for eating. Maybe become a street vendor. But what could I sell?

Back at the sleeping closet, I realized I had four pairs of yellow and blue underwear, reflector sunglasses, and, of course, the turquoise. That was more than enough to get me by for a while.

Hawking goods in the streets of Bombay is as tough as trying to sleep in the street. Even the children are con artists. I wasn't the only Westerner out of money and in the streets by a long shot. Lots of transient beach people, junkies, and hard luck cases were begging right along with the Indian professional beggars. Every ten feet a money-changer was hassling me, a beggar pawing at me, or just some panhandling freak trying to sound like a street barker.

Trying to sell anything in the street was more than challenging. Crowds of pushy people could make your merchandise disappear in a hurry. I decided before I got started to only try to sell one item at a time and to keep that one item in my hand. Of course, I had no trouble attracting would-be buyers. Everybody was interested in the crazy dancing hippie, chanting like an American Indian, swinging the underwear over his head like it was the next best thing to nudity, which it was.

It took nearly an hour, but my first sale was enough to keep me in bananas and chai for the night.

That night at the Rex was lonely. The Westerners holed up there kept to themselves. I wrote in my journal and wished I had a midnight snack or maybe a nice cold beer or even a small spliff. I went to bed hungry, both physically and emotionally.

The next morning, I was at the American Express office bright and early. Nothing had arrived for me except a notice that my father had received the telegram and money was on the way. I spent another hectic day on the street and sold another pair of underwear, my sunglasses, and a couple pieces of turquoise at below clearance sale prices. I bought myself a decent meal and a couple beers.

My third day at the Rex was the same routine. Go to American Express, find no money there, and spend the rest of the day trying to survive in the streets. I sold my last pair of colored underwear and went into a corner café to have a snack and some tea. Things were looking grim. Even the cool breeze blowing through the open windows couldn't cheer me. I stared out onto the street, wondering how long I could live like this.

That's when I saw a sight I didn't at first believe could be possible. I blinked and then realized it was true. There in the window, staring back at me, was none other than my old road brother, Peter.

"Peter!" I jumped out of my seat. "Can it really be you?"

Peter was as surprised to see me as I was to see him. He came running into the café and threw his arms around me, lifting me completely off my feet. "Hey, man, do you know where this bus is going?" He laughed, repeating the first thing he ever said to me in the bus on Mykonos.

"This bus is going nowhere." I laughed in pure joy. "I'm waiting for money to come in so I can fly home. I hope you've got some cash."

Peter roared, "I've got cash and, better yet, I've got hash!" He quickly quieted down when he realized the entire café was monitoring our boisterous reunion.

"Where's Adriana?" he asked.

I told him the whole story. He shook his head as he listened carefully. "I hate to say it," he said, "but I knew you were going to have to find out the hard way about her."

"It was the hard way that got me into trouble in the first place," I said. "Why didn't you try to talk me out of that whole scene?"

Peter put his elbows on the table and rested his head on folded hands. He sniffled and wiggled his nose. "There was no talking to you. You fell for that woman like an anchor off a ship. Besides, I could see you two were right for each other. You had a great time, yes? So what if it didn't last? Nothing lasts on the road, does it?"

I grabbed him by both forearms. "Oh, man, it is so great to see you. I figured you'd be in Tibet by now."

Peter hailed a waiter and ordered two beers before responding. "No, I traveled with the Germans all the way to Agra and then I've been working my way down here for a week. The rides are short but not much waiting. I'm headed for Goa. All I need is a beach and a little tent and I'll be happy for a while. Why don't you come with me?"

I frowned, shook my head and changed the subject. "Did you do Delhi?"

"No," Peter answered. "We were told to avoid that place, so we camped outside the city for a couple days."

"You were smart," I said. "The Crown Hotel was a pretty cool scene, but it was completely surrounded by death and starvation."

Peter sighed and returned to Adriana. "So, you left her standing on the balcony of the Crown Hotel? I'll bet she was surprised that you'd really leave her."

"I don't know, man. She got pretty crazy." The beers arrived and we toasted each other.

"She was crazy to start with," Peter said.

"Well, so was I."

"Me too," Peter agreed as we laughed together. It felt great to laugh with Peter. He still had the biggest guffaw I'd ever heard. Getting to-gether again was like we'd never been apart. Nothing had changed.

We talked about Rebekah and how neither one of us had seen her. He bought me a big lunch and several beers. Then we went to the Rex and he rolled one of his patented nine-paper spliffs.

"You know," he mused. "A week ago, I stopped smoking dope for two days and after that I got so stoned you wouldn't believe it. It's really good to stop once in a while."

"This is my first in a few days," I said.

"Oh, boy," he said. "You'd better be careful. You're going to catch a buzz like you won't believe. This is good Afghani hash. Government seal and all."

He was right. Halfway through his monster spliff, I had to wave off on a hit. He laughed and kept smoking. "See what I told you? This is great shit, huh?"

Bombay turned out to be a lot more fun once Peter was around. We explored the city and the harbor like two schoolboys playing hooky. We were both happy to have each other's company. Everything seemed hilariously funny because we were completely stoned. We ended up reuniting with several fellow travelers and having mini reunions on the docks and in the parks.

The next morning, my money arrived. Peter wasn't as happy as me to see it because he knew it meant I would be leaving soon. He tried to talk me into going to Goa with him.

"You've got some time, don't you? You don't have to quit until January, right? So why not hit the beach for a while? It'll be packed with beautiful women from all over the world."

"Don't take it personally, Peter," I explained. "It's just way past time for me to head home. "I'm really tired of all these people and being on the move all the time. And the last thing I need is another woman."

"I hear you there," Peter said as he realized there was no talking me into Goa.

Buying a plane ticket wasn't easy. I could only afford a charter flight and they were mostly filled because of the Christmas season. After bouncing from one impersonal travel agency to the next, I finally found my man. He was a topflight hustler, dealing in everything from plane tickets to hashish to World Health Organization cards with the shot record all pre-stamped.

I took a chance that he wouldn't hustle me and kept a close eye on my receipts. He had jet-black hair and a long, thin nose that looked like it had been broken several times. He wore a suit without a tie. He had an office with a secretary. But it was the mischievous look in his eyes that made me trust him as a kind of kindred spirit. He got me a ticket all the way to Montreal.

The next day, I was on my way. Peter and I said goodbye and promised to stay in touch. "Come see me in the States," I shouted to him as I jumped in a cab headed for the airport.

"I'll be there before you know it," he yelled. "Good luck with the Air Force."

I waved at him through the back of the cab, marveling at the strange ways he had come into my life. I wondered if I would ever see him again.

At the airport, my travel man got me involved in his hustle. Just before my flight boarded, he handed me a fifty-dollar bill with these instructions, "Go to the duty free shop, buy two bottles of Chivas Regal, put them and the change in a brown paper sack and deliver it to the police officer over there by the counter."

I didn't bother trying to figure out who he was bribing or for what. I wanted to get on the plane, so I did what he told me. I half expected to be arrested when I took my seat. Only when the plane lifted off the runway did I realize I was finally going home.

CHAPTER FIFTEEN

Smith vs. the USA

THE UPHOLSTERED luxury of the jet airliner felt way too comfortable as I settled in for the flight from Bombay to London. It had been months since I'd sunk into a cushioned chair that made hissing sounds as it accepted my weight.

The flight attendant looked at me cautiously as she offered a beverage. My Afro was sticking out about a foot since I'd managed to wash my hair before the trip. I wore a clean, embroidered shirt from Afghanistan, completely patched blue jeans, and a beat-up shoulder bag. My hiking boots from Austria looked like they'd been through a war.

"And for you, sir?"

"I'd like a Bloody Mary, if you've got it."

"That would be two dollars, US," she said like she thought I might not have it. I gave her the money without comment and began slowly sipping on the cocktail. It was heavy on the vodka. That was fine with me. The mix was plain tomato juice. I didn't mind. I was remembering my last flight six months earlier when Danny and I got acquainted over a couple reckless joints. I wouldn't do that now. I must have been out of my mind.

As the vodka tickled my nostrils, it occurred to me the flight would continue on to Montreal after London. *Danny lives in Montreal*, I thought. *I could look her up. She might even be happy to see me. Of course,*

I'll have to apologize for my immature behavior in Portugal. After all, I'm a different person now. Or maybe she'll hear my voice on the phone and quickly hang up.

The plane leveled off above the clouds. I had a window seat with no one else in my row. I wondered what Adriana was doing. She was probably on the beach in Goa by now and I was probably the last thing on her mind. I could almost see her bounding naked into the surf with the little feather bracelet around her ankle. It occurred to me that the road had gotten almost mystical once I left her, as though I had to rid myself of one last emotional attachment before I could be truly free.

And what about Hanna? No doubt she was back in Finland organizing some kind of political rally, probably deeply in love with some rising-star member of the Communist Party.

What a trip it had been! The road had brought me three beautiful, headstrong women who had each turned me around in her own way. Each one had taken me under her wing for a short time and demanded emotional evolution. It was as though the universe had conspired to push me into learning how to be my own man. Each woman turned my head about sixty degrees. By now, I was going home completely turned around, 180 degrees from how I had started. Much of my fear had been replaced by a faith that the road would not steer me wrong. I no longer thought of myself as an officer in the Air Force.

I took a big sip of vodka and shuddered to think what would happen if Danny and Hanna and Adriana ever got together in the same room with me. I would have trouble getting a word in edgewise. They wouldn't be fighting over me. They'd probably get along fine and go out partying without me.

Now, here I was, lonely again. I missed them all. I missed their smell and their touch and their bitchiness and their tears and their tenderness and their toughness. I missed laughing with them and exploring new territory.

I had another drink and thought about how quickly I was flying over ground that had taken so long to hitchhike. The last six months felt like three lifetimes. I was now thirty-five pounds lighter than when I began. My worldview had completely changed. I was coming back a conscientious objector.

There had been very little violence involved in my travels. I'd hitchhiked through some of the most dangerous areas in the world and no one had attacked me. I'd hitchhiked through a civil war in Afghanistan and hitched rides with both sides. Even hitchhiking through the Iron Curtain had been pretty much a friendly experience. The only bloodshed I'd witnessed was Adriana wiping off her blade after stabbing the fool who tried to rape her in a latrine in Iran.

I carried a nineteen-inch machete the entire way and never had to use it or even draw it in self-defense. I did cut my finger on it pretty badly by using it improperly to pry up a tent stake after a rainstorm in the Alps.

No, my road to decision would not make a very good action movie. Nobody got shot or blown up. Everywhere I went, people were friendly and interested in living peaceful, happy lives. For the most part, they were eager to help a wandering stranger. It didn't hurt that I was friendly and had nothing to steal.

In my mind, I was already writing my position statement for becoming a conscientious objector.

The trip had convinced me that people everywhere want to live and love and watch the sun go down with friends. The people of the world don't want to be involved in so much as a fistfight, let alone get caught up in the horrors of war.

So, how can there be so much killing and hatred if people are mostly full of goodwill?

The answer is simple. Even good people become violent when they become frightened. The world is full of fear. Personal fears paralyze most of us into mortgaging our freedom for security.

I had to overcome a great deal of personal fear to make my journey. But then there's public fear, a fear that turns farmlands into battlefields. Leaders bent on personal conquest whip up public fear to prod the peaceful masses into violence. It's the oldest trick in the book. The Crusaders had the Infidels. Adolf Hitler had the Jews and the Russians. Joseph Stalin had his theory of Capitalistic Encirclement and America had its Red Scare. Fear is the reason the history of man is written in blood. Fear is primal. It is a survival instinct. The cavemen used the evil clan in the neighboring valley as an excuse to turn hunting parties into war parties.

Truth be known, the peaceful people of the planet outnumber the violent ones a thousand to one. It's time to stop letting an angry little minority ruin everything. Violent people should be put in jail, not given medals for heroism. We fight from fear, not courage.

Some would point to Adolf Hitler and the Third Reich as reason to go to war. The point is the peaceful people stood by and allowed Hitler to bully his way into power. The violent types have to be stopped before they can gain too much momentum. Young Adolf should have been nipped in the bud by the very people who overlooked the danger of his fear and hatred.

One reason I saw no violence on my trip was because I posed no threat to the people I encountered. I was also just plain lucky. There are killers on the road. There were plenty of "troubadours who get killed before they reach Bombay," as the Rolling Stones sang in their song, "Sympathy for the Devil." I knew a few of them myself.

But now I had a little more than $100 in my pocket and people bringing me drinks at 20,000 feet. I felt vastly wealthy. It was bittersweet relief, leaving behind a world of starvation from which millions could not hope to escape. I knew I would never forget my months of poverty or take for granted the convenience of modern life.

The plane detoured to Amsterdam due to some weather issue. The airline put us up in a hotel. I had my own room with clean sheets on a big double bed. There was a flush toilet and a shower with all the hot water I could use. It was an amazingly fresh experience. The radio was playing Dr. Hook's song, "On the Cover of the Rolling Stone." There was a television and a telephone in the room. It was amazing. In only six months on the road, I had forgotten how comfortable life feels in a modern hotel.

The next night I was back on the street in Piccadilly Circus, London. We flew into England from Amsterdam. There was a sixteen-hour delay before the flight to Montreal, so I took a taxi to explore the city. I walked the historic, civilized streets until after midnight and then rolled out my sleeping bag on some cardboard in the entrance to one of the Piccadilly shops. Why waste money on a room for only a few hours?

There were no beggars or street thieves to contend with, but it was quite a bit colder than Bombay. I put on an extra shirt and my black leather jacket and cuddled up behind my pack in my sleeping bag to drift off into what I thought would be a peaceful slumber.

Shortly after dawn, the club of an English cop rudely awakened me. He hit me hard several times in the midsection before I even knew what was happening. I scrambled out of the sleeping bag with my hands in the air, shouting, "Easy! Easy! There's no need to beat me! I'm not doing anything wrong!"

Fortunately, we spoke the same language, although it was difficult to understand the patois of an excited Bobby. Once he realized I posed no immediate threat, he told me the store I had chosen as my campsite had been burglarized that very night and that I was the number one suspect for obvious reasons.

"Wait a minute," I kept my hands up in self-defense. "I'm not your guy. I'm an American citizen and I'm flying home today."

"So why did you break in?" the Bobby said, raising his club menacingly.

"I didn't break in," I said. "Here, I can prove it. Everything I own is in this pack. Go ahead and search it. There's nothing stolen in there."

Several officers assisted in a quick search of my person and pack. Finding nothing, they had a huddle to determine my fate. I couldn't risk getting dragged down to the station and missing my flight, so I continued arguing my case. "I'm not a thief. I just flew in from Bombay. Here, look at my passport. I'm completely legal and I would never break into any place. Besides that, how did they get in? I've been here all night."

The first Bobby took my passport and finally said in a sullen tone that admitted he finally believed me, "They broke in the back window."

I lowered my hands. "I doubt if whoever broke in the back would be sleeping out front the next morning."

The Bobby shook his head. "You'd be surprised how many thieves are so drunk they can't manage to leave the scene of the crime." By now, his fellow officers had moved on to other phases of their investigation. "Go on, then," he said brusquely. "Pack up and be on your way. Sorry about the beating and all that, old boy, but you were trespassing."

"Thank you so much, officer," I said, packing up quickly, amazed at the begrudging kindness of the constable. Nothing like cops on the beat to welcome you back to modern civilization.

My plane arrived in Montreal at 5 p.m. I called Danny before I even picked up my pack at baggage claim. Her mother answered the phone and handed me over to Danny, who sounded delighted to hear from me. "Where are you?" she asked in an excited tone.

"I'm at the Montreal Airport, heading for baggage claim."

"Oh, my God!" she shrieked. "I thought you'd be dead by now! Don't go anywhere. Wait for me outside baggage claim. I'll be there in ten minutes."

I had just walked out the door of the terminal when she pulled up in a new compact car, honked the horn, and came to a screeching stop. She jumped out and rushed into my arms before I had a chance to put down the pack. I held her tight for a moment and smelled her salon-styled hair. The flowery fragrance took me right back to the beach at Estoril. She pulled back to look at me and then kissed me hard on the lips. She tasted like French menthol cigarettes and peppermint.

"I'm so glad you called," she said, backing up, a little embarrassed about being so animated. "I've been thinking about you a lot and worrying about you and wondering if you ever made it through the Iron Curtain and hoping you would forgive me for being such a bitch."

"Danny, Danny." I waved off her apology. "All I remember is the great time we had together. Look at you." She had put on at least twenty pounds since I last saw her. If anything, it made her look even more voluptuous. "You're even more beautiful than I remember. And you look a lot less stressed."

"I am. I am," she bubbled. "I got rid of the men in my life and moved in with my parents and got a less stressful job. But look at *you!*" She paused to look me up and down. "Your hair and beard are so long. And you've lost so much weight. You're too skinny. Come on. Get in the car. My mother's a great cook. She's expecting you for dinner. I warned her you're a hardcore road hippie. I think she and Daddy can handle it. Wait 'til they see you. You're even wilder than I remember!"

I outlined my hitchhike to Bombay as she drove to her parents' three-bedroom apartment. She was amazed I'd made it as far as I did on so little money. Her mother met us at the door in her cooking apron as her father turned off the television to get up and greet me. The two of them couldn't help themselves. They stared at me like I was from outer space.

"Mother," Danny said, "I'd like you to meet Mark. Daddy, this is Mark, the young man I met in Portugal."

I held out my hand and smiled warmly. "I'm pleased to meet you. Thank you for inviting me into your home."

They seemed vastly relieved that I was at least well-mannered and friendly. Seeing the shocked look on their faces, however, made me realize how much my appearance had changed while on the road. I looked like the kind of person you give a little extra room on the sidewalk.

Danny's father was quick to recover and determined to be hospitable. "What can I get you to drink?" he asked.

"I was hoping you might have a cold Molson in the fridge," I said, making reference to the famous Canadian brewery founded in Montreal.

Danny and her parents laughed heartily. The ice had been broken. "I like a man who knows what he wants and where to come get it," her father said as he fetched a round of Molson from the fridge. He was a union man in his early fifties and eager to hear stories from the strange young man his daughter obviously trusted. Although their native language was French, both her mother and father spoke excellent English. They laughed at my tales of the English Bobbies in London and the street thieves in Bombay. We were really having fun by the time Danny's mother sat us down to a roast beef feast, the likes of which I hadn't seen in a long, long time.

It was good to see Danny happy and relaxed in her parents' home. She was a gracious hostess and waited until dessert to ask the big question. "So, are you still going to quit the Air Force?"

"Absolutely," I said without hesitation. "That's the reason I'm coming back."

Her father pounded the table in appreciation. "Good for you! It's about time you crazy Americans stopped that senseless war. I wish you nothing but the best. I hope there's more like you." He raised his wine glass in a toast to world peace.

"Now, dear," his wife scolded. "We don't want to say all Americans are crazy." She was a fun-loving copy of Danny with a few more pounds and wrinkles. It was easy to see how Danny came by her sense of humor and adventure.

"No, no," I said. "I don't take offense at all. I'm right there with you."

We all clinked our glasses again.

Dinner lasted until 11 p.m. I told one story after another as they kept encouraging me and refilling our wine glasses. Her father had a few stories of his own from World War II. He'd seen enough senseless violence to turn him into a bona fide peacenik. As I was telling the story about hitchhiking through the Iron Curtain, Danny's father asked to see my orders from the Air Force. I retrieved them from my shoulder bag. He examined them carefully and shook his head slowly. After some thought, he said, "I'll say this, you don't look anything like any officer I ever served under. You are a good man to stand up against all this. I wish you well."

Shortly after that, her parents said goodnight and went off to bed, leaving the dishes to Danny and me. There was no dishwasher, so I washed while she dried and put away. As the last wine glass went on the shelf, she turned to me and said, "You know you are still my guru."

I took her into my arms and kissed her, softly at first, then more passionately. Her lips were hungry and full. She seemed much sweeter and gentler than I remembered. Our angry words and nasty breakup in Spain had all been forgiven. She was not shy about wanting to reunite. Our tongues danced together as she slid her hand into my pants. "You're not wearing underwear," she said in soft surprise.

I sucked her neck in a kiss of sudden arousal. "I had to sell them in Bombay."

"That's a story I don't need to hear." She laughed as she guided me into her bedroom and pushed me down backwards onto her large fluffy bed. The girl was ready.

"What about your parents?"

She helped pull the shirt over my head. "They can't hear a thing. Their room is on the other side of the kitchen."

We made love hungrily, each of us grateful to be back in the other's arms. She was athletic to the point of being acrobatic. I did my best to keep up with her. Her moaning became much too loud, considering her parents were in the same apartment. At some point, the light from the kitchen went out and we were in total darkness. "Don't stop," she cried as I reached the point of no turning back. I could feel her nails on my back and her hips convulsing as I exploded inside her.

We rolled together in the slippery sweat of ecstasy until we had to rest and become two separate people again.

"Did you see that?" Danny asked once we were both basking in afterglow.

"I saw the whole thing."

"No, did you see the light go out?"

"The light from the kitchen?"

"Yeah, didn't you notice it got completely dark all of a sudden?"

"I guess I did, but I didn't think about it." And then I realized what had happened. "Oh, no, are you telling me your mother shut the bedroom door while we were going at it like dogs in heat?"

"That's what I'm saying." Danny laughed.

She thought it amusing. I was mortified.

I sat up in bed. "Are you sure it wasn't your father?"

"Positive." She giggled. "He would have slammed the door."

"Oh, my God, I am embarrassed now. Your poor mother."

"She'll just be a little jealous," Danny said. "She's not that old. We talk about sex."

I fell back on the pillow. "I feel bad. Here your dear mother cooks us a feast and wines and dines me and then has to shut the door on us because we're howling in the night like two cats on a fence."

Danny giggled again and rolled over on top of me. "I just wonder how long she was watching."

"Don't say that!"

Danny couldn't stop laughing. She found it hilarious that I was embarrassed about her mother. I couldn't help but laugh along with her.

"Do you remember our first time on the balcony in Estoril?" she asked like she was slipping into a dream.

"How could I forget?"

She kissed my ear and whispered. "That was the first time I ever made love on the first date."

"That was more than a first date."

"What was it?"

I grabbed her arms and pushed her up so I could look at her. "It was a date with destiny."

She thought about that for a moment and then asked, "Do you think we came together for a reason?"

"I don't know about a reason," I answered. "I'd say we both just got lucky."

"Lucky like right now?"

"Lucky is always right now."

We talked late into the night. Basically, we kissed and made up for all the drama in Portugal and Spain. "You know I haven't been with a man since you left," she said.

I looked her in the eye and smiled. "Danny, that is a sweet thing to say, but you know I don't believe you."

She rocked her head back and forth on her shoulders. "Well, there was that one guy on the beach, but that doesn't really count."

"Why not?"

She put her hands on her head. "He was so rough it felt like he was beating me up."

We laughed a little, then talked some more and finally fell into a satisfied sleep. When we awoke the next morning, her parents were already gone. "I would have loved to say goodbye to your parents," I mused. "But I wouldn't know how to act after last night."

"Don't worry," Danny said. "We're mostly French. It's different here than in the Bible Belt."

"What do you know about the Bible Belt?"

"I read *Time Magazine,*" she said with a sophisticated shake of her head. We laughed.

It was fun to be with her again. We made breakfast for each other and drank several cups of coffee. She didn't have to work until 11 a.m. so she drove me to the highway. She knew I was eager to get back home, so she didn't beg me to stay. She was pleased I had come to visit. We promised to stay in close touch. I invited her to Indiana to meet my family.

When she at last pulled the car over to the side of the road, she said, "Last time I tried to drop you off we were surrounded by Spanish soldiers pointing guns at us."

"Thank heaven we're in Canada!" I said as I got out of the car.

"You were brave that night," she said.

I pulled my pack out of the back seat and shut the car door. "I was scared shitless."

"You fooled me," she said and then blew me a kiss goodbye. We both knew a quick farewell would be best.

As I watched Danny's car disappear down the road, it occurred to me I hadn't thanked her for helping me make my decision to quit the military. I resolved to write her a letter.

Two days later, I was walking down Sunset Drive in Fort Wayne, Indiana, toward my childhood home. My sister, Terri, was coming out of the driveway in the family station wagon. She stopped and jumped out to greet me. Terri was twenty years old, almost six feet tall, and even more beautiful than I remembered.

"Mark. It's really you!" she shouted joyously as we embraced. "I can't believe it. You're home!"

"Did you ever think I wouldn't make it?"

"Well," she started off uncertainly, and then corrected herself. "No, I always knew you'd be back." She gave me another quick hug. "I'll be right back. I've got to do one quick thing and I'll be right back. What a surprise! Everybody's home. You're gonna blow their minds when you walk in. You look like you just got off the commune. You look great!"

And off she went.

Sunset Drive was a neighborhood of doctors, lawyers, and insurance execs. The homes were two stories tall and spacious, mostly thirty years old. They were built close together in a platted addition with curving streets near a park by the St. Mary's River. The Smith house was up on a small hill with a giant pine tree nearly blocking the front door and a screened sitting porch on the other side. The tree we all climbed as kids was still angling its long branches over the lawn I used to mow.

My mother screamed in delight as I walked in the back door. My sisters, Amy and Laura, 16 and 13, soon joined in an excited group hug. My father came into the kitchen with a big laugh and we had an instant family reunion. We had always had a good time together, whether at home or on extended family vacations to Florida or Colorado or New Jersey. I felt vastly relieved to be home again. There had been many times on the road when I thought this moment would never happen.

It was Sunday afternoon and a conservative couple from church was in the front room visiting. They took one look at me and left in a polite hurry.

"Your hair and beard got long," Amy said. At sixteen, she was a blond beauty and a hippie in training.

"Do you think I need a trim?"

"No, it's cool!"

"What was India like?" Laura asked. She was skinny, blond, cute, and curious.

"It was beautiful," I answered her. "Nothing like you learned in school. It's a big beautiful country."

Terri rushed in from cutting her errand short and created another family hug.

"You're going to be quite the social lion, son," my father said. "Your articles in the paper are causing quite a stir. In fact, people at church were talking about the one in today's paper. It's the one about Turkey."

"We've been so worried about you," my mother said as she hugged me again. "You have no idea how many nights I couldn't sleep, worrying that you might be injured and lying in a ditch somewhere in wherever you were."

Everybody laughed because the "lying in a ditch" line was the one she always used when any of us came home late.

It was great to be home. As the six of us sat down to dinner that afternoon at the round table in the dining room, I realized how fortunate I had been growing up in such a loving environment. "Do you realize how good we have it?" I asked my sisters.

"Listen to your brother," Mom said. "Now he knows how lucky we are. Listen, so next time you start complaining you won't complain."

"Mom," Terri said. "That doesn't make sense."

"You know what I mean," Mom retorted as we all laughed. The family dinner table had always been a center of good food and fun for the Smith kids and all their friends. It had also been the forum for many a heated debate on the Vietnam War and all the cultural upheaval of the 1960s.

My father eventually turned the conversation into a more serious direction. "I understand from your letters that you are planning to resign your commission in the Air Force."

I sat up straight in my chair and looked at each member of the family before answering in a serious voice. "Actually, I'm going to declare myself a conscientious objector." The table fell silent as we waited for Dad to respond. We all knew he'd been formulating his response for some time.

"You know, son," he began slowly. "I'm not saying this war in Vietnam is a good thing. In fact, a lot of us who supported it at first are now opposed to it. But that's not the point. As you know, I was an enlisted man in World War II and an officer in Korea. I know a lot about the military. The problem with your plan is this . . ."

He made us wait for it with a dramatic pause.

"You can't beat the United States military. They're too big and the law is on their side, not yours. As an attorney, I'm telling you this case you're undertaking is going to be a loser and it's going to cost you and this entire family more than it's worth."

I looked at my sisters. Laura's eyes were big. I heard Amy gulp. Terri was holding her breath. My mother looked at me. I didn't say a word. I knew Dad wasn't finished.

"You entered into a contract with the government. They paid your college tuition and you agreed to serve for six years. This case won't be about the Vietnam War. It will be about your breach of contract and you will lose in any court in the land."

"I plan to pay the federal government back every cent they ever gave me," I said without anger. "This case isn't about money. It's about morality. I've just hitchhiked around the world and do you know what I learned?"

I paused for my own dramatic effect. Nobody said a word until Laura couldn't take it anymore. "What?" she asked. "What did you learn?"

We all had to chuckle at her innocence and impatience. "I learned that the whole world thinks we are killing innocent people for no good reason. In fact, I met some of those innocent people and there is no way I'm going to drop bombs on them."

"Will they throw you in jail?" Amy asked anxiously.

"No, they won't because I'm going to win my case."

"Will you defend him?" Terri asked Dad.

He looked at me and said sadly, "I wouldn't represent you if you weren't my son."

He meant, first, that being my father might keep him away from the case. Representing a close family member can be difficult because it's hard to maintain a professional objectivity. Second, he was saying that even if I were a regular, prospective client, he wouldn't take the case because it was such a loser.

"Max," my mother said, "you've got to help him."

I put my hand on my mother's shoulder to reassure her. "No, Mom, he doesn't. I've got to fight this battle on my own. Dad and I have to agree to disagree on this one."

Everybody looked at Dad for his response. "That we can do," he said magnanimously. "We can agree to disagree, for now."

The entire family breathed a sigh of relief. The argument had been tabled, put off for another time. Dad had taught us all how to agree to disagree. He'd tried many cases with good attorney friends representing the other side.

"So, let's open up a bottle of wine," he said. "Let's not spoil your coming home party with politics. I'm ready to hear some stories. I'll bet your sisters have a couple to tell as well. I might have one or two myself, and I know your mother has a lot to tell you."

That was by no means the end of my father trying to talk me out of my position. Even so, he always said he respected me for standing up for my beliefs. Unfortunately, the United States Air Force and many self-proclaimed patriots in my home city weren't so open-minded. News of my decision spread quickly and every day somebody in the family was confronted about my lack of courage and patriotism.

Shortly after my return, *The Fort Wayne Journal-Gazette* gave me an entry-level job as a reporter, which meant I began my journalistic career as the Death Editor, writing obituaries. It was exciting, working in the newsroom and seeing what you wrote appear in the paper the next morning.

In January 1973, I headed off to Grissom Air Force Base in Peru, Indiana, to declare myself a conscientious objector.

I was driving my father's 1968 Buick Riviera. It was a big white boat of a car with a huge engine and a top speed of 130 miles per hour. I was passing cars and trucks on the two-lane highway like a fighter pilot in a dogfight. Nothing beats the thrill of speed when you want to forget your troubles. Now that the moment of truth was upon me, I was nervous and apprehensive.

There was no rush to get there. I had no appointment. In fact, I had no idea what to do once I arrived on base. All I knew was there would be no turning back from this afternoon. All my dreams of flying jet planes were going to crash and burn. There would be no heroic climbing into the cockpit for me. There would be no high-speed acrobatics, no fighting of G forces. I had wanted to fly since seeing my first jet plane at the age of seven. The Air Force theme song kept running through my head.

Off we go into the wild blue yonder,
Climbing high into the sun;
Here they come zooming to meet our thunder,
At 'em boys, Give 'er the gun! (Give 'er the gun now!)
Down we dive, spouting our flame from under,
Off with one helluva roar!
We live in fame or go down in flame.
Hey! Nothing'll stop the US Air Force!"

Now, it was time to declare my independence. What would I say? What would they do? Would they throw me in jail on the spot? *It's not too late to turn the car around and drive back home,* I told myself. *No, there will be no turning back.*

I was amazed that, after all I had been through, I was still having moments of self-doubt about my decision.

The guard at the security gate waved me through without asking for so much as an ID. That was odd since I didn't look at all like military personnel. I had shaved off my beard, but my hair was still way too long to be regulation. I was wearing my black leather jacket.

I drove around and followed the signs until I got to what looked to be headquarters. I parked the car in a nearly empty parking lot and walked through the unlocked glass doors. No one was there to greet me. The facility was not guarded. I wandered down the hall to where an officer was sitting behind a desk. He watched me coming and waited for me to identify myself as I stood in front of him.

I couldn't help but come to attention. "I'm Second Lieutenant Mark Paul Smith, and I'm here to declare myself a conscientious objector."

It took a while for my words to sink in. I could see the officer was a first lieutenant as he sized me up. He wasn't unfriendly, but he did seem slightly amused by my presence and stated purpose. He looked over the desk at my shoes. I was wearing my hiking boots. He looked into my eyes like he thought I might be playing some kind of Candid Camera joke on him. I didn't smile. Finally, he said, "I don't believe you. I don't believe you're a second lieutenant."

Without saying a word, I handed him my orders. He read them carefully, then looked back at me and said suspiciously, "I don't believe you're Mark Paul Smith."

I handed him my Indiana driver's license, which he examined closely. As he handed it back, he said, "Are you Max Smith's son?"

"Yes, I am. How would you guess that?"

"I know Max. I'm an attorney myself in Fort Wayne. I'm in the reserves. And I know you from your articles in the newspaper. You've had one helluva trip."

I relaxed in surprise that he knew who I was. "Yes, it was an amazing time, but I'm glad to be back home again in Indiana."

He laughed briefly at my reference to the song "Back Home Again in Indiana." Then he sobered and asked, "Does your father know you're doing this?"

"Yes, he does."

"Does he approve?"

"No, he doesn't."

The officer stood up slowly. "Maybe you should listen to your father and go home and think about this. You can't just walk in and quit the United States Air Force. I don't even know how to process this kind of thing."

"No, I've thought about it too much already," I said. "This is something I'm quite determined to do."

He held out his arms like he was ready to welcome me into a private club. "You know it's not so bad being an officer. As you can see, I'm not exactly slogging through the jungle in Nam."

I could see he was really only trying to keep me from doing something he thought I would later regret. "Thank you, sir," I said. "But I really do have my mind made up about this."

Our eyes met. He studied my face. I smiled tightly. "All right," he said with a sigh. "Let me call somebody to see what to do."

I ended up driving home that day with a note to call a captain in the Judge Advocate General's Corps. I would have to complete three interviews with Air Force officers: one with the captain, who was an attorney for the government, one with a chaplain, and one with a psychiatrist.

Fortunately, I secured the services of a bright young lawyer before going to those interviews. He took my case without asking for a retainer fee. In our initial session, we talked for more than two hours about my decision and its legal consequences. He was sympathetic to my cause and pleased to get a case that didn't involve more boring corporate contracts. He acknowledged he had never done a CO case before, but I felt certain he would be up to the challenge. He did not accompany me to the officer interviews, but he prepared me well.

The interview with the attorney captain began quite formally. He was a tall thin man with a wry smile. I knew right away he was no spit-and-polish career military man. A civilian court reporter was present to record the session.

The captain began speaking formally into a tape recorder microphone. "My name is Captain John L. Tison. I have been appointed to interview you, Lieutenant Mark Paul Smith, on your application as a conscientious objector. Let the record reflect it is now 1500 hours, 22 January 1973."

He looked up at me and spoke in a more friendly voice. "Do you desire to have a civilian counsel present at your own expense?"

"No." I kept my answer short as I had been coached by my attorney.

"I have reviewed your statements on your application, and I wondered if you could briefly describe when you began to have your present views?"

"I feel like I became a conscientious objector during the first few months of my travels, which started in June. My doubts began to crystallize while traveling."

"Where did you travel?"

"California to Montreal, Lisbon to Austria, through the Iron Curtain to Hungary, back to Italy, Greece, Turkey, Iran, Afghanistan, over the Khyber Pass to Pakistan and finally to India."

"What event or thing made you become a conscientious objector?"

"Self-awareness that traveling creates."

"What did you become aware of?"

"My motivations for being in the military were flying, money, and job security. I began to think I didn't want these considerations to be my guiding force. I have seen too much suffering. The world is in a deplorable state. You go to India, they are in a famine; and here, we are eating like kings. My belief is in the brotherhood of man. Everybody should have an equal opportunity to become a human being."

"What does equal opportunity have to do with being a conscientious objector?"

"If you think everybody should have equal opportunity, you are not going to kill him."

The captain seemed to think that made perfect sense, but he couldn't agree with me on the record. He focused on my ROTC experience. "At what point did you begin to have doubt about serving in the Air Force?"

"I started thinking it was wrong during my studies in Vienna and Budapest during my junior year at DePauw University. My roommate in Vienna was a CO. What really changed me, though, was talking to the communist students in Budapest. I began to see that communism isn't the enemy. Communism is an economic model that calls for the state to own the means of production, not private owners. It's not the anti-democratic menace that demagogues like Senator Joseph McCarthy would have us believe. That means trying to stop the spread of communism in Southeast Asia is not a valid objective or reason for invading the country. You can't bomb an economic ideal back into the stone age."

"Didn't you notice when you were in Hungary that the Russians colonized that country by military force?"

"That's true," I said. "But the Eastern Bloc isn't a 'bloc' at all. The people of Hungary won't need our help to break free of Russia. They hate the Russians. So do the Chinese and the North Vietnamese."

"How do you know this?"

"I talked to these people on my hitchhike to India. I'm telling you, the whole world knows the United States war machine is the problem, not the solution."

"Well, you're certainly entitled to your own political opinions. But we're not here to talk politics. Didn't the Air Force pay for your tuition and books while you were studying abroad?"

"Yes, they did. And I intend to pay them back every cent. I could say their investment in me was a good thing if it turned out that they educated a conscientious objector. But I don't want to confuse the issue. This is a moral and ethical issue, not a financial one. I can repay the Air Force. I won't be able to take back the napalm they want me to drop."

"Have you had long-standing doubts about your military commitment?" He asked the question that had been important in court rulings on previous CO cases.

"Yes," I answered. "As I'm sure you know, my ROTC professor at DePauw has written a letter which documents the fact that I tried to quit the Air Force at the beginning of my senior year."

"But you didn't quit at that point?"

"No, they started handing out flight suits and private pilot lessons. I wanted to fly so bad I couldn't quit. I got my private pilot's license and logged about eighty solo hours in a Cessna 150. I was hooked. I was ready for jet school."

"So, you took the money and now you don't want to live up to your end of the bargain?"

"I was bribed, and it was wrong, and I want to repay the money. No amount of money could make me kill innocent civilians. The war is wrong. All wars are insane."

The captain sighed heavily. "What finally happened to make you resign your commission? Did you have a crystallizing moment?" Again, he was using key words from previous court decisions. My attorney had prepared me for these questions about "long-standing doubt" and "crystallizing moment."

Not that I needed to fabricate answers on these topics. I had agonized over my military service since I first put on a uniform. I'd paid a taunting price for wearing that uniform on campus for four years in the heat of the anti-war movement. In those days there was no way to be cool with short hair.

"I stayed with the Air Force because of the full-ride scholarship and the dream of flying jets. Even so, the evidence kept mounting that my country had gone horribly astray in Southeast Asia. In June of 1972, I graduated from college and accepted my commission. That very month, the horrific photo of a naked Vietnamese girl screaming and trying to run from her own napalm burns was seared into the worldwide consciousness."

I answered the captain's question about "crystallizing moment" by carefully telling the story of the grieving North Vietnamese man who had sobbed in my arms near the fountain in Debrecen, Hungary. "His girlfriend was a nurse in a hospital in Hanoi. She died in a US air strike. The American people didn't even know we were bombing civilians in North Vietnam," I concluded in disgust.

The captain shook his head sympathetically. He could feel me. He knew I wasn't playing games.

The interview continued halfheartedly for another twenty minutes. He had a checklist of questions. When he asked if I would have killed Hitler in order to avoid World War II, I answered, "I have been instructed not to answer any hypothetical questions."

"Oh, so you've already retained legal counsel," the captain correctly deduced.

"Don't you think that's a good idea?" I asked.

Before answering my question, the captain concluded the interview and made sure the reporter was packing up and we were off the record.

"I think it's a very good idea." The captain smiled. He was a kind man who was just trying to do his job as an attorney for the Air Force. He confided his own opposition to the Vietnam War and clued me in to the importance of doing well in my next two interviews. "Be nice to those guys, like you have been to me. The three of us are each going to write a report on you that will have tremendous impact on your case should it go to trial."

"You mean go to trial in a military court?"

"No, this case is now in administrative review. That's what the interviews are about. Once the Secretary of the Air Force reviews the case, he decides if you are a conscientious objector. If you don't like his decision, then you and your lawyer will likely have to sue the Air Force in federal court. It's been happening a lot lately." The captain was clearly trying to be helpful.

"What do you think my chances are?"

"I can't answer that. All I can say, and I'm only saying this off the record, is that I think you are sincere. I'll write you a good report."

I thanked him profusely and went back to being a journalist for another couple months before reporting to Grissom Air Force Base for my next interview.

The chaplain was a colonel and a career officer in the Air Force. He was bald and square-jawed and wore his uniform crisply. He put me on the spot right away.

"Do you believe in God?"

"Yes. God is the force behind me."

"You believe in a benevolent God?"

"God is beyond my comprehension."

"If you don't understand me, am I God?"

"I have the potential to understand you."

"Do you believe God is in everything? Do you believe man has a soul? Do you believe in life after death?"

I should have objected to the multiple form of the question, but I answered simply, "No."

"You believe in reincarnation?"

"No, but I don't discount the possibility."

The chaplain began to loosen up and his questions became more open-minded. We ended up having quite the conversation about Jesus Christ. He didn't like it much when I said, "I don't believe God only had one son and that He only wrote one book and that there's only one way to get to heaven."

Seeing the look of disapproval on the chaplain's face, I quickly backpedaled. "I'm not saying Christianity is bad. It's given a lot of hope and comfort and compassion to millions of people. I am saying that my opposition to war is an ethical objection, not an objection based on religion."

I knew that's what the cases on conscientious objection had recently relied upon. The law had evolved through previous decisions to the point where you didn't need to be a Quaker or member of some non-violent religious sect to qualify as a conscientious objector. My attorney had informed me the law said you needed only an "ethical opposition to war in any form" to qualify for CO status.

The chaplain didn't care about the law. He was more concerned with saving my soul. I wasn't having it. "The way I see it, all Christians should declare themselves COs," I said brashly. "Jesus talked about 'love thy neighbor' and the Bible is pretty clear on 'Thou shalt not kill.' How could any good Christian go off to war? And what gives with that song about 'Onward Christian soldiers, marching off to war'?"

The chaplain smiled patiently and said, "War has been a sad fact of life for men of faith for as long as history has been written. Are you saying you are above basic human nature?"

"No, I'm not saying that at all. I'm saying it is the basic nature of humans to want peace. I've been around the world with no maps and no money and I'll tell you this, the people of the world do not want war or even violence. They want peace and prosperity and time to spend with their grandchildren. Everywhere I went people were good-hearted and ready to help if they could. It's time for the peaceful people of the world to unite against war and stop it forever."

"Do you think God created war for a purpose?" he asked.

I tilted my head and smiled. "Is that one of the questions you have to ask?"

The chaplain laughed slightly. We were starting to get along. "Yes, it is. But it's a great question, don't you think?"

"Yes, it's a great question," I said, relaxing a little. "For starters, I hate the word 'God.' It got pounded into me as a kid like there was some kind of Santa Claus up there, making a list and checking it twice."

"Gonna find out who's naughty or nice," the chaplain chimed in, almost singing the children's song. We laughed together. I could tell he was a bit of an iconoclast himself.

"So, let's call it the universe," I suggested.

"Fine with me." The chaplain rubbed his hands together like he was sitting down to feast.

I got as honest with him as I could. "I've got to say mankind has no clue about the universe. We don't know where we come from, we don't know where we go when we die, and we don't have any idea what we're doing here in the first place. The human race isn't really that intelligent. We've got enough brains to ask the questions, but we don't have enough to come up with any decent answers."

The chaplain's eyes lit up. "Isn't that where faith comes in?"

I leaned across the desk and spoke in a conspiratorial tone. "You know what I developed faith in?"

"What?"

"The road."

The chaplain leaned back in his chair, clearly interested. "How so?"

The interview was making progress. "I began to see that the road would lead me where I needed to go as long as I surrendered and let it take me where it wanted."

"Some people call that surrendering to God's will."

I had to think about that for a moment. "I doubt if God is a sentient being with a will or plans for my life or a system of punishments and rewards like heaven and hell."

"But isn't the point to believe in something outside yourself?" the chaplain asked. "I mean, if you believe in 'the road,' isn't that the same leap of faith the Christians talk about when they come to believe?"

I had to admit he was making excellent points. By the time the interview ended, the chaplain and I had reached a lot of common ground. And while he never came right out and said it, I could tell he was strongly opposed to America's terrible crusade in Southeast Asia. I knew he would write me a good report.

About two months later, I reported back to base for my third interview. The psychiatrist was a major and every bit as interesting as the chaplain colonel and the attorney captain. He took his thick glasses off when I entered the room and squinted at me like my very presence caused him intellectual pain. He started off discussing Joseph Heller's book *Catch 22*.

"You know the story," he started. "Damned if you do, damned if you don't. In the book, pilots could only get out of combat by saying they were insane, but if you said you were insane everybody knew you were sane because you were trying to get out of flying combat missions."

"Don't you think all war is insane?" I asked.

"Oh, no you don't." He chuckled patronizingly. "You don't ask the questions here. I do."

He then asked a series of questions that I answered as honestly as I could.

"Have you participated in demonstrations?"

"Yes."

"Have you been arrested?"

"No, but I was tear gassed at the 1969 Peace March in Washington, DC."

"What would you have done in World War II?"

"Been a conscientious objector. I'm against war, against competition, and against violence, which is the most radical form of competition."

"So, what you're saying, then," he concluded, "is that you're ethically opposed to the entire twentieth century?"

"It's been pretty much a senseless slaughter, hasn't it?" I asked. He looked up and over his glasses but did not respond with anything but a cryptic smile.

He carefully took notes the entire session even though the interview, like the others, was being recorded by a court reporter. I thought we were nearly finished, but then he asked, "Do you believe in the devil?"

"No."

"Evil?"

"I don't know. I think evil comes from fear and much of mankind's motivation comes from the fear of death. Freud talked about it in sexual terms, Marx talked about it in economic terms, but they were both hip to the fact that fear runs our lives. In fact, I think I stayed in the Air Force for fear of not having something else to do."

"What other fears do you have?

"Fear of not being accepted, not being successful, being alone."

"Is that all?"

"I guess I'm afraid of being thrown in jail by the United States government. But I'm not ruled by fear anymore. Traveling made me face so many fears that fear no longer controls my life."

He started to ask another question but caught himself beginning to treat me like a patient. He closed his notebook and ended the interview rather abruptly. As the court reporter was packing up, the psychiatrist looked at me over his glasses and shook his head affirmatively to let me know he would write a good report on my sincerity.

I thought I had the case in the bag. I went back to the newspaper and told everyone I was going to win the case because three out of three interviewers were writing favorable reports on me.

More than six months after my three interviews, I received a letter from the Secretary General of the Air Force. I hoped it would say something along the lines of granting me an honorable discharge from the military. I was nervous yet confident as I opened the highly official envelope. After all, each of the three interviewers had found me to be sincere.

A bell of impending doom began ringing in my head as I read the bad news. The highest-ranking officer in the Air Force was disagreeing with his three investigating officers and basically calling me a coward. I sat down on the sofa in shock and thought I would never be able to get up. The weight of the world was suddenly on my shoulders.

"What did I tell you?" my father said as he reviewed the letter. "You can't beat the government. They're too damn big and they write the laws to make sure the law is always on their side."

I was in a state of emotional shock until I got to my lawyer's office two days later and showed him the bad news. I was relieved to hear him say, "This is not the end. This is just the beginning. Don't panic. The cases say the Secretary General has to follow the recommendations of his investigating officers. Look here, he even states in the letter he's overriding their recommendations. You're going to win this case."

A week later, we filed a writ of habeas corpus action in federal court. We asked that a stay be issued so I wouldn't be in jail awaiting the outcome of the legal action. The court granted the stay and I had my freedom, at least for a while.

Meanwhile, my case became headline news, much to the chagrin of my editors at the paper. Fortunately, the publisher of *The Fort Wayne Journal Gazette*, Richard Inskeep, was a man of moral and political courage. He stood by me and let me keep writing as the case progressed. A wave of angry letters to the editor hit both our paper and the competing daily paper, *The Fort Wayne News-Sentinel*. Most of the letters focused on the fact that I had taken scholarship money from the government and not lived up to my end of the deal.

It took some talking, but I finally convinced my attorney to file a motion in federal court requesting that I be allowed to pay back the federal government.

"There's no way you have to pay the government back any money," my lawyer argued.

"That's not the point," I said. "I don't want to confuse the moral issue with the financial issue. Besides that, a deal's a deal. If I'm not going to be a pilot for six years, I want to repay them every cent they ever gave me."

The court took my motion to pay back the government under advisement, along with the case itself. Meanwhile, my family and friends and fellow reporters watched me take an occasional beating in the Letters to the Editor section of the paper. This went on for months and into years. It wasn't easy being publicly called a coward. I took solace in becoming a competent investigative reporter as the nation watched President Richard Nixon being run out of office by Woodward and Bernstein of the *Washington Post*.

An amazing thing happened while I was working at the newspaper and waiting for my case to be adjudicated. Adriana came to visit. I was totally surprised when she called on the telephone and said she was in Fort Wayne. Nearly two years after our dramatic breakup, it was wonderful to hear her voice.

I went to pick her up right away. She looked more tired than when

I last saw her, but she was still using a piece of gum for a canine tooth. She needed a place to land for a while to recover from the rigors of the road. I invited her to move into my apartment and we were back to making love like we'd never said goodbye. What she was really doing was touring the United States. I was not so much a destination as a convenient stop on the journey.

"I waited for you for a week at the Crown," she said. "I never thought you would actually leave. I know I got a little crazy, but we were both crazy then."

I didn't argue with her. It was fun to show her my new life as a journalist and introduce her to my friends and family. I knew she needed a break from the road, and I was only too happy to be able to offer a little Hoosier hospitality. She had lost some weight since we'd traveled together. I made sure she had plenty to eat and drink. Her independent spirit was as dominant as ever.

My father asked her during a cocktail party at Sunset Drive how she liked American beer. She gushed like she'd been waiting for someone to ask the question. "It tastes like horse piss! But I do like the red wine from California."

Adriana stayed with me for two weeks, during which time it became increasingly obvious to both of us that we were destined to be more friends than lovers. Besides, she could see I was falling in love with a beautiful young art teacher named Jody Hemphill, who lived downstairs.

"You treat her like she is already your wife," Adriana observed one day. I had no idea at that point how right she was.

Eventually, Adriana and I parted on good terms. She told me I was her last stop on the way back home. The road was finally taking her full circle. "I had to make sure you were all right," she said with genuine affection. "I was sure you would starve to death in India. Of course, I knew better. I just had to see you one more time."

We hugged each other for a long time at the bus station before saying goodbye. She waved to me through a side window as the Greyhound pulled away. It felt good to rewrite our final scene.

In April of 1975, Federal Judge Jesse Eschbach of United States District Court for the Northern District of Indiana, Fort Wayne Division, ruled in my favor and against the federal government. The case was captioned United States of America, ex rel. Mark P. Smith v. Lyle Stockton (or his successor), as Commander of Grissom Air Force Base, ET AL., Civil No. 73 F 63.

There was no hearing. The judge simply ruled on the motions. I wasn't even in the country when the ruling came down. I was in Mexico doing a series of hitchhiking stories for the paper. I learned about the decision when I arrived back in the country by way of Chicago.

Jody picked me up in her TR6 convertible at the Chicago Art Museum. I was taking a hit of marijuana, roaring down Michigan Avenue, when she told me the news. "By the way, while you were gone, they ruled on your case. You won and you don't have to pay them back and the court didn't order any alternative service."

She stopped for a red light. I screamed in pure joy and rolled out onto the pavement. Drivers in many lanes of traffic must have wondered why the crazy man was shouting and dancing in glee. I couldn't believe it. I was finally free.

"I'm free!" I shouted to the skies and to the wide-eyed drivers watching. I danced circles in the street until the light changed. I got back in the car and asked her if she was really sure about everything she told me. She kissed me and breathed on me and looked me in the eye and smiled magnificently. In that moment, I knew everything was right in my world. The long night was over. The weight of the world had been lifted off my shoulders. I hadn't fully realized until that moment how much psychic dread the pending litigation had caused.

On April 26, 1975, Karen Walker wrote the following article for *The News-Sentinel* under the headline, "Judge Orders War Objector Discharged":

Federal Judge Jesse E. Eschbach has ordered the Air Force to grant Fort Wayne resident Mark Smith's application for conscientious objector status and to discharge him from military custody.

Smith filed suit in federal court Aug. 3, 1973, claiming he is a conscientious objector and that he was unlawfully denied discharge from the Air Force.

In 1969, while a student at DePauw University, Smith joined the Air Force Reserve Officer Training Corps, Eschbach explained in his order. Smith received a ROTC scholarship during three of the years he was in college.

Following graduation, he was ordered to report for active duty in August 1972.

Smith received an extension of time before he had to report then on January 22, 1973, filed application for discharge as a conscientious objector setting out in detail his opposition to war in any form.

Smith claimed, according to Eschbach's order, that he had doubts about his military commitment while still in college.

Smith also claimed that after traveling abroad just before he was to report for active duty, he came to adopt an "anti-materialistic, anti-capitalistic view of life with competition replaced by cooperation." Smith said he sees violence and war as the extreme form of competition.

The CO application filed by Smith was investigated by three commissioned officers, who recommended approval because Smith's "beliefs were sincerely held."

However, on May 11, 1973, after review of the application and record, the Secretary of the Air Force refused to reclassify Smith as a CO.

The Secretary concluded Smith was not sincere but was seeking CO status to avoid military obligations after he received a "free ride" through college.

Eschbach concluded the Air Force did not have the evidence to support its finding that Smith has not painted a complete or accurate picture of his activities and beliefs.

Smith has offered to repay the scholarship, Eschbach pointed out, but the judge did not order such repayment.

The judge's ruling and the news coverage led to another storm of public controversy and criticism. I didn't pay it much heed. I was grateful to be fighting against war and winning at least a small victory. There were plenty of people climbing on the peace bandwagon. By 1975, the Vietnam War was over except for the ignominious final flail of an exit from Saigon.

On May 5, 1975, a dear friend of our family, Carmen Nicklin, wrote this letter to the editor of *The Journal-Gazette* on my behalf:

Gentlemen:

A word in defense of Mark Smith's stand as a CO must be said. Having known Mark for at least thirteen years, and having heard, in person, his thinking and reasoning on the subject of war, I can and do vouch for his sincerity. He was ready to pay the price for his decision ... even imprisonment if necessary. And he has paid a price in facing the scorn, ridicule, anger and attacks on his honesty from peers and respected elders.

How many of us, having embarked on a certain course,

MARK PAUL SMITH   399

and finding ourselves gravely doubting its worthiness, are willing to reverse our decision?

I am more than willing to pay my share of Mark's education (which couldn't be more than 1/100,000 of a cent, in view of the national defense budget). Have we not ALL taught our children, Thou shalt not kill? Then should it shock us when a young man suddenly becomes acutely aware that his own action WILL cause countless deaths? Should it shock us that he is horrified at that very stark realization? Let's be grateful that he is! How many of us have asked ourselves, "Could I kill? Would I kill?" Many conclude that they can and will in the name of national security. That is an individual answer to one of the world's hardest questions. If someone decides that he cannot and will not . . . should we debase him? That too is an individual answer to a very hard question.

Mark did nothing illegal or immoral. He did not desert . . . he took his case to the courts of our land. He was obedient to the law and justice was served.

For centuries mankind has sent its most promising, most able-bodied, and intelligent young men into battle for what seemed at the time, a very worthy cause. History is strewn with repetitions of battle after battle and war after war. Have we learned nothing? Isn't that Mark's question? Could it be time to at least listen to the Marks of this century? Could mankind possibly be ready for a more humane way of dealing with adversaries? Is our ideal of Peace really brought about by killing through war, or, could it be . . . is it possible . . . is it just too naïve to believe that Peace will be brought about by Peace Makers?

I loved the way she capitalized "Peace."

It took a couple weeks for the federal court victory to sink into my consciousness. I hadn't realized what a heavy emotional burden the case had been until the load was lifted. I was walking on air. I was free. For the first time in my life I felt free. I could go anywhere and do anything I wanted. I had been working six- and seven-day weeks as a reporter, waiting for the judgment to come down. Now, nearly two and a half years since the case began, it was over. No more worrying about doing time in prison or what life might be like as an exile in Canada or Finland or wherever.

For many mornings after the decision came down, I woke up and had to remind myself that my case was over, and I had won. My friends and family and people I didn't even know seemed to be congratulating me all the time, although there were many who thought I had pulled a major scam on the government. Many who congratulated me to my face ran me down behind my back. I learned to not rely on the judgment of others. I knew what I did was right.

My father was the biggest fan of the decision. "It restores my faith in the system," he said one day when he took me out to lunch in the middle of his legal day. "After thirty years of practicing law, your case and your determination have restored my faith in the rule of law. I've won a lot of cases I should have lost and lost a few I maybe should have won. But this case I never thought you could win has brought back my pride in the American system of justice. And I want to say it now." He raised his glass and his voice in a toast. "I'm proud of you, son."

It's a fortunate son who receives that kind of reaffirming praise from his father. I toasted him back. "I'm proud of you, too, Dad."

What I didn't say to my father was that I was still appalled by our nation's foreign policy since World War II. I also didn't try to explain the guilt I felt at having been so lucky in my dealings with the United States military. More than 58,000 Americans lost their lives in Vietnam and more than 300,000 were wounded. Most who returned from combat operations would never be the same.

I also didn't try to explain, even to myself, why millions of Vietnamese had to die at the hands of foreign invaders.

Often at night, while falling sleep, images of the hitchhike to Bombay drifted into my dreams. I was dancing with Danny in a fishermen's restaurant, swimming with Hanna in the sunrise, and riding across the Khyber Pass with Adriana. I could hear monks wailing in minarets, John Lennon singing in the sun, and oceans thundering to shore. The smells of beach fires and opium smoke and slum slime filled my head. Peter was rolling nine-paper spliffs, Canaga was giving tours of Herat, and the Sikh truck driver was blowing his low horn to clear cows from the road. An emotional kaleidoscope of fear and courage spun the light of lies and truth into confusing patterns. Through it all, the road made me a believer, strong enough to leave my military mind behind and become a musician and a writer.

One night while celebrating the court's decision once again, I managed to blurt out the truth. "It's time for the peaceful people of the planet to get together and put an end to war." I pounded my empty beer glass on the table for emphasis. "It's not enough to 'Give Peace a Chance.' We've got to make peace happen. And we've got to do it now!"

As I stumbled out of the bar, I looked up at the same stars that had guided me across Spain and Italy and Turkey and Afghanistan. I was now a free man. Free to realize my journey had not ended. It was just beginning.

THE END

About the Author

Mark Paul Smith has been a trial attorney for 37 years. Before law school, he played in a rock band in New Orleans, which became the inspiration for his novel *Rock and Roll Voodoo*. His second book, *Honey and Leonard*, comes straight out of his law practice. *The Hitchhike* is a memoir of an officer in the Air Force hitchhiking around the world and coming back a conscientious objector.

He and his wife, the artist Jody Hemphill Smith, own Castle Gallery Fine Arts in Fort Wayne, Indiana.

Other Books By Mark Paul Smith

ROCK AND ROLL VOODOO

During the 1970s on a magic mushroom harvesting adventure in the Bayou, a young, aspiring rock and roll musician discovers the voice of voodoo, which not only alters his life, but the life of his band, the Divebomberz.

When the band is on the verge of making it big, tragedy strikes and Jesse is confronted with the hard truth that life is often a spiritual obstacle course designed to see if you can get over yourself.

A book for rock and rollers of all ages and for restless souls who have chased a dream only to discover that what they really needed was with them all along.

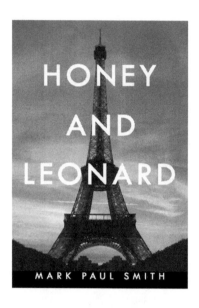

HONEY AND LEONARD

Honey and Leonard are in their seventies when they fall in love. Leonard is in the early stages of Alzheimer's and Honey thinks her love will cure him.

When their heirs try to keep them apart, they flee to France in violation of court orders. Pursued by police, press, and private investigators, they become an international media sensation. In a time just before cell phones and the Internet, they become the Bonnie and Clyde of love.

Their whirlwind romance encompasses arsenic poisoning, elder law, Alzheimer's, an Eiffel Tower arrest, and a Paris jail break.

And through it all Honey is in the middle of the difficult process of discovering that love does not conquer all. Or does it?